THE ROAD FROM THE PAST

The Road from the Past

TRAVELING THROUGH HISTORY
IN FRANCE

INA CARO

NAN A. TALESE

DOUBLEDAY

New York   London   Toronto

Sydney   Auckland

PUBLISHED BY NAN A.TALESE
an imprint of Doubleday
a division of Bantam Doubleday Dell Publishing Group, Inc.
1540 Broadway, New York, New York 10036

DOUBLEDAY *is a trademark of Doubleday, a division of*
Bantam Doubleday Dell Publishing Group, Inc.

Book design by Marysarah Quinn
Map by Jackie Aher
Illustrations on pages 11 and 251 by Martie Holmer

"Château de "Rocamadour" by J. T. Arms: The Metropolitan Museum of Art,
Gift of John Taylor Arms, 1942 (42.21.34); "Bourges" by J. T. Arms: The Met-
ropolitan Museum of Art, Gift of John Taylor Arms, 1942 (42.21.29).

"Blowin' in the Wind" by Bob Dylan. Copyright © 1962 by Warner Bros. Mu-
sic. Copyright renewed 1990 by Special Rider Music. All rights reserved. Inter-
national copyright secured. Reprinted by permission.

Library of Congress Cataloging-in-Publication Data
Caro, Ina.
The road from the past : traveling through history in France
Ina Caro. — 1st. ed.
p.   cm.
"Nan A. Talese."
Includes index.
1. France—Guidebooks.   2. Historic sites—France—Guidebooks.
I. Title.
DC16.C37   1994
914.404'839—dc20   *93-34636*
CIP

ISBN 0-385-26672-3

FOR BOB

SAINT-GERMAIN FOREST

Maisons-Laffitte

SEINE R.

Saint-Denis

Saint-Germain-en-Laye

Paris

MARNE R.

CHEVREUSE VALLEY

Versailles

Sceaux

Orly

Rambouillet

Dampierre

Vaux-le-Vicomte

RAMBOUILLET FOREST

Chartres

Fontainebleau

SEINE R.

North

⑤

SEINE R.

Paris

MARNE R.

Chartres

⑤

SEINE R.

Orléans

LOIRE VALLEY

④

LOIRE R.

LOIRE R.

CHER R.

Bourges

Chinon

INDRE R.

Loches

VIENNE R.

Conques (Romanesque pilgrimage church)

DORDOGNE R.

Sarlat

③

Rocamadour

GORGES OF THE TARN

RHÔNE R.

DURANCE R.

GARONNE R.

CAUSSE DE GRAMAT

Albi

TARN

Millau

GARD R.

①

Toulouse

②

Béziers

Nîmes

Arles

Carcassonne

Montségur

AUDE R.

Massif de la Clape

CORBIÈRES

Narbonne (Archbishop's Palace, Saint-Just Cathedral, Robine Canal)

Fontfroide

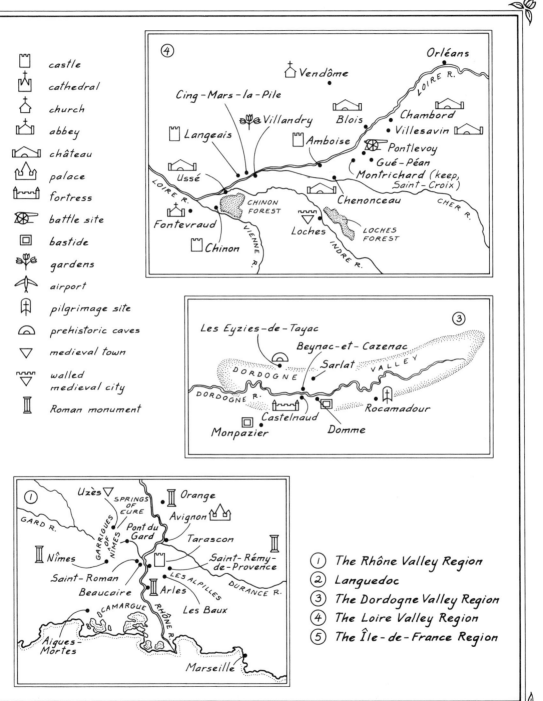

castle
cathedral
church
abbey
château
palace
fortress
battle site
bastide
gardens
airport
pilgrimage site
prehistoric caves
medieval town
walled
medieval city
Roman monument

④

Orléans

LOIRE R.

Vendôme

Cing-Mars-la-Pile

Villandry

Blois

Chambord

Langeais

Amboise

Villesavin

Pontlevoy

Gué-Péan

Montrichard (keep,
Saint-Croix)

Ussé

LOIRE R.

CHINON
FOREST

Chenonceau

CHER R.

Fontevraud

VIENNE R.

Loches

LOCHES
FOREST

Chinon

INDRE R.

③

Les Eyzies-de-Tayac

Beynac-et-Cazenac

Sarlat

VALLEY

DORDOGNE

DORDOGNE R.

Rocamadour

Castelnaud

Domme

Monpazier

①

Uzès

SPRINGS
OF
EURE

Orange

Avignon

GARD R.

GARRIGUES OF NÎMES

Pont du
Gard

Tarascon

Nîmes

Saint-Rémy-
de-Provence

Saint-Roman

LES ALPILLES

DURANCE R.

Beaucaire

Arles

Les Baux

CAMARGUE

RHÔNE R.

Aigues-
Mortes

Marseille

① The Rhône Valley Region
② Languedoc
③ The Dordogne Valley Region
④ The Loire Valley Region
⑤ The Île-de-France Region

ACKNOWLEDGMENTS

I would like to express my thanks to all who have helped me in one way or another to write this book: to my editor and publisher, Nan A. Talese for her enthusiasm and belief in this book; to my copy editor, Bob Daniels; to my agent, Wendy Lipkind Black; to Marion Fourestier at the French Government Tourist Office; to Katherine Hourigan; to Cynthia Cupples; and to Nancy Evans. However, I can never adequately thank Robert A. Caro, my husband and my traveling companion on all but one of my trips to France these past seventeen years. When I told him my idea of driving through history in France—originally from the Roman ruins of Provence to the World War II invasion beaches in Normandy—he was skeptical but drove. Afterward he thought it was such a great way to travel that he urged me to write this book and helped me every step of the way. Without his advice, encouragement, and unwavering faith in me, this book would not have been possible. As his researcher on *The Power Broker, The Path to Power,* and *Means of Ascent*, I learned the importance of visiting places you write about. As my husband and traveling companion, he has turned every one of our trips into a magical experience. This is not an age when prince charmings, idealistic knights, and true love at first sight are taken seriously. When I was still in my teens, I fell in love with Bob, and he has been my prince charming for over thirty years. And I want to thank him for never once changing into a frog, and for visiting with me the castle of Sleeping Beauty which lies in an enchanted valley filled with a thousand castles and food so magical that fish and asparagus taste better than cake.

CONTENTS

THE ÎLE-DE-FRANCE

INTRODUCTION

Pâté and Palaces

M ost people return from Europe with a memory of the places they have visited that is very much like a salad after it has been put through a Cuisinart. They have been to so many countries and heard so many dates and names of kings that when they return, the trip is all a blur. When I see the typical American tourist, I feel like yelling out, "Don't do it that way, it's no fun. Do it my way."

If you do it my way, you will rent a time machine—available at any rent-a-car agency—and drive through history. Our time machine can't take us into the future any faster than a minute at a time, but we can, if we properly plan our route, actually simulate the sensation of traveling through several centuries of the past on a magical vacation in France. If you follow the route I describe from Provence to Paris, traveling to some of the most magnificent and beautiful monasteries, churches, châteaux, and towns built in France over a period of nearly two thousand years, and visit these sites in the order they were built, you will feel almost as if you are traveling through the past, through the history of France.

To an American, a tour of this type may seem like whimsy, not only because our history is relatively short, and Americans generally have little sense of history anyway, but also because we have simply leveled too much of our past—to make way for newer, more profitable buildings—for us to travel from one age to another. But it does work in France, where coliseums, cathedrals, keeps, fortresses, and castles decorate the landscape of a Frenchman's life and are concrete reminders of his historical and cultural past. France is so abundant in such remembrances, so rich in a past that is forever embedded in the present, that we are able, while traveling there, to transform dry memories of facts gleaned from books into substance and reality.

I have found that there are only three essential rules to follow to create the sensation of traveling through the past. The first is to visit sites in chronological order. The order in which we see the sites is as important, if not more important, than the sites themselves. If on our road map we place an overlay of time, really a route we will follow which takes us to the sites in the order of their construction—arranging our visits to temple and fortress, palace and château so that we begin with those structures built earliest and continue architecturally through the ages—as we travel we cannot help but feel the flow of years passing by rather than the miles. The reason we feel this flow of time is this: architecture has evolved. One period has developed from another. The architecture of ancient Rome became Romanesque. The Romanesque style evolved into the Gothic, the Gothic into the Renaissance, and the Renaissance into the Mannerist and the Baroque. Each style incorporated certain aspects of its predecessor and eliminated those aspects which had become unnecessary or undesirable.

For example, as we travel through time, we can see arches change. We see the grandiose rounded Roman arch, created to overawe, slowly transformed into the austere rounded arch of the early Christian Church; transformed again from austerity and simplicity to the elaborate storytelling beauty of the twelfth-century Romanesque arch; and then, at the very pinnacle of this beauty, transformed again into the simple Gothic arch—which again evolves over the years from simplicity to flamboyance. Not only does the architecture of the Church change during our travels through the centuries, but so, too, does secular architecture. The somber fortress, encircled by ramparts and moats, with its narrow slits in the walls for defending archers (the only openings to the outside world and to light), its battlements for crossbowmen to stand behind, its machicolations from which other defenders could pour boiling water and hot oil, its watchtowers where sentries awaited besieging knights with their catapults, battering rams, and assault towers—a fortress like Chinon, Castelnaud, or Beynac—changes with the years. As we travel through time, from one castle to another, we see the walls open up to light and air. The moats become mere decorations and then landscaped reflecting pools created to delight the eye rather than to defend against attacking Vikings, Magyars, Saracens, or another noble's knights. At first the battlements are retained as fantasy designs, and then they disappear altogether. We see the awkward proportions of feudal castles dissolve into harmony and perfect proportions during the Renaissance, then change again in the seventeenth century, when the castles of kings were meant to impress and overwhelm, when the French monarchy was at its height. We can, in fact, see the growth of royal absolutism mirrored in these castles. Visit Chinon, Loches, Langeais, Amboise, Blois, Chambord, Fontainebleau, and Versailles in the order in which they were built, and know only that these were the successive residences of the Kings of France, and you will understand—quite deeply—what is meant by the growth of French absolutism.

But visiting sites in chronological order is, by itself, not enough to create the sensation of traveling through the past. Next we must select sites on our map of time that not only represent a particular age but are among the best, most aesthetically pleasing embodiments of its spirit. We should seek out not just representative architecture, but wonderful architecture: châteaux, cathedrals, and monasteries that are beautiful in and of themselves—stunning works of art set down against the background of the beautiful French landscape. And each of these sites should bring to life its age as does the Pont du Gard (near Nîmes), whose hugeness and classical proportions can overawe us today with the power and rigid rationality of mighty Rome just as it did the Celtic barbarian two thousand years ago, or the Cathedral of Conques, whose Romanesque mystical beauty can make the most agnostic of us feel the Age of Faith. In other words, the site should possess that indefinable quality which makes us classify a work of man as Art, that quality which gives one of man's creations life enough to survive through the years, a quality that made it please not only the generation of its creator but future generations as well. (However, some places, while architecturally stunning, are not pleasant to visit. There are places such as Les Baux in Provence, Langeais in the Loire, and Versailles in the Île-de-France, which are marvels but where the guides or the townspeople embody those traits of arrogance and rudeness which Americans who think they hate France identify with France. Since there is no shortage of aesthetically wonderful, architecturally stunning sites in France where the people are gracious, charming, and hospitable and where the tourist—regardless of his accent—is treated like a welcome guest, I have tried to avoid those places where, no matter how renowned the town's tourist attraction may be, the American tourist is likely to be arrogantly or rudely treated. I have tried to direct you to places that are not only aesthetically pleasing but are also enjoyable to visit.)

And lastly, to understand the centuries through which we are traveling, we must know something of the kings and counts, the queens and courtesans—some famous, some not—connected with building the structures we will visit and in shaping the significant historical events that took place within their walls. Since this is a vacation and we want to be amused, there is no need for us to be bored in France by choosing figures from what I call the "begot" school of history—someone like Louis the Fat, also known as Louis the Wide Awake, whose major accomplishment apparently was to stay awake long enough to "beget" an heir, and who happened to be King of France merely because he was "begotten" by a King of France. France has as many engrossing historical figures as it has castles to visit. We have Julius Caesar and Vercingetorix, France's first hero, to explain Gallo-Roman France; Saint Bernard to lead us through the Age of Faith; Foulques Nerra, Eleanor of Aquitaine, Henry Plantagenet, and Richard the Lion-Hearted to help us see the various stages of feudal France; and Joan of Arc to lead us through the endless Hundred Years War. We have the plump and sinister Catherine de' Medici and her rival, the beautiful Diane de Poitiers, who charmed a king twenty years her junior into giving her both castles and crown jewels, with whom to see the Renaissance; and the poignant story of Fouquet and Louis XIV to understand absolutism at its height.

In order to understand what I mean, let us visit the eleventh century at the ruins of the Castle of Cinq-Mars-la-Pile, in the Loire Valley. This castle—fortress really—is not usually listed on any tour, Michelin gives it no star, and Fodor's ignores it completely. However, its romantic garden, filled with a profusion of wisteria in the spring, provides a lovely place for a picnic lunch, and the fortress itself, while not grand, fits to perfection the type of building fashionable in 1050, when feudalism was the rage. Feudalism, you will recall, was the political-military-economic system of relationships between lord, vassal, and peasant—its values best expressed in the *chansons de geste,* popular songs of the time that told of faith, of deeds of valor and chivalry, and of what we might today call "machismo."

As we enter the village of Cinq-Mars, on our way to this feudal fortress, we see, as clearly as in the pages of a book, but with substance and reality, how this structure tells of life in the early Middle Ages. Approaching the fortress, we first see the peasants' huts, huddled for safety inside the crumbling outer walls, as close to the fortress as they could get. Since peasants were always the first to be killed, raped, and looted, they tilled the land of the Marquis of Cinq-Mars in exchange for his protection. This land, in turn, had been given to Cinq-Mars by his lord, the Count of Blois, in exchange for his services as a knight in wartime. The land would by tradition become the inheritance of Cinq-Mars's son—never of his daughter, since daughters did not go to war—and of his son's descendants. Across a wide moat we see fortifications: two austere rectangular towers, called keeps (or donjons), topped with crenelated battlements. We know instinctively, just by looking at these structures, that they were built for defense and for defense alone. The eleventh century was a time of constant war and pillage, and these grim fortifications and the huts huddled around them bring the insecurity of the Middle Ages to life in a way we can understand and never forget.

But that is only the beginning of what this fortress can tell us. As we cross the moat, we see walls decorated with a stringcourse (a horizontal line of stone whose height from the ground indicated the owner's rank in the social order). If we ask ourselves what kind of society would mark *in stone* a member's position in its hierarchy, we cannot but conclude that the society we are visiting was as calcified as the stone itself, as indeed feudal society was. In feudal France, people were not expected to raise or lower their respective social stations during their lifetime or during the lifetime of their heirs. Their position was believed to have been ordained by God. The height of the stringcourse at Cinq-Mars also tells us that the rank of the lord we are now visiting was below that of a king, duke, or count—in fact, he was a minor lord, a marquis, who was the vassal of the Count of Blois. That means that when the Count of Blois went to war, the Marquis of Cinq-Mars was under his command.

As we climb one of the two tall towers of the fortress, we find ourselves inside exceedingly cold and gloomy rooms, rooms of bare stone walls, vaulted with ribbed ogival arches, rooms that lacked windows because windows might let in attackers as well as light and air. Because this structure was built for defense, there are no decorations. When we reach the top of the tower and look out over its battlements, we are overwhelmed by the beauty of the landscape spread before us, a panorama that includes the golden Loire as it meets the River Cher, the lush greens of the Forest of Chinon, and châteaux, and hints of other châteaux, everywhere. But we cannot really understand this fortress, nor can this fortress come alive for us, until we know something about the marquis who built it and the circumstances that caused him to build it the way he did. To understand the eleventh century, we need to know something of the Marquis of Cinq-Mars, as well as of the man whose life exemplifies and explains this age, whose life was consumed by murder, lust, avarice, and piety—eleventh-century emotions we in the twentieth century can relate to and understand. We need to know something of the man the fortress was built to keep out, Cinq-Mars's fearsome enemy—a warrior feared the length of the Loire Valley: Foulques Nerra.

In fact, standing behind the battlements atop one of the two rectangular towers, we can see both the land that comprised the domain of Cinq-Mars and, if we look to the west, the Château of Langeais. And it was to the west and Langeais that the sentries of Cinq-Mars's fortress watched, watched in fear from its battlements for the enemy to attack, watched for Foulques Nerra and his knights. For in 987, at the age of seventeen, Foulques Nerra, translated Black Falcon and meaning "bird of prey without pity," succeeded his father, Geoffrey the Grey Coat, as Count of Anjou and ruler of half the Loire Valley. From the very moment of his succession until his death at the age of seventy—he would outlive four Kings of France—Foulques devoted his life to increasing the land under his control. He did so by constantly waging war, mostly, it seems, against the rulers of the other half of the valley, the Counts of Blois, whose land he wanted, and by marrying at least two heiresses whose dowries consisted of large segments of the Loire. After obtaining Vendôme—the dowry of his first wife, Élisabeth—he disposed of her by falsely accusing her of adultery, and then by burning her at the stake (after dressing her in her best clothes), so that he could marry another heiress. However, we know he wasn't all bad, because after murdering the Count of Blois and driving his widow with her six small children from their home, he took up the pilgrim's staff and journeyed for the first time to Jerusalem to be redeemed for his sins. In fact, he made four pilgrimages to far-off Jerusalem; he returned from one of the trips with a piece of the "True Cross," which he said—and people who knew him believed him—he had bitten off with his teeth.

Knowing a little about the Marquis of Cinq-Mars's conflict with Foulques Nerra, the function of the fortress of Cinq-Mars as an outpost becomes clearer. It is positioned so that the marquis could give early warning to his lord at Blois of an attack by the Black Falcon. Looking out over the battlements of Cinq-Mars, we cannot help feeling the insecurity of the early Middle Ages. In the area that now is France, the eleventh century was, in fact, a time of constant warring and whoring and praying. Warring over land, land that was the only source of wealth and power in this moneyless, tradeless time, land that was acquired either as a fiefdom, in return for services as a knight, or by marriage, or by war. And praying to be forgiven for both the warring and the whoring. Everything about the fortress of Cinq-Mars tells us of feudal war: the width and depth of the moat; the solidity of the bare stone walls, in which the only openings are narrow arrow-slit windows; the height of the towers; the total lack of amenities. The man who built this fortress centered his life around the defense of his stronghold, and had time for little else.

From Cinq-Mars the road to confusion is easy, since in the Loire Valley alone there are more than one thousand châteaux and fortresses. And if you follow the road from château to nearest château, as most tour books suggest, the road leads not only to confusion but to repetition and boredom. For example, Langeais is only three miles away, and in the garden of the royal palace there you will find the remains of a keep, or fortified tower, quite similar to the one at Cinq-Mars. There is another keep at Montbazon, another at Montrichard, and another at Loches. In the eleventh century Foulques Nerra built twenty-three of these keeps, one day's march apart from one another, so that no matter where in his realm he and his knights found themselves at nightfall, they would always have a safe place to spend the night.* Other keeps were built by Foulques's enemy Eudes, Count of Blois. The method of design and construction was basically the same for each of them, none varying much from the keep at Cinq-Mars. Since these keeps provided their owners with few amenities, their internal inspection provides the tourist with little aesthetic pleasure. Therefore, if you know what these structures are, who built them and why, you certainly don't have to visit them all to understand the fractious age in which they were built. If, in fact, you visit the keep of a minor lord, such as the one at Cinq-Mars, which has a fabulous view of the valley from its watchtower, where you can stand, just as sentries stood over a thousand years ago watching and waiting for Foulques Nerra to attack, and if you then visit briefly the keep at Loches, which was the center of Foulques's offensive system, it is quite enough. It is enough if you know that these keeps were all built alike and were spaced one day's march from one another. It is enough if you know that Foulques Nerra, Count of Anjou, considered himself the equal of the King of France. It is enough if you know that he built not only twenty-three keeps but châteaux, monasteries, and churches as well. If you know something of Foulques Nerra and visit one of his fortresses, you need not visit the other twenty-two that he built. One is exciting and thrilling. More would be redundant and boring. But it is good to know what these struc-

*The king, Hugh Capet, who was not given to construction, could not travel throughout his realm without being robbed.

tures are and who built them, since you will pass one or another of them on almost any drive you take in the Loire Valley.

There is another reason for visiting the eleventh-century keep at Cinq-Mars aside from its being a typical fortress of the early Middle Ages whose lord was consumed by a bloody little civil war similar to the bloody little civil wars that were occurring throughout France at the time. Cinq-Mars is a convenient place from which you as a tourist can visit other châteaux in the area. And not far away is the Abbey of Fontevraud, where Eleanor of Aquitaine spent her final years, and close by is the marvelous medieval Château of Chinon, built during a slightly later age, a château that became the residence of the Kings of France and where Joan of Arc urged her dauphin to let her relieve the siege of Orléans. And the road from Chinon is on the road to visiting the growth of royal power in France. It is not far to the royal château at Loches, and from Loches it is only twenty-five miles to the royal residence at Amboise and the beginning of the Renaissance, and only seven miles to Chenonceau, the most perfect Renaissance château with the most perfect Renaissance love story.

In other words, the castles and other sites I have chosen will take the tourist chronologically—and pleasantly—through the history of France. Not only do they architecturally represent the ages in which they were built, but they are aesthetically beautiful in themselves and possess historically significant stories that make the structures come alive. I have tried to find places that seem frozen in time rather than places where the twentieth century intrudes upon the visitor. I begin with the Gallo-Roman Arch of Triumph in Orange and end with Napoleon's Arc de Triomphe du Carrousel in Paris. Architecturally the two arches are quite similar, and once I saw and understood the two-thousand-year-old Roman arch in Orange, I understood more about why Napoleon had built his triumphal arch in Paris and was thrilled by it in a way I had never been before. In fact, after seeing each age separately, in settings practically frozen in time, in splendid isolation, then to see all the ages splendidly thrown together in Paris is an incomparable experience.

Provence

A FUNNY THING HAPPENED TO ME
on My Way to Marseille

I had originally come to Orange by accident. I was on my way to Marseille in quest of the perfect bouillabaisse and could drive no farther. Actually, since it was a shift car—which I was unable to drive—my husband could drive no farther. His enthusiasm for bouillabaisse had never been as great as mine, and had disappeared completely after lunch and the beef bourguignonne two hundred kilometers before. That was 1974. It was a different time. It was a time when there weren't so many tourists, and vacations didn't have to be planned in advance, and you could stop driving when you found a great beef bourguignonne or felt yourself getting tired. There was a sense of freedom and adventure driving through the French countryside, deciding that in an hour you would like to stop, turning to the red Michelin on your lap and finding a hotel with a red bird on a rocking horse, ending up unexpectedly in a delightful place like the little city of Orange, and deciding that the hotel was so charming, the owner so gracious, the food so delicious, that you would stay the week. Which is what we did.

Up until the day we arrived in Orange, our "grand tour" of France had been a tour of sheer gluttony in which we drove through the country eating at one starred restaurant after another. Seeking out and enjoying the food and wine in France's great restaurants were the natural result of my youthful and hedonistic outlook on life, which philosophized that eating is like sex: if you don't like it, you're just not doing it right. In my attempt to do it right, I not only had set out for Marseille in quest of the perfect bouillabaisse but had also spent hours swimming laps in Lake Annecy so that I could work up enough of an appetite to enjoy both lunch and dinner at Père Bise, the famous restaurant in heavenly Talloires. (That would have been fine had I swum the laps in August, but our two-week vacation at that Alpine resort was in May—before the glacial snow that feeds Lake Annecy had melted. And though I did work up enough of an appetite to enjoy both meals, I think only a polar bear would have felt that the effort was really worth it.)

Luckily for my figure, gluttony came to an end after coffee and croissants in Orange the morning after our arrival, and starred restaurants became a delightful bonus but never again the object of a major detour. For it was in Orange that I discovered how much more France had to offer than perfect meals. It was in Orange that I discovered the magic that occurs when the past within us meets the past without. I discovered how the remnants of the past that decorate the landscape of a Frenchman's life—the coliseums, castles, cathedrals, fortresses; the architecture the French have so magnificently preserved—can bring to life events and people of the past that I had only read about. The faded pages in my mind found a fuller substance as I walked in the places where these ghosts once walked. It was a marvelous experience, a magic nearly transcending the dimension of time. I have felt it so many times as I have traveled through the countryside of France, but I experienced it for the first time in Orange.

It happened quite unexpectedly. After dinner on the evening we arrived, Bob and I walked through the little city and discovered one delightful café after another, each with a terrific pinball machine—which is a pleasant exercise for the competitive well-stuffed traveler. The next morning I turned to my guidebook to see if there was anything worth seeing in Orange. The only local offerings mentioned were some "vestiges of ancient Rome": a Roman triumphal arch "built to commemorate Julius Caesar's conquest of Gaul" and later rededicated to Tiberius, as well as a Roman theater "built during the reign of Augustus." Even though the guidebook stated that the arch was the best preserved of its kind and one of the first triple arches to be built, and that the theater was not only the best preserved but the most beautiful in existence, Henry James had not waxed ecstatic about these vestiges, so I was not particularly eager to see them. There were, however, three hours before lunch, and it was either the triple arch and the theater or three hours of pinball. I opted for the "vestiges of ancient Rome."

THE ARCH OF TRIUMPH

at Orange

I decided to try the arch first. On the map of Orange it appeared in a circle at the end of a long promenade. I decided to walk, presuming I would have an increasingly dramatic view of the arch as I approached it. However, as I walked down what I thought was going to be the "promenade," I wished had taken the car. Unlike the rest of Orange, which is a bustling provincial town filled with delightful cafés and restaurants, the area leading to the arch was unpleasant: noisy with traffic, hot, smelly with fumes from cars and buses, a route crowded with gas stations and nondescript structures that made it impossible to get a good view of the arch from a distance. The arch was located in the middle of a traffic circle at the end of a broad street, and as I approached it, I could see big tour buses circling the traffic island on which it stood. I also noticed that although the buses were circling the arch, they were not bothering to stop. The fact that they were circling but not stopping led me to believe that I should have spent the morning drinking coffee and perfecting my pinball technique. However, having invested nearly an hour walking to the arch, I decided I might as well take a good look at it. Besides, it was a very hot morning, already in the high eighties, and the only shade—and I was in need of shade by this time—was under one of the three arches.

So, dodging buses and trucks, I ran across the road to the grassy island on which the arch was standing and found myself face-to-face with a sculptured relief that in all honesty is the cause of this book. Since I had come on a sunny morning, the entire arch had a golden glow, and the sculpture on the eastern wall was brilliantly illuminated. I think the morning sun must have been important, because without it these reliefs on the eastern face would have been in shadow and hard to see, but with the sun spotlighting and illuminating them, they were so powerful that I was completely overwhelmed. In fact, I don't think any American, with his feelings about individual freedom—feelings that come close to religious passion—could help but be overwhelmed by the carving on the eastern wall.

What I saw was two captured Gauls chained to a tree: a man and a beautiful woman. The woman is still beautiful after two thousand years. Her head bent slightly forward in despair, she is obviously yearning to be free. She is the most poignant captive I have ever seen. Above the two captives is a Roman legionnaire, his arms stretched wide above his head in victory like a tennis star who has just won the U.S. Open, holding not a tennis racket but two captured Gallic shields, one in each hand: arrogant and cruel in his victory. While the original intent of the arch was obvious—to impress the barbarian with Roman superiority—what I felt upon seeing this frieze was something more, transcending its original intent. What I felt must have been the emotions experienced by the artist who carved this work into stone two thousand years ago: compassion for the captives suffering the humiliation of subjugation; hatred for the Roman legionnaire so obviously elated by victory and domination. I had always thought of the advance of the Roman Empire as the advance of civilization. Not once before seeing these carvings had I thought of what it must have been like to lose one's freedom to a people as arrogant as this triumphant Roman soldier. I actually found it rather peculiar that a Roman Arch of Triumph commemorating and celebrating a Roman victory over the Gauls should arouse such strong feelings of compassion for the Gauls and corresponding feelings of hatred—rather than admiration or awe—for the Romans. I later learned a very poignant fact that explained my odd reaction: although the arch was designed by the Roman conquerors, it was executed and paid for by the defeated Gauls. The fact that the friezes were carved by native Gallic, rather than Roman, artisans explains why I felt such compassion for the Gauls' loss of freedom. And in this carving the artist had expressed his suffering so well that it was still vivid to me looking at it two thousand years later.

Gallic artisans were able to execute the Roman designs with such fine craftsmanship because they had been trained by Greek masters. As early as 600 B.C., Greek merchants began establishing peaceful trading posts, first in Marseille and then farther inland along the banks of the Rhône, intermarrying with the barbarians who were the forebears of today's Frenchmen. By the time the Romans came to the area now known as Provence and forcibly made it a province of Rome, it had already been Hellenized and part of the Greco-Roman world for centuries. Its citizens dressed in Greco-Roman togas, attended schools established by the Greeks, and studied under Greek masters who taught, among other things, the art of sculpture.

The arch is a monument both to the melding of three cultures and to Roman political sophistication. In addition to commemorating the victory of the legions that had conquered Gaul, it was built to both impress and overawe the citizens held in subjugation. And not only did the Roman conquerors force Gallic artisans to carve the friezes on the arch; more subtly still, they forced the citizens of Orange to pay for the arch by having them hold a referendum authorizing funds for its construction. By holding this "election," the conquered people of Orange showed their "willing" submission to Rome.

If the Arch of Triumph at Orange was built to impress, it certainly must have done so. I was impressed, not only by its carvings but, when I started to think about it, by the fact that the Romans built so grand and majestic a structure in what was a very remote part of their empire. I was impressed—and I had just left a modern hotel. How must a Gallic barbarian have felt when he first saw the gleaming white marble triple arches of this Imperial structure, so Roman in nature. A barbarian arriving from the north would have just left his mud-and-wattle hut in the forest. That was what his civilization knew how to build. He must have been awed. Was he also grateful, as I had read in history books for years, for the generosity of the far-off and mysterious emperor in having bestowed on his city this monument with its graceful Corinthian columns and tablature and magnificent coffered vaulting. The barbarian would not have needed a guidebook to tell him that this was a triumphal arch, that this was a monument to victory, the victory of Roman legions over his fellow tribesmen. The Romans designed the arch to tell the illiterate barbarian of his defeat and to impress him with the civilization of his conqueror. The message was as clear today as it was when the arch was built two thousand years ago.

As I walked around the arch, I realized that the entire structure was covered with friezes: friezes of naval trophies symbolizing Roman supremacy at sea; friezes depicting Roman legionnaires defeating naked, hairy Gauls; and a collage of trophies from these battles hanging from trees to symbolize Roman supremacy on land.* All the friezes celebrated Roman victory, and each would have evoked meaningful stories to the citizens living at the time during which the Republic of Rome was becoming the Empire, stories that began with Caesar's war in Gaul and ended with Actium, the great naval battle at which the forces of Augustus defeated those of Antony and Cleopatra.

I stopped and looked at the long bas-relief collage of captured trophies: torques (the bands of precious metal that Gallic warriors wore around their necks), shields, swords, and Gallic trousers. The Romans hung everything they captured from trees, including the pants worn by the Gauls. These trousers were actually quite a novelty to the toga- and tunic-wearing Romans. Only the Gauls living in the north of France wore trousers.† At the time that Caesar came, saw, and conquered Gaul, France was divided into two parts—the north and the south. The south, or Provence, had long been

---

*The carvings were not done by one artist but by a number of artists over a period of years, which explains why the style of the carvings differs from face to face.
†Capturing a pair of trousers may seem an odd trophy to the twentieth-century tourist, but to my mind it was definitely preferable to the favorite trophies of the Gauls—severed human heads, which they hung from their saddles or from lintels in their temples, or kept (embalmed in juniper oil) in chests in their homes, where they displayed them to unsuspecting guests. This Gallic obsession with the human head, which the Gauls felt contained the human spirit, was first noticed by a horrified early Greek colonist and was later chronicled by Caesar.

a fashionable and favorite resort for political exiles of the Greco-Roman world, Hellenized by the intellectual Greeks who had first settled there. It was prized for its climate, its wines, its fish soup, and its olives and spices. In the rest of France the Gauls still dressed unstylishly in trousers instead of the more chic white toga, didn't shave their faces, and wore their hair much too long and shaggy to be socially acceptable. Some of the ancients derisively referred to the northern half of France as "the trouser-clad place." It was Julius Caesar who arbitrarily labeled the area, which now contains northern France, Britain, and Belgium, "Gaul," which he divided into three parts and where he won the victory this arch commemorates. (This is a fact I wish I had known during my first year of Latin, when as a ninth-grader I parsed my way through Julius Caesar's *Commentaries on the Gallic War.* I was unable to find Gaul in my atlas and, considering the barbaric nature of the places Caesar described, could not figure out why he came, saw, and conquered it.)

In 36 B.C. Augustus gave Orange to the veterans of Caesar's Second Legion as a reward for their service in the Gallic Wars.

These wars, which lasted eight years, had begun in 58 B.C. Gallic chieftains asked Rome for help in driving off a tribe of 368,000 Helvetii who had migrated into France from Switzerland. For two years Republican Rome had ignored the request: in Republican Rome only defensive wars could be fought—wars of expansion were illegal, and the Helvetii posed no threat to Rome. But when Caesar became proconsul of Provence in 58 B.C., he realized he could use the two-year-old request to enrich and advance himself by conquering Gaul. He led ten thousand of his fierce, disciplined veterans against a huge horde of the Helvetii, killing 238,000 of them before he drove the rest back to Switzerland.

Vercingetorix, chief of the Averni, one of the many tribes of Gaul, watched Caesar's slaughter of the Helvetii and realized that although the Helvetii were gone, Caesar's legions were not. Vercingetorix realized that Caesar's "aid" meant the end of Gallic freedom. Traveling from tribe to tribe, appealing to his fellow Gauls' love of freedom, telling them "it was better to die fighting than to forfeit their ancient military glory and the liberty their ancestors had bequeathed them" (and cutting off ears and gouging out eyes when that appeal failed), he was able to unite the independent tribes of Gaul to fight Caesar and the Roman legions. His father, previously chief of the Averni, had been condemned to death for attempting to unite and make himself the king of these tribes, who shared a common culture and language. But Vercingetorix succeeded where his father had failed.

The Celts had defeated the Romans once, but that had been in 390 B.C., almost four hundred years before Caesar renamed them Gauls. At that time they had burst out of Central Europe, vanquishing and intermarrying with each of the tribes they encountered as they conquered western Europe and Britain. They were able to vanquish everyone because they had invented the double-edged sword, the atomic bomb of the Iron Age. Putting the second edge on a sword doesn't seem like much of an invention today, but twenty-four hundred years ago it gave the Gauls a definite edge over their enemies. (The double-edged sword symbolizes the Gallic double-edged temperament: warlike on the one hand and poetic on the other. Warlike, they learned to extract iron ore from stone and turn it into this new kind of sword; poetic, they saw the taking of iron from stone and transforming it into a sword as a magical act—one that, as the centuries passed, was transformed into marvelous tales of chivalry in which God gives the hero a great sword—always embedded in a rock—with which to defeat his enemies. As time passed, pagan legends became Christian miracles: Roland, the personification of the perfect Christian knight, is able to hold off a hundred thousand Saracens because of the divine properties of his sword, Durendal, which—to prevent its capture by the infidels—he flings into the air before dying; it magically lands embedded in a rock at the pilgrimage site of Rocamadour. Across the English Channel, King Arthur proves his right to the throne by removing Excalibur, the magic sword, from a stone.)

But in 58 B.C., when the tribes of Gaul, united under Vercingetorix, faced Caesar's legions, the Romans were the superior military force. Vercingetorix realized he couldn't defeat them in open battle—he had witnessed Caesar's cunning and siegecraft when the Romans slaughtered the Helvetii and knew that unexpected tactics had to be devised. Vercingetorix's strategy was brilliant: a combination of modern guerrilla warfare and scorched-earth policy, in which he convinced his fellow Gauls to burn over twenty of their cities to deny the Romans shelter and food, and then to attack the Romans as they searched for food. He must have been a very charismatic leader to have convinced the peasants to burn the homes, crops, and villages that lay in the path of the Roman advance. According to Caesar, Vercingetorix told his people that "these measures might be thought to be unfair and even terribly cruel; but . . . the alternative was infinitely worse: slavery for their wives and children, death for themselves—the universal fate of conquered peoples."

He almost succeeded in defeating Caesar and his invincible legions. However, when fellow Gauls begged him not to burn Bourges, their most beautiful city, he gave in. Since Vercingetorix did not burn Bourges, he had to defend it. He couldn't. Vercingetorix's defeat is brilliantly described by Caesar. Before the battle of Bourges, the Romans had been close to starvation and defeat, but Bourges's capture gave the Romans its stores of food and gold. Accused of cowardice in refusing to meet the enemy in open battle—Vercingetorix had argued that "the Romans had not won by courage in the open field, but by cunning and expert knowledge of siegecraft, with which the Gauls had not much acquaintance"—Vercingetorix finally was forced to fight a pitched battle against Caesar on the field of Alesia, outside Beaune. Vercingetorix watched the Roman legions slaughter his one hope for victory, the Gallic calvary, as well as thousands of his fellow tribesmen, and realized that the eight-year struggle for freedom was lost.

On the following day Vercingetorix addressed a meeting of Gallic chiefs and explained that "he had embarked upon this war not for private ends but in his country's cause. 'Now,' he said, 'I must bow to the decrees of Fate.' "

To prevent more of his men from dying, he bravely dressed himself in his best armor, rode into Caesar's camp, and gave himself up in exchange for an end to hostilities. When Vercingetorix offered himself to Caesar, he had expected—and wanted—instant death. But Caesar was the brilliant politician. Not only had he seen in the conquest of Gaul the source of the fame and wealth that would gain him control of Rome, but he also knew that the Gauls believed in instant reincarnation—they believed, he wrote, that "souls do not die but after death pass from one another"—and that the death of Vercingetorix would have to be delayed until he was forgotten. So Caesar kept him in a cage in Rome for six long years before having him strangled.

The bravery and love of freedom of this first great leader in the land that became France were not forgotten. Two thousand years later, during the Second World War, Vercingetorix would become a symbol of French resistance to the Nazi invaders.

The Roman Theater

OF ORANGE

I hurried back to our hotel to wake Bob. I was sorry I had seen the arch alone, and didn't want to visit the Roman Theater without him. As I recall, he had very little trouble persuading me to delay my visit until after he had had his breakfast at the hotel—after all, I could hardly expect him to eat alone. Although it was already lunchtime for me, I wanted to be companionable, and ordered the most breakfastlike dish on the menu—an omelette Provençale. To be honest, I don't know if my omelette was as delicious as I remember it. I still have the recipe, which our waiter was happy to get for me, but no matter how many times I make it, the combination of eggplant, tomatoes, truffles, black olives, and fresh spices, never tastes as good as I remember it tasting that day in Orange seventeen years ago.

We have been back to Orange many times since then, and each time we return, more of the ancient Roman city (Arausio) has been uncovered. As we entered the theater on our first visit, we passed a mysterious pile of stones, a city block wide and city block long. There was no explanation telling why the stones were there or, for that matter, why a perfect Roman theater was sitting here in southern France. Today, the stones are taking on a definite shape. A miniature ancient Rome is emerging from the rubble, painstakingly pieced together by French archaeologists. A gymnasium and temple now have enough stones back in place so that even someone not familiar with archaeological digs can discern what they are. Perhaps soon a forum and baths will emerge from the rubble as well. This is because the Orange of two thousand years ago *was* a miniature Rome, complete with many of the public buildings that would have been familiar to a citizen of the Roman Empire, except that the scale of the buildings had been reduced—a smaller theater to accommodate a smaller population, for example. The same was true of the nearby cities of Nîmes and Arles; and it was true of many of the cities built in France by the Roman legions after the first century. In addition, each of these cities was laid out on a typical plan so that a Roman citizen—whether traveling over the two hundred thousand miles of roads connecting the cities of the Empire or by boat across the Mediterranean Sea, from whose shores the Empire had spread—would feel at home.

If you have trouble imagining what Orange was like when France was part of the Roman Empire, you can visit the tiny museum located across the street from the theater. It contains a small painted model of Roman Orange. In the museum you can also begin to understand how seriously the Romans took their colonial cities. Hanging on the wall, like a giant jigsaw puzzle, is a tax map *(cadastre)* carved in marble, showing the plots of land that were allotted to the veterans as the sites of their retirement homes. During the reign of Augustus, who reformed the army, each soldier who completed his twenty-year tour of duty was given both land and Roman citizenship. Before retirement, soldiers were kept occupied in times of peace by constructing huge public-works projects like these marble cities, complete with triumphal arches, coliseums, theaters, forums, circuses, temples, baths, and fountains. Not only did this keep the citizens in the provinces happy and grateful to the emperor in far-off Rome, but it kept the soldiers too tired to cause trouble. For these landless, impoverished veterans, Provence must have been what America was for my grandfather in the nineteenth century—a chance to start over and raise a family on his own land.

While you need a bit of imagination to visualize the gymnasium and temple that greet you at the entrance to the Roman Theater of Orange, very little imagination is needed when you visit the theater itself. It was built for entertainments for the veterans of Caesar's Second Legion, who were given Orange, and enough of the theater remains to give you an idea of what it looked like during the Age of Augustus. No storm or hurricane these past two thousand years has disturbed the carefully laid stones of its towering tiers of seats.

Before entering the theater, we stopped at a café across the street. I wanted to take a good look at the exterior wall of the theater facing the street. Louis XIV, whose reign is often compared to the Age of Augustus, had called it "the finest wall in my kingdom," and I felt I should try to understand why. My first reaction upon seeing the wall was that this was some "vestige." The wall was huge—an immense rectangle 118 feet high and three times as long. Not until the Romans revolutionized architecture with their use of the arch could a wall this high have been constructed: the arch could support heavier weights than the post-and-lintel system used by the Greeks. The only decoration was the rough texture of the stones, the hints of false arches near the top of the wall, the straight lines of lintels, and, far overhead, a row of corbels that once supported awnings to block the sun. A row of arches marched along the street to support the huge rectangle. It was a sunny July afternoon, and the entire length of the wall was bathed in sunlight, so that the stones seemed golden. Sitting there for an hour or two, drinking coffee and watching the sun play with the textured stones, I was reminded of Monet's paintings of the Cathedral of Rouen, in which he captured the illusion of changing color as the sun moved across the sky. I found this aspect of the wall very appealing and began to view it as a giant impressionistic sculpture. However, I knew that color and natural illusion, though appealing to me and my generation, would not have appealed to Louis. It was the wall itself he admired. This immense structure would not have been possible without the arch.

And in a way, not yet clear in my mind, perhaps because I lacked Louis's dreams of empire, the Roman Empire would not have been possible without walls like this.

Then we entered the theater. Standing in the pit at the foot of the stage, I saw the towering scene wall—the last surviving one in Europe—behind the stage. This was the interior of the wall I had been contemplating from across the street. It was the Romans' architectural contribution to Greek theater design. Once, it was faced in gleaming green marble, and columns rose in tiers along it. Three of the columns are still intact, and portions of many others hint at the ornateness of decoration, which must have dazzled first-century audiences. I could now see that the wall had at each end a large rectangular tower containing storage areas for scenery. Actors could come out not only on stage level but also on a higher platform for scenes in which pagan gods were portrayed.

High above us, in a niche in the center of the wall, above the mortal players on the stage, above the platform where the gods played out their scenes, towering higher yet, gleaming in the hot sun of Provence, we saw a white marble statue of the emperor Augustus, who, like Louis, took as his symbol Apollo, God of the Sun. Staring out at the audience, Augustus, dressed in the tunic of a Roman general, rests his weight on one foot; the contrast between tensed and relaxed limbs gives the figure a feeling of potential movement and vitality. The statue is larger than life, two times larger than life. Godlike, you could say. And I believe most people living in Gaul did say so in the first century. As I looked up at the statue, I wondered if my guidebook had been mistaken about the side of the wall that Louis liked. This was definitely a statue of a man to whom Louis could relate. There is nothing "first among equals" or democratic about it. And if you had seen the statue in the first century, when a carved figure of a Gallic slave (now lost) kissed Augustus's foot, it would have seemed even less democratic. There was a pretense of retaining the Republic back in Rome when Octavian became known as Augustus and was *imperator.* He said:

In my sixth and seventh consulships, after I had stamped out the civil wars and at a time when by universal consent I was in absolute control of everything, I transferred the *res publica* from my own charge to the discretion of the Senate and the People of Rome. For this service I was given the name Augustus.

There was, however, no pretense in the provinces. Personality cults, which worshiped living men as gods, may have been abhorrent to Romans, but they had long been accepted in those provinces recently added to the Empire. Yet even in Rome, where his formal deification took place when he died, Augustus during his lifetime was revered as the "Divine Son" of Julius Caesar (who had been deified at *his* death) and as the "Savior who brought peace" (because it was Augustus who ended nearly a hundred years of civil war). In the provinces, especially the eastern portions formerly belonging to the Ptolemys of Egypt, which became part of the Roman Empire after the Battle of Actium, people were accustomed to worshiping their local rulers as gods, so the transition to emperor worship was easy. Augustus encouraged his deification in the provinces just as he encouraged the preservation of religious beliefs (whatever they were) throughout the Empire, because he believed they kept the masses obedient. Looking up at this statue, I had to say it was godlike—wise and beneficent. And Augustus had proved to be a wise and beneficent ruler of the provinces: instead of seeing them as a source of riches to be looted (as had been the case during the Republic), he saw them as an extension of Rome, a valve to regulate excess population, and he pursued a policy of huge public works in which theaters such as the one at Orange were built.

Standing in the center of this huge, majestic theater, I thought of the theaters that had preceded it—and how the Romans transformed everything they touched with their passion for unity and order and drama and grandeur, and their genius for physical construction.

This theater's ancestors began hundreds of years before in the pagan world: as little altars in secret grottoes where the annual harvest of the vine was celebrated with drunken, orgiastic revelry. Bacchanalian celebrants marched into sacred grottoes, playing flutes and cymbals, and formed a circle around their priest, who sacrificed a goat to show Dionysus, God of the Vine, their gratitude for magically transforming the juice of the grape into wine. Under the Greeks the altar on which the goat was sacrificed bisected the circle and became a stage; the priest began telling the legend of Dionysus in a more formal manner, and part of the chorus with whom he conversed became actors. The musical procession evolved into the orchestra, and you might say the goat (tragos in Greek) became tragedy, and the religious pretext for drunken revelry became comedy. Finally, the Feast of Dionysus became a competition in which poets vied with one another in retelling well-known tales of gods in dithyrambic verse intoned by choruses.

But the Greek theaters were small and intimate, and the emphasis was on the content of the play. The first audiences sat on bare hillsides; later on, the slopes were tiered with wooden planks, which gave way to seats made of stone or marble slabs.

Then came the Romans. Behind the stage they added an element all their own, the scene wall, which unified the structure architecturally. With their engineering skill at constructing walls of superimposed arches, they created freestanding tiers of seats, and were thus able to take theaters from natural hillsides and make them part of their cities. Rome was also order. The seats were divided into three sections so that the three classes of Roman society—the aristocracy, the middle class, and the slaves—would be separated.

People from Orange and the nearby villas came to the theater to be entertained. They came to see their favorite comedy or tragedy, or the popular troupes of mimes, acrobats, marionettes, and singers that toured the provinces. The audience sat under awnings protecting them from the rain and sun, eating fruit and sausages bought from hawking vendors, being sprayed with showers of perfumed water on hot days, watching actors whose masks were amplifiers. But though the design of the theater stayed the same for three centuries, Roman culture changed. Plays dwelled less on affairs of state or the complexities of human relationships. Entertainment became increasingly more lavish, bawdy, and obscene. Even simpleminded family farces, concerned with drunkenness, greed, and adultery, popular in first-century Rome, were, by the later years of the Empire, replaced by half-naked acrobats and mindless spectacles. And all during this passage of time, these passing centuries, while generations of people watched—the aristocracy from the bottom tier of seats, the middle class from theirs, and the slaves from the upper tier—it would have been unavoidable for them not to have been aware of the emperor's presence looking down on them. For this was a public place with a political function, and the dynamic statue of Augustus, with the Celtic slave kissing his foot in devotion to the Imperial regime, was a constant reminder of this fact.

As I sat in one of the best seats in the house, a seat once reserved for the aristocracy, drowsy in the warm Provençal sun, I was not the least bit sorry I had missed the last performance. To me, it is one of the ironies of history that it took six hundred years for the theater to evolve architecturally into the shape it finally became at Orange, and that by the time the Romans perfected their acoustical technology and engineering skills so that they were able to build theaters seating eleven thousand people in a setting grand enough for the tragedies the Greek playwrights had written in the fifth century B.C., there was, as on television, nothing very much to watch. I thought of the Roman general who, during the reign of Augustus, in some remote province of the Empire, sat listening with pleasure to his Greek slave recite Euripides, and I wondered why those ancient people who made up audiences for five hundred years, crying and laughing at the psychological dramas and political satires of Aeschylus, Sophocles, Euripides, and Aristophanes, the comedies of Menander and Plautus, stopped crying and laughing and began to demand mindless spectacle.

By the time—on that day in 1974—that I left the theater, I felt like Alice when she followed the white rabbit into Wonderland. I couldn't wait to see anything and everything that would tell me about that world of two thousand years ago. And while I was to find that there was no single town in Provence that possessed all the buildings which would have made up a typical provincial Roman city in the first century—many buildings had disappeared, their stones quarried to make newer buildings—I was to learn that by traveling to Nîmes, Arles, and Glanum in the Rhône Valley, which are all quite nearby, I would be able to see just about every type of building that would have made up a typical Roman provincial city.* Even though I couldn't see everything in one place, I could stay in one place and, by making day trips, never packing or unpacking, never driving more than an hour and usually quite a bit less, see the entire world of provincial Rome.†

---

*Roman ruins are being found throughout France. For example, there is a theater in Autun, also created during the reign of Augustus. The most exciting Roman baths I've come across were uncovered in the town of Metz while the museum directors were extending their fabulous museum downward. Narbonne, long the capital of the Roman province, is still in the process of uncovering its Roman ruins, and may have the best collection of mosaics, statues, and frescoes anywhere in France.

†Orange is not the most centrally located place to stay. Saint-Rémy-de-Provence is. Not far from Saint-Rémy is Les Baux, where, if you like being insulted, you can stay at a three-star Relais & Châteaux hotel with other Americans who are being insulted and overcharged for everything, including the spectacular view. I found the town bland, crowded, and commercial. The last time I was in the area, I stayed in a very romantic hotel outside the medieval town of Uzès, called the Hôtel Marie d'Agoult (after Franz Liszt's mistress, who was once its owner).

The Pont du Gard

That evening, I wanted to have dinner at the Vieux Moulin, a country inn from whose walled terrace, I was told, there is a spectacular view of the Pont du Gard, the aqueduct the Romans had built to carry water to the fountains of Nîmes from the springs of Eure thirty-one miles away.

We left Orange and headed south, by mistake taking the A7, which goes to Avignon, instead of the A9, which goes to Nîmes and the Pont du Gard. Worse things can happen. We got off the autoroute at the Avignon Nord exit and drove along a local road that runs along the banks of the Rhône. As we passed the Palace of the Popes in Avignon, I told Bob, who was driving in heavy local traffic, about the impressive walled city he was missing. Only after we crossed a modern bridge right next to "le Pont d'Avignon," which I had sung about in French class, were we able to pull

off the road so that he could look back across the Rhône at the walls surrounding the late-medieval palace and fortress. Several weeks later we visited the empty palace. It had been looted during the Revolution. Looking
at it from a distance was better.

Heading for the dinner and the aqueduct, we then took the N100 south
through a gently rolling valley of pale green hills buttoned with dark green
cypress trees. At first the drive seemed strangely relaxing. Then it dawned
on me: there were no other cars on the road. They were all vying for position on the autoroute.

We arrived at the restaurant about eight o'clock.

From our table on the terrace we had a perfect view of the aqueduct,
which runs across a wide gorge. The Pont du Gard is awe-inspiring. It is
truly one of the wonders of the world. In its hugeness, in its majesty, in the
regimented discipline of its three towering tiers of arches marching im-
placably across the river, it is the very essence of all that "Roman" means to
me. As the sun began to set, I began to understand why the Romans, unlike so many conquerors after them, were able not only to conquer Gaul
but to rule it for centuries. Capturing the hostile Gallic armies was the easy
part. Capturing the imagination of a defeated people was the hard part.
The legions that built the aqueduct are gone, but the arches remain—as if
the arches and not the legions were the real conquerors of Provence.

As the sun set, the rosy hue of the stone turned gray and military, and
then the arches began to fade into the night, as they had for nearly a million evenings before.

Just when the light was nearly gone, most of the men sitting on the terrace, including Bob, jumped up and ran toward the street, on the other side
of a low stone wall bordering one side of the restaurant. I had been looking
in the other direction, toward the craggy ravine carved by the Gard River,
watching the departing campers on the sandy beaches far below collect
their belongings, and the ordered, proportioned arches vanish one by one
into the night.

As I was watching the arches disappear, a Frenchwoman sitting close
to the entrance to the terrace saw her pocketbook disappear. Two men had
driven up; one got out, leaving the door of the car open and the motor running, walked into the restaurant, took her purse, ran back to the car, and

drove away. As a New Yorker, I hardly consider the theft of a pocketbook worth mentioning, except that the Frenchwoman's reaction was so different from what mine would have been. I would have felt a sense of violation, anger at myself and anger at the thief, as I had once when I found someone's hand in my purse. But she was furious at the restaurant owner for allowing such an incident to occur. I never would have thought of being angry at him. But she felt (and, I could tell by the level of her voice, very strongly) that it was his responsibility as a restaurateur to make sure she could concentrate on her food and not on her purse. I could hear her shouting at the poor man for at least fifteen minutes before he was able to get her inside the inn and close the door. As I tasted my second course, I thought it a shame that her energies had been wasted on the theft rather than on pointing out the kitchen's deficiencies. I don't mean to say the food was bad—my timbale of scallops was actually quite good—but the rest of the meal was not worthy of the view.

Since the twentieth century had intruded on my visit to this Roman structure, the following day we had our hotel (the Marie d'Agoult) pack us a picnic lunch, and we set off again for the Pont du Gard. We turned off Route D981 into a parking lot, where we left the car. After walking a short distance, we were able to leave the twentieth century completely behind. (This may not be possible in the near future. There is horrifying talk of turning this area into a theme park, a Roman Disney World, since the Pont du Gard isn't producing enough tourist dollars.) We walked along the shore of the Gard River, which flows through a heavily wooded and craggy ravine. And suddenly, as we came around a turn in the path, there in front of us, crossing the wild gorge, were three tiers of huge arches, one atop another, towering in the sky. Our view would have been little different from that of a Gallic tribesman when he came across it, or of Julius Fontius, a first-century Roman engineer and general who was given the post of water commissioner and who, inspecting the aqueducts under his command, exclaimed, "With such an array of indispensable structures carrying so many waters, compare, if you will, the idle Pyramids or the useless though famous works of the Greeks."

The great aqueduct—with its thirty-one miles of connecting covered canals—was built by Marcus Agrippa during his two-year governorship of

Gaul, 20 to 19 B.C. Nîmes already had enough drinking water for its fifty thousand inhabitants, but Agrippa, victor over Antony and Cleopatra at Actium, wanted the city that had been given to his veterans to have as many fountains as there were in Rome. At first I couldn't believe that Agrippa had built this aqueduct, considering everything else he accomplished in his life. Agrippa had been Octavian's close friend at school when, on the Ides of March in 44 B.C., the future Augustus learned of his uncle's assassination. It was Agrippa who urged his friend to go to Rome and claim his rights as Julius Caesar's heir. As great an engineer as he was a general, Agrippa restored Rome's aqueducts, cleaned its sewers, constructed its baths, laid out its parks, and designed one of the most beautiful buildings in the ancient world—the Pantheon—which he dedicated to his dear friend Augustus, who had by then become his father-in-law.

It seemed impossible that this colossal structure standing in the wilderness of southern France was built by the same man, that he had sat here, near this rock where Bob and I were picnicking, and, with his wax tablet, abacus, and level, determined that the springs of Eure were only fifty-six feet higher than the city of Nîmes, and then calibrated the descent of connecting canals at .34 meter per mile—so that the twenty thousand cubic meters of water that would rush into the city each day would not flow so fast as to destroy the aqueduct or so slow that limestone deposits would build up and block the canal. So accurate were his calculations that the Pont du Gard carried water to Nîmes for nine hundred years. So precisely were the blocks of masonry cut—some weighing as much as six tons—that they were laid, after being hoisted into place by hundreds of legionnaires and slaves, without mortar or cement, and they stand as solidly today as they did two thousand years ago, when they were put into place.

Incredibly, during those nine hundred years the canals didn't leak. Learning the recipe used to waterproof and seal the canals—lime, pork fat, and the latex of unripe figs—I jotted it down, and will give it to my superintendent if he fails again *this* year to fix the leak in my apartment ceiling.

The Pont du Gard continued to be used as a bridge centuries after the stones of the connecting aqueducts had been carried off to build other structures. During the Middle Ages the Romans and their engineering methods were forgotten. Men attempting to span the wild Gard River saw their modern bridges repeatedly—actually, until 1958—swept away. However, the Pont du Gard continued to stand. On one of its blocks is a bas-relief of a phallus, which the Romans believed warded off the evil eye and which, therefore, was carved on public buildings. A local legend, inspired by this strange symbol, and later written down by the poet Frédéric Mistral, explained why the Pont du Gard did not fall. According to this story, the devil constructed the bridge in one night in exchange for a promised soul. When the soul turned out to be a rabbit, he flung it against the bridge. The phallus was said to be the rabbit.

The miles of arches of the connecting canal marching across the countryside provide other benefits. On another day, Bob and I were on our way to the Pont du Gard with a picnic lunch when Bob noticed a sign to the Pont Rou. Turning off D227, we came to a little circle that seemed to be in the middle of nowhere, followed the road just a little farther, and parked. Across a field was a row of Roman arches. Happily, the wind that was blowing that day was not the unpredictable mistral, but a delicious breeze filled with the aroma of wild rosemary and thyme. We spread our blanket on top of one of the arches. I don't know if it was the scent of wild spices, the feel of the ancient bridge, the wonderful pâtés, salads, cheeses, bread, and Rhône wine we had purchased, or the wild loneliness of the place—but it was the most perfect spot for a picnic.

The Provincial City of Nîmes

On our first trip to Provence, like most tourists we visited and loved Arles: spent sunny sleepy days ambling along its narrow streets; visiting its Roman theater, coliseum, and Baths of Constantine, its museums of pagan art and early Christian art, and its subterranean granary, or cryptoporticus; and eating lunch in one of its many lively restaurants or sipping coffee at the bustling Place du Forum. However, on succeeding visits, as the Arles van Gogh painted disappeared year by year into a city jammed with tourists and their cars, and the scaffolding covering the façade of the Romanesque Cathedral of Saint-Trophime remained, we transferred our affections to Nîmes, a city to the southwest, which possesses not only the most impressive Roman monuments in France but also life and vitality beyond tourism.

While we have never stayed in Nîmes itself, the Hôtel Marie d'Agoult in Arpaillargues, just outside Uzès, my favorite hotel in the Rhône Valley, is admirably located for taking trips there. A country road winds its way from the d'Agoult for seventeen miles through the nondescript town of Blauzac and then, on Route D979, dramatically through craggy limestone hills, called *garrigues,* toward the gorge crossed by the Pont Saint-Nicolas, a Gothic arched bridge built by the Frères Pontifes, a religious brotherhood of bridge builders. At one end of the bridge stands a ruined tower where during the Middle Ages the local lord stationed armed sentries to collect tolls from anyone who wished to cross; at the other end is one of the few places wide enough to park a car on this isolated, narrow, twisting road, and the view there is worth stopping for. (I mention this so that if you are approaching the bridge, you will know when to signal the French driver who appears to be attached to your rear bumper that you are about to pull off the road.)

The view from the bridge changes dramatically with the seasons. In July the river is sand and a puddle, and it is hard to imagine why anyone on foot or horseback would have needed a bridge—and have had to pay a toll—to cross. However, in May, when we saw it, the Gard River is full of itself; then it is the raging river that chiseled and hacked away at the soft limestone *garrigues* over centuries to create the deep gorge crossed by the bridge. The landscape, with the carved gorge and the unweathered shapes of hills thrown up by nature thousands of years ago and untouched by man or God since, is spectacular. As we got out of the car, we could smell wild lavender, thyme, and rosemary in spite of the fumes from the long line of cars that had passed us, and from the center of the bridge I could see miles and miles of a wild countryscape of steep cliffs and jagged white-topped hills, with scraggly bushes clinging to whatever crevices their roots could find.

Beyond the bridge the road twists and turns some more, and then, suddenly, we were out of nature's *garrigues* and in the bustling Mediterranean city of Nîmes.

Nîmes, like Arles, had been a Gallic fortified settlement, and then a trading post in the Greek colony that slowly spread north along the Rhône from the major Greek port at Marseille (Massalia), established in 600 B.C. For the next four centuries Provence remained a Greek colony, and the Romans had little interest in this sunny land along France's Mediterranean crescent. In Republican Rome the Senate could not authorize wars of expansion, only defensive ones. Colonies outside Italy were established mainly as buffers and protection for Italy itself. Since Greece was then an ally of Rome, the Romans viewed the friendly Greek colony in southern France as ample protection—particularly since between it and Italy lay the formidable barrier of the Alps. Hannibal, the great general of the Carthaginian army, taught the Romans that they were wrong.

Instead of attacking Rome by sailing from Africa as his father, Hamilcar Barca, had done when he lost the First Punic War (264–241 B.C.), Hannibal, a military genius, attacked Rome by taking a route I would have thought only a travel agent would select, the scenic route, across two seemingly impassable mountain ranges: the Pyrénées and the Alps. Hannibal crossed these mountain ranges as a psychological ploy—an early recorded instance of psychological warfare. According to myths believed by the Romans, the hero Hercules could never be defeated. Hannibal wanted his contemporaries to compare him with Hercules, wanted to be thought of as the hero's equal; since Hercules had crossed both the Alps and the Pyrénées, Hannibal felt that if he, too, crossed them, his enemies would believe that he, like Hercules, could never be defeated, so why try. And he furthered the comparison with another psychological ploy. Hercules had brought with him the oxen of Geryon (the monster with three heads, six hands, and three bodies). Hannibal brought his own monsters: elephants—fifty-eight of them. (The elephants' attitude toward this trek was not improved by the narrowness of the mountain passes through which they had to squeeze or by the Gauls, who were whooping and hollering on the far shore of the Rhône as the Carthaginians tried to float the huge beasts across on rafts.)

Hannibal brought the elephants to awe and frighten the Gauls and Romans: to awe the Gauls so that they would join forces with him; and to intimidate the Roman soldiers so that they would be too afraid to fight. The ploy worked with the Gauls, who hurried to join Hannibal's army; but in the centuries of Rome's glory, no one intimidated Rome. Roman senators countered with their own psychological strategy. They staged a circus in

Rome and invited their legions to attend. During the circus a mere hand-
ful of slaves armed only with prods directed a great number of tame elephants in the arena so that the soldiers would not be frightened by these
strange beasts when they encountered them in battle. (At the picture-per-
fect castle at Tarascon, which you pass if you cross the Rhône traveling
from Arles to Nîmes, you will find a series of tapestries depicting Hannibal's trip across southern France and his battle with the Roman general Sci-
pio. While the Greeks were unable to defend Gaul from Hannibal's army,
they did warn Rome so that his attack was stripped of the element of surprise.)

Hannibal's war with Rome lasted fifteen years, and although he won
many great battles, he eventually lost. As a result of the Second Punic War
(218–201 B.C.), Spain was annexed to Rome. The Third Punic War followed, and when it ended with the total destruction of Carthage, in 146
B.C., the Romans wanted to make sure that their border with southern
France and their lucrative trade route with Spain were secure. Hannibal
had demonstrated that the Alps could be crossed and that the Greeks could
not defend the area, so the Romans turned southern France into a Roman
province. They stationed garrisons in towns between the Alps and the
Pyrénées, an area that became the Province of Gallia Narbonensis, or "the
Province." Its capital was Narbonne and it included the areas now called
Provence, Languedoc, Roussillon, and Savoy. During this early period of
Roman occupation, southern France was viewed as a source of slaves, trib-
ute, extortion, and plunder. Its Roman governors were noted for their cor-
ruption.

However, after the Battle of Actium in 31 B.C., when Octavian became Augustus and the Republic became the Empire, Roman policy
changed toward settlements outside Italy. Augustus conceived of a simple
solution to socioeconomic problems that had been causing civil war and
unrest in Italy for over a hundred years: landless peasants, idle and rebellious veteran soldiers, and insufficient food for a growing population,
which, spoiled by a growing dependence on slaves, no longer wanted to
work. The provinces, previously regarded as a source of wealth, became
under Augustus an extension of Rome, where landless citizens not only
could be removed from Rome and settled far away but could produce

food and goods for the Italian peninsula. The aging legionnaires could also be settled there, removing them as a source of unrest in Rome and at the same time expanding the Empire and protecting its borders. The emperor reduced the number of legions from sixty to twenty-eight and gave each retiring legion a city and the surrounding countryside, whose land was divided among the veterans as reward for their years of service and their victories. The Second Legion of Julius Caesar, we saw, was given Orange. His Sixth Legion, which had been victorious over Pompey at Marseille, was given Arles. And the legions that had defeated Antony and Cleopatra at Actium—the legions that had given Augustus absolute control of the Empire—were given Nîmes (Nemausus) and twenty-four surrounding cities subject to Nîmes's control. Augustus used the wealth of the Ptolemys, which came to him after Cleopatra's death, to purchase land for his veterans. But the brilliant emperor knew it wasn't enough merely to settle these veterans in the provinces. Soldiers who had returned from years of looting wanted the comforts of Rome, the free entertainments of the circus and the arena, the free food they felt had become their due. Augustus had the genius to build theaters and arenas in these far-off places and make the provincial cities clones of Rome, or as Livy, a friend and protégé of Augustus, wrote, "more like Italy than Italy."

The old Herculean route that Hannibal had taken became the Via Domitia, connecting Nîmes with Spain and Italy, a small part of thirteen thousand miles of roads the Romans built in Gaul, which in turn was a small part of the two hundred thousand miles of roads they built throughout the Empire to connect the new marble cities.

Nîmes, once a Gallic settlement, then a Greek trading post, then a Roman outpost, became a jewel in a necklace of provincial cities that adorned the Empire of Augustus. The emperor was lavish in the construction of public works in this provincial city given to the veterans, building the Pont du Gard, public baths, temples, a forum, a coliseum, and a circus. An inscription carved on the architrave above the gateway, or Porte d'Arles, says that the gates and adjacent walls were a personal gift: "The Emperor Augustus Caesar, son of god, consul for the eleventh time . . . gives these walls and gates to the colony."

It was not difficult for the soldiers settled here, who had spent so much of their lives in Egypt, where the pharaoh was worshiped as a god, to worship Augustus as a god as well. The Imperial cult flourished here with a new priesthood—the Augustales—seventy-five strong in Nîmes, for the service of the new divinity.

The Maison Carrée

In Nîmes there is a temple similar to the Temple of Apollo that Augustus built in Rome when he took the Sun God as his patron. Nîmes's temple, now called the Maison Carrée, was built in memory of Augustus's grandsons, Gaius and Lucius Caesar. The emperor had hoped that these young princes, the sons of his daughter Julia by Marcus Agrippa, the victorious general at Actium and builder of the Pont du Gard, would succeed him as emperor. But, like each of the several heirs he chose, they died before he did. Only Tiberius, whom Augustus hated, survived. After the two young princes died, monuments were erected to them throughout the Empire.* To honor his sons' memory, Agrippa built the Maison Carrée, the most perfectly preserved Roman temple in existence.

---

*In this area there is a beautiful mausoleum outside Saint Rémy at Glanum, one of several Roman monuments referred to in tour books as Les Antiques.

It is built in the "hexastyle pseudoperipteral style"—a convenient phrase to know if you take tours, as we once did, with guides who turn to their group and say, without further explanation, "Here we have a perfect example of the hexastyle pseudoperipteral style used by the Romans on all their temples after the Augustan principate." The term simply refers to the adaptations made by the Romans to Greek temple design. The Greek temple, like the Parthenon, was open and surrounded by a peristyle, or row of columns. The old-style Roman temple was enclosed by a wall. And, based on ancient Etruscan designs, it was set on a huge raised podium so that it towered over and impressed the worshiper, who was forced to look up as he approached the broad front steps. The Romans liked the Greek columns but wanted to keep the temple enclosed, so they placed columns only in front to create an open porch, its six *(hexa)* front columns and two side columns forming three open bays. Because the main hall was still enclosed, the worshiper was forced to enter through this front porch. To keep the Greek peristyle look, the Romans attached "pseudo" columns, not totally round and not weight-bearing, to the solid walls.

As I looked at the Maison Carrée, I could see the Greek influence on Roman architecture. I could see how the Romans took the beautiful Greek peristyle and created the illusion of surrounding the temple with Corinthian columns, flattening and squashing them on the sides of the *cella,* the main room. The Maison Carrée has inspired generations of architects and rulers. French architects studied and copied it during the French Renaissance. Louis XIV liked it so much that he wanted to move it to his gardens at Versailles. Napoleon used it as a model for the Madeleine in Paris. Thomas Jefferson used it as the model for the State House in Richmond, Virginia. But as much as I had been looking forward to seeing it (and as glad as I naturally was to see a concrete example of the hexastyle pseudoperipteral style), my only feeling on my first visit was that it was perfectly unexciting.

I tried to be excited by the Maison Carrée. I had read how perfect it was, how beautiful it was. Perhaps I had read too much, or seen too many imitation classical temples. Perhaps my disappointment was caused by the temple's location in the center of a bustling modern city, rather than facing the open space of the Forum. It was impossible for me to step back and look at it as I approached from the direction the Romans had intended me to use. I believe that the twentieth century must have invaded too much of the space around it, because a woman describing her "summer ramble" in 1842 wrote, "Italy does not possess a gem of antiquity more perfect than the famous Maison Carrée. Its peculiar form and dimensions, the delicacy of its sculptures, and the magnificence of the ornaments that adorn it, combine to render it a chef d'oeuvre of art . . ."

When I said that I liked Nîmes because it has a life beyond tourism, I didn't mean to imply that there was no desire to make its Roman vestiges, such as the Maison Carrée, appeal to a greater number of tourists. The last time we were in the area, in July of 1991, we watched an event called the Via Tegulae. It may have been an expression of civic pride—or simply a failed but blatant attempt to attract the tourist trade. Whatever, those participating in it seemed to have a ball. Two hundred men and women dressed in Roman togas and Gallic costumes, some on foot, others riding in ox-drawn chariots, and twenty-five others in brightly colored ass-drawn carts, made their way from the city of Millau to the Maison Carrée. The caravan stopped at several towns along the way, celebrating with a spectacle each night. The ostensible purpose of the trip was to carry tiles from Millau to Nîmes. These tiles were copies of the ones that had covered the Maison Carrée in the first century. Archaeologists had recently discovered one of the originals, which had been made in Millau by ancient Gallic potters. Now the caravan bore new tiles, made with the same materials and methods those Gallic potters had once used, along an old Roman route (Via Tegulae) joining the two cities. During another parade, which I think I'm glad I missed, men from Nîmes dressed themselves as Roman soldiers and rode motorcycles surrealistically disguised as crocodiles.

The Roman Amphitheater

Although in 1991 we visited Nîmes in July, we usually take our vacations in May, when the Pentecostal Feria is held. The first time we attended this festival, which lasts for ten days, we were carried through the city on a tide of people who had come to see the bullfights. All along the boulevard leading to the Roman Amphitheater, there had sprung up brightly colored tents selling paella from large round pans, as well as other local foods. Music was playing everywhere. Every corner we turned seemed to hold a delightful surprise, and every square had been turned into a stage. We encountered a mime, then a puppeteer, a group of folk dancers, Gypsies, musicians dressed in peasant costumes playing music native to Languedoc, others from neighboring Provence. We were literally caught up in the *abrivado,* the ritual in which bulls are chased into the arena, and we had to scramble to the top of a TV truck as a wild horde of young men chased some very scrawny bulls through the streets. The only thing I did not enjoy was the actual bullfight. (I prefer the Courses Provençales, which also takes place in Nîmes. It is like a pizza without hot pepper, since the bull is not killed. The spectacle consists of extremely agile men *(razetteurs)* trying to seize a cockade from between the bull's horns. The fun in the sport is watching the *razetteurs* try to avoid the horns of charging bulls by leaping over the barricade that surrounds the arena floor.) The bullfights and the Courses Provençales take place inside the ancient coliseum, or amphitheater, which today, as in the first century, holds twenty-four thousand people.

Once, while attending a bullfight with a French guide, it occurred to me that the present-day spectacle was quite similar to a ritual practiced in this area during the first and second centuries A.D. The Roman soldiers, who had spent so much of their lives in the east before being settled in Nîmes, brought back with them not only the tractability to worship the Roman emperor as a god but other eastern religions as well, including Mithraism. In the ritual of this cult, a priest representing the savior Mithra would plunge his curved sword into the bull in such a way that the blood would erupt and cover him, purify him—purge him and all the world of sin. While watching the matador plunge his sword into the bull, I happened to mention to my guide that perhaps there was a connection between this bloody spectacle, at which I was about to throw up, and the long-forgotten religious ritual. The guide, an erudite Frenchman, glared at me. I was feeling too ill to figure out whether he was angry at the comparison or, once again, at my accent. He pointed out that during the Gallo-Roman period the ritual of Mithra was performed in secret grottoes outside Nîmes, while the amphitheater was where Christians were killed by charging bulls. I stood corrected.

The amphitheater, the Arènes of Nîmes, was built approximately eighty years after the theater at Orange. Roman engineers were by that time adept at using the arch and a new quick-drying cement discovered in the first century, and were thus able to design freestanding structures. As the word implies, the amphitheater architecturally completes the semicircle the theater had begun. Two tiers of sixty arches each circle the coliseum in Nîmes, as opposed to the eighty arches at the Coliseum in Rome. Since the spectacles at that time were free, provided by the government to keep the colonials happy, each of the sixty arches on the ground level provided an entrance and exit for the spectators. (Today most of the arches are fenced off and people are herded through the main arch so that admission can be collected.)

Seating, divided into four sections, reflected the hardening of the class structure that took place during the relatively short time that had elapsed since the theater of Orange was built. The great wealth that resulted from both the conquest of Gaul (51 B.C.) and the conquest of Egypt (31 B.C.) was not evenly distributed throughout Roman society but flowed into the hands of a very few. Those few, of course, did not view the new situation pejoratively; however, a huge gulf was created between the very rich and very poor. Previously, even the distinction between slave and master had not been as great as vocabulary would suggest, and a degree of class mobility existed. Slaves, particularly Greek slaves, who were considered intellectually superior to their Roman masters, could gain both their freedom and Roman citizenship. Social mobility gradually decreased as the gulf between rich and poor became impossible to cross, and class lines hardened. The change in society was reflected in the seating in the amphitheater, which was far more segregated than in the theater built only eighty years earlier. The amphitheater was so arranged that each class—the senatorial, the equestrian, the plebeian orders, the slaves—could enter and leave without coming into contact with the other classes. They poured in and out of their own (I love this visually descriptive Latin word for exit ramp) *vomitorium* into separate circular corridors and terraces. The design was originally intended to further the comfort of the spectator. Vitruvius, the great Roman engineer and architect who would become the idol of architects during the Age of Louis XIV, wrote:

> It is necessary to spread out the numerous and spacious access ways, so that those coming from above do not meet those coming from below; it should be possible to reach them from any seat, by direct link and without returning, in such a way that . . . people are not squeezed together, but that each one finds, no matter which seat he has occupied, a separate exit which presents no obstacles.

The comfort of the spectator was taken into consideration in other ways. As at the theater, people did not sit in the sun or rain; they were protected by huge canvases that, like sails, were manipulated by cables supported by wooden poles.

The symbol of Nîmes was the crocodile of the Nile in chains, symbolizing Cleopatra's defeat at Actium. The coin minted in ancient Nîmes showed the faces of Agrippa and Augustus on one side and a crocodile chained to a palm tree on the other. There are hints that it was not only Roman veterans of Actium but Egyptian captives who were brought to this city. The Egyptians, however, were not given grants of land, nor did they live in villas. They came to Nîmes in chains, as slaves. It was slaves who fought as gladiators in the Arènes. While a few men became gladiators out of destitution, most gladiators had once been free men: Picts and Celts captured in Britain and northern Gaul, Germans captured in battles along the Rhine, Moors captured in battles in the Atlas Mountains, and later, much later, Goths, Franks, and Saxons who had fought the spread of the Roman Empire into their homelands and, having lost, had been condemned to spend their lives fighting for the entertainment of the masses in arenas throughout the Empire, provincial copies of the Coliseum at Rome.

In the beginning, the spectacles had a strict formality, and schools sprang up to train contestants. The most famous school for gladiators in France was in Autun. In A.D. 21, Julius Sacrovir, a Gallic nobleman from Provence who hated Roman "pride and arrogance," led a revolt against Roman taxation—and placed gladiators trained at Autun in the front ranks of his army of forty thousand. Sacrovir also had a secret weapon, developed at Autun—armor made of a single plate of iron—but his weapon misfired. Tacitus, unable to restrain his amusement, tells us that their "armor was impenetrable to the stroke of the enemy, but at the same time rendered the men too unwieldy to move." (Since they were unable to move, the Roman legions of Tiberius defeated them. However, when Tiberius rededicated the arch of Orange to himself, natives of this area carved Sacrovir's name on it, a form of Gallic graffiti.)

Schools like the one at Autun trained the slave to be not just a gladiator but a charioteer, a *retiarius,* or a *secutor.* For example, in a contest between a *secutor,* who was armed with a helmet, sword, and buckler (round shield with a strap for the arm), and a *retiarius,* who was naked and armed with a large net and a trident, the object was for the *retiarius* to entangle the *secutor* with his net and then kill him with the trident. If he missed his first throw, he was usually in trouble, obliged to "fly from the pursuit of the *secutor* 'til he had prepared his net for a second cast." One *retiarius* became so popular with the crowds at Nîmes that when he was finally killed, his epitaph was carved on the wall of the Arènes. The most popular gladiator was Faustus the Arab, a charioteer who won thirty-seven crowns.

The spectacles in the amphitheater were staged with great pageantry. One in particular has a note of poignancy, given the history of the men who were watching it. Nîmes's arena could be flooded by subterranean pipes with water brought there over the aqueduct built by Agrippa, the general who had won at Actium. The water would turn the fine-grained sand that had soaked up the blood of defeated gladiators into a red sea on which Egyptian-style ships, manned with Egyptian slaves, would fight, over and over, the battle Cleopatra had lost. And among the twenty-four thousand people cheering the spectacle and turning thumbs up or down were the descendants of the Roman legionnaires who had been victorious over the Egyptians on that day.

Les Alpilles

AND THE END OF ANTIQUITY

B ob and I had been staying outside Uzès at the Hôtel Marie d'Agoult, which we love so much, dining each night in its romantic garden and making daily trips to the world of provincial Rome, never driving more than an hour, and usually quite a bit less. We had visited Orange, Nîmes, the Pont du Gard, Arles, and Glanum, and had seen just about every type of structure that would have been found in a typical provincial Roman city. Since the Romans built each city in the provinces alike so that a citizen of Rome would feel at home no matter where he traveled throughout the Empire, each city was laid out in a similar manner—on a rectangular grid, the center of which was supposedly fixed according to a sighting on the sun on the day the town was founded. Each city had its forum, temple, theater, circus, public baths, and triumphal arch—modeled on its counterpart in

Rome but scaled down in size. And in every city the location of each building was the same in relation to the others. Therefore, a Roman merchant
traveling from city to city in the first century could have found his way to
market, theater, or temple without the fatigue that strangeness causes. A
traveler today, while unable to see an entire provincial Roman city in one
place, can, by taking day trips, acquire a mental image of what such a city
was like, at the same time having the pleasure of visiting the delightfully
different towns built along the Rhône.

I wanted to visit the Roman ruins in France not just to visualize a
provincial Roman city but to visit the foundations out of which France
emerged. For example, while the Arch of Triumph at Glanum (21 B.C.) is
typically Roman, the Arch of Triumph at Orange (A.D. 21), completed
about fifty years later, is already altered by the soul of France. The coliseum
and the Maison Carrée of Nîmes are the best-preserved coliseum and temple from this period; after seeing them, you understand how they inspired
architects in the centuries that followed. Visiting Nîmes, you see the past in
the city's present, a Roman heritage echoed in modern sculptures and fountains and, of course, arches—arches in the façades of banks and office
buildings and in parks and plazas, nineteenth- and twentieth-century
arches found everywhere throughout the city, a rondo of modern variations
on the great Roman theme. Roman cities may have been stamped out as little clones of Rome, but, like Nîmes during the intervening twenty centuries, they evolved in different ways.

Much as I enjoy traveling through the world of provincial Rome, however, the Roman era was only a brief phase in French history, and it was
time for us to leave for the next phase: the period of violence and anarchy
once known as the Dark Ages. The Dark Ages began when the barbarians—the Ostrogoths, the Franks, the Huns, the Saracens, the Vikings—
swept down upon France and drove the Romans out. This was the first period of the Middle Ages, during which France was plundered and pillaged.
Roman theaters, sewer systems, and schools disappeared. The seas were
closed to commerce, first the Mediterranean by the Saracens, and then the
Atlantic by the Vikings. Cities atrophied as France was forced to turn in on
herself and commerce between cities virtually came to an end. The emperor Charlemagne (768–814) provided a brief period of peace and order by

uniting France and organizing it into counties under his central administration. But weak descendants and subsequent wars of succession resulted in the gradual dissolution of Charlemagne's empire until there was no central authority, and the entity known as France splintered into scores of independent feudal domains, each ruled by its hereditary lord.

These lords were constantly engaged in petty wars primarily designed to increase their domains. It was a time of disorder in which the only unifying force was the Roman Catholic Church. During this time, sometimes called the Age of Faith, the Church built a system of monasteries throughout the countryside. As commerce revived, the Church erected cathedrals in the cities. Although it is difficult to date precisely the beginning or end of the Middle Ages (the term merely refers to a span of time between the end of the ancient Greco-Roman world and the beginning of the Renaissance) because the dates change from historian to historian and from province to province, the Middle Ages lasted approximately a thousand years, ending in France in 1494, after the end of the Hundred Years War. (This description of the Middle Ages, is, of course, a terrible oversimplication, as we will see vividly on our subsequent travels in France.)

While the Middle Ages may not have been a terrific period to have lived through, especially if you liked to bathe frequently, or to read, or were opposed to rape, pillage, and plague, it is certainly a visually exciting period to visit. The medieval architecture of France, with its turreted and moated castles, its soaring cathedrals and fortified monasteries, evokes a time of wandering troubadours and chivalrous knights, of pious monks and avaricious priests.

Bob and I were about to head northwest into the Middle Ages, to visit the medieval monastery of Fontfroide, the fortified medieval city of Carcassonne, the fortified medieval cathedral at Albi, the pilgrimage sites of Conques and Rocamadour, and the feudal castles of Beynac and Castelnaud, as well as a soaring Gothic cathedral at Bourges. While I couldn't wait to enter this medieval world, I hated to leave my hotel and Provence. Each time we stay at the d'Agoult, I'm afraid it will be the last time, since it is so out of the way: the last time I will have dinner under the spreading fig tree in the pebbled garden, served by friendly waiters who always suggest some wonderful inexpensive local wine to sip with dinners that, no matter how long we stay, are always delightful. On our next-to-last night I became teary as I sat at our table facing the garden, with its mysterious little fountain hidden in a paganlike grotto. I began to miss my room—where, I imagine, Marie d'Agoult once entertained her lovers—with its antique secretary and marble fireplaces, its shabby oriental rug, its mysterious little door, its bathroom with the almost life-sized mosaic of Venus rising from the sea. That evening as I descended the stairs to get our bucket of ice, I fondled the large stones hollowed by centuries of footsteps with my bare feet. I got up early the next morning to take a swim by myself in the oversized pool, where water spouts from bronze dolphin heads.

I couldn't bear to leave without taking one last drive through the Alpilles, a range of limestone cliffs whose white shapes against blue skies look like monstrous ocean waves thrown into motion by hurricane winds, yet seem to shelter the many little towns nestled in valleys that stretch from Avignon to Arles. And on this drive we discovered by accident, even before we left Provence, a wonderful hint of the Dark Ages we were heading into.

Languedoc

Saint-Roman

AND THE DARK AGES

Practically every day of the two weeks we had been in Provence, we had passed a sign pointing to "Saint-Roman" when we drove through the town of Beaucaire. (Because of the location of the Hôtel Marie d'Agoult, no matter where we were going, we almost always had to drive through Beaucaire.) I had never noticed the sign on previous trips, so out of curiosity I bought a local guidebook and learned that Saint-Roman was an abbey that during the fifth century had been carved by monks out of a cave in which ascetic hermits, fleeing from civilization, had lived for two centuries before that.* Since the guidebook said that most of the abbey had been destroyed over the centuries and the main reason for tourists to visit it now was its panoramic view of the Rhône Valley, I had decided to give it a miss; I had already seen a sufficient number of panoramic views of the Rhône.

*You will see the word "troglodyte" used in guidebooks to describe this abbey and other sites. All "troglodyte" means is that the site is in a cave.

On our sentimental last drive through the Alpilles, however, we found ourselves behind an excruciatingly slow truck in a traffic jam outside Beaucaire—and there again was the "Saint-Roman" sign. We impulsively turned off the road and headed for the abbey, hoping the traffic would disappear by the time we finished our visit. The first thing to disappear, however, was any sign leading to the abbey. Then the road to which the one and only sign had pointed disappeared. It became narrower and narrower, then turned into a gravel path, and then even that path came to an abrupt end. We got out of the car. Far above us, dismayingly far above us, on a rather rugged limestone *garrigue,* too far away for us to see it clearly, was something that might have been an abbey (but probably was just a wall-shaped limestone outcropping). We climbed a dirt footpath for over an hour, during which time the path became narrower and steeper and my shirt became wetter and wetter with perspiration. Then the path disappeared. (The supposed abbey disappeared, too, since turnings in the path and a heavy growth of scrub brush had caused it to vanish from our sight.) As we walked single file through the brush, I kept assuring Bob, whose shirt was even wetter than mine, that we must be heading in the right direction, because each time we looked back, the view of the Rhône Valley was better. However, I finally had to give up because my sandals couldn't handle the loose pebbles of the rocky slope (which—although I did not feel it necessary to mention this to Bob, who had fallen somewhat behind—was about to descend into a gulley). We turned back without having come anywhere near the hilltop.

On our final day in Provence we were driving once again through Beaucaire but this time on another road (Route 999). We passed still another sign reading "Saint-Roman," and perhaps because I was now about to enter the Age of Faith, we turned off the highway and onto a one-lane paved road that wound up the steep slope of another limestone *garrigue.* Halfway up the slope, we came to a tree-shaded parking lot, where a large placard told about the excavation of the Abbey of Saint-Roman and gave directions for getting to it—on foot. Luckily, we happened to be properly shod with sneakers this time, and we set out on a bulldozed and graded path definitely more well-trodden than the one we had taken the day before. As we climbed, the path became rockier and more sunbaked, the trees that had provided shade at the beginning of the walk gave way to scrub, and the dry white soil reminded me of Texas caliche. After only a half hour, and before we were sweating too badly, we came to a broad terrace on which stood the remains of a magnificent wall; above us we could see the entrance to the abbey itself. But there was no sign of life. About ten minutes later an elderly couple came up the path. We would have asked them whether they knew when and if the abbey opened, but they were quite pink from the sun and panting too hard to answer.

The entrance to the cave was in the rock still some distance above our heads. That entrance was reachable only if we climbed a rather crudely hammered-together set of wooden steps, with a loose guard rope on one side, that led to a makeshift plywood platform, also with a guard rope. At the base of the steps there was a large wooden sign: "Danger Do Not Enter." It seemed like good advice. As we strolled along the terrace around the top of the *garrigue,* from which the abbey had been hollowed out, we found extensive views of the Rhône Valley, including Avignon, Mont Ventoux, the Lubéron, the Alpilles, and the castle at Tarascon, spread out below us. Although the temperature when we began the climb was well into the nineties—it was July, and in Provence it is always hot in July—the wind here felt as if it was blowing at gale strength, and it was pleasantly cool. While wondering what I was supposed to do now that we were in this remote, isolated place that was so hard to get to that someone had had to bulldoze a path to it, I looked around. Across a valley I saw another *garrigue,* on top of which I could make out another cave carved into the limestone, perhaps leading to the abode of a third-century hermit. And suddenly I found it quite dramatic to be sitting up here on top of this *garrigue* where hermits had carved living spaces out of the rock in the third century, and looking down upon the twentieth-century smokestacks in the valley below. It was like sitting in the past and being able to see the civilization that was to come.*

*While those in charge of the excavation had dated the abbey from the fifth century, the first hermits began living in caves in this area as early as the third century, when the ideas of the Eastern asceticism widespread in Egypt first reached the Mediterranean shores of Gaul and sent religious fanatics off in search of isolated desert places like this. The ascetic ideal had been brought back by pilgrims to Jerusalem who wanted to duplicate the models of monasticism they had observed. Renouncing the physical pleasures of life, they fled from the degenerate to live a life of perpetual solitude.

Shortly after ten o'clock a thin, long-haired, serious-looking young man arrived with a knapsack on his back. He walked past us, his eyes, behind thick glasses, glued to the pebbles at his feet, like a waiter avoiding the eyes of diners wanting service. He raised the large wooden DANGER sign, and it became the roof of his shabby tourist booth. Opening his knapsack, he took out hand-typed guides in French and laboriously translated English and laid them on a board that served as a counter. Like the medieval pilgrims who had paid their tithes, we modern pilgrims paid ours and silently passed inside the troglodyte abbey, wondering at what point, and how, the medieval pilgrim had been asked to cough up. What you walk into is a natural grotto that had been enlarged to create various rooms of an abbey. Since everything that could be carried off had been removed from the abbey over the centuries, the only interesting room that remains inside the grotto is what I assumed was once the Chapter Room, where the abbot would have sat and read aloud to the assembled brethren a chapter each day from the Book of Saints. In this room, primitive Romanesque arches had been carved into the walls to create niches, the largest of these containing what is called the Abbot's Seat, a primitive eleventh-century throne with ornamented elbow rests and a relief of tiny arches at its base. It would have been in this seat that the abbot sat and read while, in the other niches, the brethren sat and listened. There is also a chapel, but with so much removed that it looks as much like a pagan basilica as it does a Christian church. Elsewhere, carved out of another part of the *garrigue*'s limestone crown, are the cells in which lived the hermits who came to this remote hilltop before the abbey was built.

It is at present believed that these early ascetics fled here with their relics—Saint Romanus's right hand and a fragment of Saint Trophime's right foot—in the third century to escape the waves of barbarian invasions that laid waste to the valley below. On hilltops all through the Alpilles are similar caves. Men escaped to these isolated places and carved out of the limestone primitive hermit cells, accessible only by ladder. They climbed this and other steep and rocky hills, denied their passions, mortified their flesh, and fasted to near starvation, either in search of eternal happiness or to escape from service in the Roman army. As times became worse, and more and more men fled to these hilltops, the caves were enlarged into hidden abbeys. By 1008 the Abbey of Saint-Roman had come under the jurisdiction of the Archbishop of Arles. When men retreated here, they turned over their worldly goods to the abbey, and by 1102 it had become independent and mildly prosperous. By 1269 the abbey was sufficiently prosperous, and times sufficiently settled, so that the abbot was able to buy himself a house in the town of Beaucaire. In 1363 the Pope, under whose ultimate jurisdiction all monasteries and abbeys fell, set up on the Saint-Roman hilltop a school where impoverished teenagers could receive free education, clothes, and food from the religious community. Later on, a fortified castle was built on top of the abbey, hidden in the caves below. The wall we passed when we first arrived is all that now remains of the castle. When times became even more settled, defensive castles became unnecessary, and the stones used in the construction of the abbey and castle were pried loose and used for construction in nearby Beaucaire.

Once we climbed out of the caves on the far side of the abbey, we emerged into the light and onto a stone terrace. Numerous graves of hermits, monks, and abbots had been carved into the stone. It was while I was sitting on this terrace, staring across a valley at another hermits' refuge and looking, beyond it, at still other *garrigues* crowned with other caves, that in my travels through the history of France I came closest to experiencing that period of history known as the Dark Ages. Periods of disintegration are very difficult to visit in the imagination. Few architectural sites evoke the rape, pillage, ravaging on the one hand, and the decline in literacy, commerce, and art on the other, that characterized this period. This is especially true of a period in which the primary building material was wood and the primary means of devastation was the flaming arrow, and fire in general. Most aesthetically memorable objects which have survived from this period are small, ornately decorated objects, such as Bibles with covers of carved ivory, objects which could be carried as the population fled in terror from whichever barbarians were attacking, and which are now found in museums such as the Louvre in Paris. But here, to lonely hilltops like this, not to museums, is where men fled, carrying their small treasures, and hid like animals in caves, watching wave after wave of barbarian invasions wash over the Roman world, battering at the walls of civilization. Watching their little cities, the little Romes of which they had been so proud, being destroyed one after another. There was no year, no day, no solitary event that signaled Rome's end and the beginning of the Middle Ages; rather, the Roman world merely faded over centuries into places like this. Charlemagne temporarily plugged the dike, driving the Saracens and the Vikings from France, but his descendants could not keep out the invaders, could not keep France unified, and with the crumbling of Charlemagne's empire and the division of France into warring feudal states, the high-prowed Viking ships were free to use the rivers of France as arteries of destruction.

Sitting here on this isolated cliff, just as men must have done centuries before, I watched a flock of birds fly overhead. Even birds were a source of terror in those years of the Viking raids. When the men in these hills saw birds migrating south, their hearts were filled with dread, because they had come to know that Viking navigators used migrating birds to guide their way south across the seas from Denmark. And soon after they saw the birds fly overhead, the men in these hills would have seen Viking ships coming down the Rhône in the valley below. From this very terrace they could have seen the Viking encampment on the island in the river where the invaders stayed from 859 to 862. From here they could have watched and, over the centuries, seen provincial Rome pillaged and destroyed. All over France— in the Dordogne, in Normandy, in the Loire at Saint Radegund's Chapel of Chinon—are caves similar to these, where men of the Dark Ages fled in terror.

Narbonne:

ROMAN CAPITAL, BARBARIAN KINGDOM

We left Provence for Narbonne on Autoroute 9, the modern highway paralleling the ancient Via Domitia, which once linked Rome with Spain. While I would like to say I selected Narbonne as a stopping point in our travels to the Middle Ages because it was both the first city in Gaul to be colonized by the Romans and the first city the Romans abandoned to the barbarians when the Empire began to contract, I actually selected it because we were passing it at lunchtime.

Leaving the autoroute, we faced a sign with two arrows, one pointing north to the city and another south to the *plage*. Since it was another very hot July day—over 100 degrees on the car thermometer—we headed south. I was thinking in terms of a swim in the Mediterranean.

As we drove toward the beach, the landscape changed dramatically: the road began to wind through limestone canyons and gorges of fantastic and chaotic shapes. I suddenly had the discombobulated feeling that I was not in a car but in Captain Nemo's submarine, traveling through an underwater seascape. Later I learned that the feeling was not so far-fetched after all: the land between the autoroute and the beach had once been the bed of the sea. The cliffs beside the road are part of the Massif de la Clape, which is itself the southernmost edge of the vast limestone tableland known as the Massif Central. Because of the dryness of the air, the limestone sculpted by the sea into strange, fantastic shapes has not weathered and thus remains unchanged.

The beach lying at the foot of the hills turned out to be a long, wide strip of pinkish sand decorated with the yellow-and-white-striped umbrellas of French middle-class families. While we ate chilled seafood salad at La Caravelle, a restaurant across from the boardwalk with a view of the sea, families pedaled back and forth along the boardwalk in bicycle buggies with fringed awnings. The beach community was immaculately clean and reminded me of my summers as a child along the New Jersey shore, but the hoped-for sea breeze never came; the heat was simply oppressive.

Not too far away is a fishing village called "picturesque" by Michelin; it was so hot that day, however, that Bob and I drove back to Narbonne without visiting it. Next time.

Narbonne itself, like its beach, turned out to be a very pleasant surprise. We parked our car near the Robine Canal, lined on each side with four rows of trees, creating long, shaded alleys. Fountains, statues, flowers, and beautiful lampposts, all immaculately kept, added to the charm of the city. The canal itself duplicates the one built by the Romans where ships both from sea and inland river once docked. When it was recently dredged, it yielded up many of the statues and artifacts now found in Narbonne's marvelous museums. The canal is beautiful and clean. In fact, as we walked through the city, I felt as though its residents had just scrubbed the pavements and the streets. No sooner had that thought crossed my mind than we passed a shop in front of which a woman was actually scrubbing the sidewalk with a long-handled scrub brush.

But Narbonne is more than a pleasant visit. We may have chosen it merely by accident (because we happened to be passing it at lunchtime) but Rome didn't; the Romans never did anything by accident.

Its location was the reason that in 118 B.C. the Roman Senate selected the inland Celtic settlement to be the first Roman colony in France and the capital of Roman Provence. Although the Republic had for some time resisted establishing colonies in Gaul, in that year two roads built for the swift movement of troops—the Via Domitia, linking Rome with Spain, and the Via Aquitania, which ran west from Narbonne as far as Toulouse—had just been joined up at Narbonne. Since Hannibal had shown Provence's vulnerability a hundred years before, the Senate decided to protect the new roads by creating a colony. The junction of the roads made Narbonne (Narbo Martius) the most strategic site.

I find what the Romans did after deciding to colonize Narbonne absolutely thrilling. They didn't just choose the little settlement; they transformed it, in a way that revealed their determination to impose their will on the natural world, to let no obstacle stand in their way—to order and plan not only roads but every aspect of life. They turned an inland town into a seaport, one of the great ports that made the Mediterranean into the Mare Nostrum—"Our Sea," the Roman sea. And in so doing, they displayed Rome's remarkable ability to impose the will of man on his environment.

Commerce in the Roman world was conducted primarily by ship, but Narbonne was not a seaport. It was not even on the Mediterranean. It was, though, only about twelve miles away, and some of the intervening miles were already under water, a marshy, mosquito-infested saltwater lake that had been left by a retreating ocean. So the Senate at Rome sent a proconsul and a legion to create a harbor large enough and sufficiently well sheltered for both military and commercial fleets. Using their administrative talents, engineering skills, and slave labor, the Romans turned the marshland into a harbor and made the new colony an important commercial center, an integrated link in a sophisticated economic empire. The marshy lake was dredged, lined with stones, and transformed into connecting lagoons and a harbor. A canal approximately three miles long, connecting Narbonne to the harbor, was dug and also lined with stones. The nearest source of water other than the sea was the Aude River, which flowed several miles north of Narbonne and emptied into the Mediterranean on the other side of the Massif de la Clape. By building a dike, the Romans diverted the course of the river so that it flowed where they wanted, through Narbonne, into the

canal, filling the artificially created lagoons and harbor to a desirable depth
for their ships. And suddenly Narbonne was no longer an inland town but
a seaport, a great one rivaling Marseille, linked as it was with inland Gaul,
Spain, Egypt, and Italy by the great Roman roads already in place. By the
time the overall plan was completed, the Romans had transformed an inland settlement in the wilderness of Gaul into a crossroads of the ancient
world. Chariots and troops could travel over a fifty-thousand-mile network
of paved and well-drained roads. Barges from the interior of Celtic France
and seagoing vessels from all ports on the Mediterranean were able to dock
at Narbonne and use its new storage facility.

To our surprise, this storage facility—the Horreum—still exists. And
we got another surprise when we visited it. The Horreum is a huge under-
ground warehouse, built during the time of Augustus, and similar to, but
far more extensive than, the cryptoporticus in Arles. I don't know whether
I would have found this ancient depot as exciting as I did had I visited it
during the winter instead of on a day when the heat was over 100 degrees.
But as I descended the sixteen feet below ground, my homesickness for
American air-conditioning was replaced with amazement. The subterranean galleries were quite cold, providing natural refrigeration—and I
was definitely in need of refrigeration, natural or otherwise.

While not all of the vast subterranean quadrangle had been uncovered
when we arrived, the galleries already opened seemed endless. Each type of
goods was stored in little rooms specifically allocated for the particular
item—pottery, marble, cloth, perfume, olives, goblets, casks of oil, honey,
wine. A design carved above each cubicle indicated the item once stored in
it. As I walked through the maze of cubicles, the maze of provincial Roman
society began to untangle to some degree. I began to see these cubicles not
just as storage bins but as opportunities for the landless but ambitious men
who had joined the Roman legions. The Roman Senate had promised land
and citizenship to every soldier who completed his tour of duty, and the
veterans of Caesar's Tenth Legion were given land in Narbonne and citizenship in the Roman Empire.* Those veterans—or their heirs—who became merchants grew wealthy as Narbonne grew wealthy. They bought

*Those looking on the darker side of this episode emphasize that the land given to the legionnaires had belonged to
Celts who probably carried out the dredging of the harbor and the digging of the canals.

goods cheaply, stored them here, and sold them when they could make a profit. In the north wing we found ancient stones carved in low relief, depicting scenes of the Narbonne of two thousand years before. One relief shows a man in a tub about to be eaten by a huge bear at the coliseum—Narbonne's coliseum. A poem carved on the wall celebrating Narbonne's beauty—its shops, its markets, its forum, its theater, its temples—tells how proud these battle-scarred veterans were of the city they had carved out of the wilderness.

Yet, the Horreum, while revealing the commercial nature of Narbonne, was the least interesting part of our visit. At the Archbishop's Palace is an exhibit of Roman paintings and mosaics that archaeologists have reconstructed from fragments found in the city. Have you ever wondered exactly what a Roman villa looked like? In that museum you can find out. A tiny theater showed a documentary film explaining how the archaeologists put together a jigsaw puzzle of fragments, using knowledge gained at the ruins of Pompeii to fill in the gaps. The exhibit contains authentic frescoes from Roman homes here in Narbonne, plus models of what the city and the homes might have looked like when they were built. Having seen the excavations of Roman homes at Glanum, where hints of frescoes remain on sunbleached stones, as well as the triumphal arch and theater at Orange and the temples and coliseum at Nîmes, I was able to mentally reconstruct and visualize the Roman town I was visiting.

Narbonne's museums contain unexpected treasures from both the ancient world of Rome and the early Christian world that developed out of it. Among them are statues and artifacts found when the Robine Canal was dredged. One, a Roman copy of a Greek statue of Silenus, Dionysus's fat, old tutor, depicted as gross and in his usual state of drunkenness, alone is almost worth the trip to Narbonne. In fact, much of the art concerns drunkenness—perhaps because Narbonne was the center of a wine-producing region (or perhaps, as some local historians suggest, because it was with wine—one Roman sneered that a Gaul liked his wine so much that he would trade a slave for a vintage amphora—that the Romans subdued the Gauls).

Narbonne was for centuries the seat of the Roman proconsul in Provence. When Constantine converted to Christianity in the fourth century, Paulus, one of the seven bishops sent to Gaul to convert the heathens, was stationed in Narbonne, and an archbishopric was founded here. For over a hundred years the two leaders—secular and religious, Roman and Christian—ruled jointly over the area. The administrative, or episcopal, structure of the Catholic Church was modeled on the Imperial Roman administrative structure; its language was the Roman language. When the barbarian invasions began, Narbonne was one of the first cities abandoned by an Empire unable to defend its frontiers in the west. The emperor had moved from Rome to Constantinople; the Empire contracted eastward. Arles, east of the Rhône, replaced Narbonne as the region's commercial center. Abandoned by the Empire, the Church, while barbarized, continued to exist, continued to keep its personnel, its land, its schools. The Church baptized the barbarian, who gradually barbarized the Empire.

It was after A.D. 410 that the Visigoths replaced the Roman rulers. Alaric, their king, swept across France and Italy, sacked Rome, and took the emperor's half sister, Galla Placidia, hostage. Since the legions were unable to drive the barbarians out, as they had previously done, all the land west of the Rhône was ceded to Alaric* and the Empire contracted east of the Rhône. Whereas Glanum no longer existed following the barbarian invasions of A.D. 270, Narbonne now suffered another fate: to become the capital of a Visigoth kingdom.

The Visigoths were impressed with the Empire they looted. Wanting to continue it, they dressed like Romans, ate like Romans. Alaric's successor, King Athaulf, married Galla Placidia, whom the barbarians had taken back to Narbonne by wagon train. The wedding took place in the house of a Roman nobleman in Narbonne with as much "Roman" pomp as the Visigoth king could muster. Athaulf dressed himself in Roman robes, adorned the house with the Roman loot he had plundered, and emphasized his relationship to the emperor in Rome by forcing Galla Placidia to lead the wedding procession. (At her first opportunity to escape, she fled to Arles, where she married a Roman general.)

The Visigoths wanted to enjoy the sumptuous life of the Romans; not destroy it. But they did not know how to administer the complex society

---

*You may notice a sign pointing to Mount Alaric as you drive along the autoroute to Narbonne.

they had conquered, or how to maintain the sophisticated physical plant created by the Romans. Illiterate, they could not read or understand the Latin laws; they did not know how to collect taxes or keep accounts. Ironically, it was because of the Visigoths' inability to collect taxes that Narbonne's Roman citizens, happy not to pay, accepted the barbarian rulers. Without the taxes, however, the barbarians were unable to maintain the city's roads, canals, aqueducts, water supply, sewers, public baths, schools, and libraries. Learning became the province of the Church as the rest of the physical plant underwent a slow process of decay.

The Visigoths barbarized the Roman civilization they had conquered, but they were probably unaware of it. A hundred years later one of their chroniclers wrote that the king dined every Saturday night at a royal table "served with the elegance of Greece, the plenty of Gaul, and the order and diligence of Italy."

In 719 the capture of Narbonne, along with other French cities on the coast, by the Saracens meant that France was cut off from the Mediterranean; its trade with the south and the east came almost to an end. Unlike the invaders before them, the Saracens failed to see any of the positive virtues of the cultures they overran. Pepin the Short recaptured Narbonne in 759, but even then the sea remained closed to trade. Charlemagne, Pepin's son, made Narbonne a duchy, creating three lordships for the city: one for the bishop, one for the Frankish lord, and one for the Jews. In the fourteenth century a storm sent the Aude River back to its natural bed, the lagoons and harbor silted over, and the sea abandoned Narbonne—as the Romans had so long before. And man, no longer dominating nature in the Middle Ages the way the Romans had in the first century, was unable to redirect the river for another three hundred years. The city suffered a period of total economic decline.

Visiting first the Archbishop's Palace at Narbonne, which was inspired by the Palace of the Popes at Avignon, and then the Bishop's Palace at Carcassonne and then the Bishop's Palace at Albi, you cannot help but be overwhelmed by the wealth required to build these palaces. Walking through the palace at Narbonne, I was not surprised to learn that in the year 1200 the archbishop was cited as an example of "clerical depravity" and called to Rome by the Pope, who admonished him "to show less interest in money and more in souls." Twelve years later, having failed to change his ways, he was removed because of "avarice."

Visiting Narbonne, Carcassonne, and Albi, each with its cathedral and its ecclesiastical palace (the bishops were made princes of the Church during the Carolingian Empire; the cathedrals were built in the thirteenth century), you also begin to understand the administrative and hierarchial legacy left by the Roman Empire to the Catholic Church. You can see the hierarchy of one slipping into the abandoned hierarchy of the other like a hermit crab twisting its body into the abandoned shell of a sea snail. In this area of France the administrative system of the Roman Empire remained in place—but it was used to administer a Catholic archbishopric. The Roman unit of the city and its surrounding countryside (the *civitas*) was replaced by the episcopal see. The hierarchy of the Archbishop at Narbonne, the Bishops of Carcassonne and Albi under him, and the Pope in Rome above him replaced the hierarchy of consuls, with their allegiance to the emperor. Traveling from Narbonne to Carcassonne and then to Albi—each only an hour's drive from the other—you sense the continuity of the Roman organizational structure as carried on by the Roman Catholic Church, as well as the fabulous wealth the Church once possessed in southwest France. You begin to understand that a new civilization—a Christian civilization— was born long before the Roman civilization died. You become aware of how large a part of ancient Rome was absorbed by emerging France.

The Roman heritage at Narbonne is very much in evidence as you wander through the apartments of the Archbishop's Palace, now a friendly, uncrowded museum with a remarkable collection of old masters. The floors of several of the rooms incorporate ancient Roman mosaics found in the city. The best mosaic illustrates the myth in which Bacchus, kidnaped by pirates while sleeping, awoke and turned the mast of his kidnaper's boat into a strangling tangle of grape vines. When you look at the portrait of Louis XIV hanging in this museum, you realize that it was not only the architecture of Rome which was incorporated into the architecture of France, but the idea of Rome as well. Louis XIV is portrayed dressed as a Roman emperor. French kings considered themselves "the successors of the Caesars."

THE TWELFTH-CENTURY ABBEY
of Fontfroide

At Narbonne the tourist has one foot still in ancient provincial Rome and the other in the emerging Middle Ages. But when you leave Narbonne, you leave Rome behind for good. If you drive out of Narbonne for seven miles, through deserted hills of scrub oak—passing no town, no gas station, no cars, no people—you will come to a secluded valley in the Corbières region where the medieval Abbey of Fontfroide lies hidden in rugged, wild hills, nestled in the mothering arms of surrounding cliffs, offering a place of refuge both from invaders and from the world. Fontfroide is not spectacular like the Abbey of Mont-Saint-Michel in Normandy, or even as dramatic as the nearby pilgrimage site of Conques, which rests atop a rocky cliff like an eagle's nest, but it is precisely how I had always pictured a monastery in my mind's eye: a place to which men fled from one world in order to create another, closer to God, an island in a wilderness.

The Abbey of Saint-Roman in Provence is also isolated and remote, of course, but it is at best only mildly interesting as an example of a troglodyte abbey to which solitary ascetics fled and from which they watched the destruction of the ancient world around them. Little remains there of buildings constructed at a time when regimented communal prayer replaced solitary asceticism. Fontfroide, on the other hand, is intrinsically beautiful. All its buildings have been exquisitely restored, and the warm rose of the stone from which the abbey is made is soothing during the day and a palette of reds at sunset. A chapter house, a monk's dormitory, a chapel, and a refectory enclose a serene cloister under whose roofed arcade monks once walked in silent meditation around an open garden. From other gardens, now filled with roses from different countries, you can see the massive buttresses and walls. The only openings in the walls are arrow-slit windows, indicating that this place of God, like the fortresses of the period, was not free from assault. The elegant simplicity and purity of the Cistercian architecture fill you with peace and serenity—as well as with a sense of what the Cistercian Order, which built Fontfroide, is all about.

The growth of the Cistercian Order began about 1098 as a reaction to the corruption and secularization in Cluniac monasteries (which had been established in 910 as a reaction to corruption and secularization in the Benedictine monasteries before them). Although both orders began by seeking reform and a return to the strict observance of Saint Benedict's rule, there were significant differences between them. Unlike the hierarchical structure of the Cluniac Order, in which all the houses were under the Abbot of Cluny, who was under the Pope, the Cistercian abbeys were independent, each under its own abbot. And unlike the Cluniacs, who emphasized scholarship, the Cistercians discouraged learning and forbade the writing of verse. The new order continued to copy manuscripts, but these were predominately religious in nature, and monks were forbidden to embellish them, lest decorations detract from the sacred text. The historian Charles Homer Haskins has written of monasteries, "Set like islands in a sea of ignorance and barbarism, they had saved learning from extinction in Western Europe at a time when no other forces worked strongly toward that end"; it was not Cistercian monasteries to which he referred, however. The major contribution of the Cistercians came from their emphasis on manual labor. They often settled on marginal land, which they made valuable by hard work and efficient methods of agriculture. It was Cistercian monks, for example, who introduced the heavy wheeled plow, capable of breaking up deep bottomland, and a new harness for attaching the plow to a horse instead of an ox. These innovations made it possible to replace the two-field Roman method of crop rotation with a three-field system, which resulted in increased agricultural production, which in turn resulted in increased population and prosperity.

The brethren at Fontfroide followed a highly regulated and austere life of prayer and hard work. Monks rose at 2 A.M. to chant nocturn, the first part of matins. At six came prime; at nine, terce; at noon, sext; at three, none; at sunset, vespers; and at bedtime, compline. They took vows of chastity and poverty on entering the order—but were given a year to change their minds. They ate nothing before noon, and, unlike the regime at the Cluniac monasteries, meat and wine were forbidden. Aside from the hours spent every day in communal prayer, their days at Fontfroide were filled with silence, and silence pervades the place still; indeed, there is such persuasive stillness that Bob and I found ourselves whispering to each other, and I was amused to see that the few tourists who arrived after us were also talking in hushed tones.

As you walk through Fontfroide, you will see no carvings of fantastic creatures, supposedly symbolizing evil, such as those incorporated in the architecture of Saint-Trophime at Arles and in the abbey church at Saint-Gilles. The simplicity of the architecture here is a visual manifestation of the ascetic religious fervor that swept through France in the twelfth century, at least in part because of the teachings of Saint Bernard. Bernard was a Burgundian aristocrat, born near Dijon, who exchanged his sword for a cross and became a militant soldier of God. His golden hair was matched by a golden tongue and a burning mystical passion for God that inspired men from the best families of France to renounce their parents, their brothers, their friends, their possessions, and "the vain empty glory of this world" and accept "all the hardships of the monastic life" or set off on a crusade to fight the infidel. By the time he died, 350 Cistercian monasteries had been established; by 1300 the number had reached 693.

The simple elegant architecture that you see at Fontfroide is expressive of Bernard's belief that church funds should be spent on the poor, not on beautifying places of worship. It is also expressive of the mystical asceticism that found the ornate decorations of the Cluniac monasteries a distraction from prayer. Just as the books they copied were unadorned, so were their places of prayer. Bernard said it better than I can:

> ... so many and so marvelous are the varieties of shapes on every hand that we are more tempted to read in the marble than in our books, and to spend the whole day wondering at these things rather than in meditating the law of God. For God's sake, if men are not ashamed of these follies, why at least do they not shrink from the expense?

Much about Fontfroide was typical of Cistercian abbeys. Benedictine monks had been allowed to settle here in 1097 by the Viscount of Narbonne as he was leaving on the First Crusade. Sixty years later, however, the viscount's descendants became disgusted with the depravity of the Benedictines, and a formal and large donation was granted to the religious community only on condition that the brethren shed the black cowls of the corrupt Benedictine Order for the white of the pure and simple Cistercian.

Fontfroide was popular with the people of Narbonne when it was a collection of monks living simple lives devoted to turning the barren hills surrounding the abbey into fertile pastures. In its early years, when the citizens felt the monks to be chaste and pious, they lavished gifts upon the abbey. Its popularity led to extreme wealth; its wealth eventually led to materialism; and its materialism led to Narbonne's hostility.

The abbey became rich first of all because of the rule that enriched all monasteries, the one requiring those who entered to renounce all worldly goods. It was, after all, to the monastery that these possessions were turned over. Wealth also came when local residents died. As a medieval observation went, "When a man lies down to die, he thinks not of his sons. He summons the ... monks ... and gives them his lands, his revenues, his ovens, his mills. The men of this age are impoverished and the clerics daily grow richer." Generalizations are interesting, but specific events show precisely how Fontfroide fell out of favor with the people of Narbonne.

During the bloody Albigensian Crusade, which will be discussed when we visit Carcassonne and Albi, the number of monks at Fontfroide grew because the abbey provided a place of refuge for fleeing heretics. Its wealth expanded during the Inquisition, which followed, when wealthy heretics were convicted and lost their possessions to the Church.

As the Cistercians became more interested in money than in saving souls, their relations with their major patron, the Viscount of Narbonne, became increasingly strained. In 1252, for example, the viscount decided to exploit a silver mine located near Fontfroide, but when he arrived at the mine with a large party of knights, serfs, and townsmen from Narbonne, he found that the abbot and his monks, carrying the relics of the monastery, had preceded him. The monks claimed the mine as theirs, and in the ensuing brawl, the viscount charged that many of the monks had taken their vows only to avoid being charged with heresy. Infuriated, the monks knocked him off his horse.

Donations, which had been generous, decreased. But by the time they came to a virtual end, they no longer mattered. The abbey already had sufficient wealth to purchase income-producing properties. Bernard had specifically forbidden the purchase of property; his intention was that the order be impoverished and totally dependent on hard work. However, by the first half of the thirteenth century, the abbey had tremendous sums of cash. Ignoring Bernard's prohibition, it purchased three income-producing seigneuries, complete with castles, northwest of Narbonne, as well as milling rights in Narbonne itself. Its right to measure and weigh grain caused friction between the abbey and the townspeople, exacerbated when the monks required permits for cutting wood on the abbey's land. Once, the Cistercians had simply given this right to the citizens of Narbonne. Now they began to charge for the privilege.

The popularity of Fontfroide hit bottom on April 8, 1333, when the poor of Narbonne gathered at the abbey's gates to receive the bread customarily distributed on Easter Sunday. Cistercian abbeys were popular because of their work in feeding the poor. During a famine in 1197, for example, one Cistercian monastery "had slaughtered its herds, and pawned its books and sacred vessels to feed the poor," while another fed fifteen hundred people a day until the harvest brought relief. But by 1333 such charitable endeavors were no longer a high priority to Fontfroide's monks.

When the poor gathered before the abbey, the monks barred the gates. In the ensuing crush, more than two hundred people were trampled to death. Enraged Narbonne officials charged a servant of the abbey with deliberate slaughter, but when the viscount conducted a personal investigation, he found the monastery guilty only of negligence.

The extent of the hostility toward the Roman Catholic Church that came to prevail in this area—hostility to the materialism of the Church which erupted in outright revolt—was expressed by a writer of the era:

> High felons are they who sell God and men undo! They color their perfidy under the cloak of honest seeming, they preach unto men telling them they are to lead holy lives. . . . And robbers are they, who over us rule . . . abounding in covetness, and spare of kindness, affable of mien, but monstrous of heart.

But if, despite their repeated attempts at reform over the centuries, French monks ate meat washed down with good wine, and preferred silks and velvets to hair shirts, and baths to vermin, we should remember, as Edward Gibbon so perceptively pointed out, "because of the voracious appetites of the Gauls, asceticism and fasting was never as popular in the areas which became France as it had been in places like Egypt."

(Thank God!)

THE FORTIFIED CITY OF

Carcassonne

We left Fontfroide for Carcassonne, sixty-one kilometers to the west in Languedoc. I had put off visiting Carcassonne for years because I had been told that it was touristy, over-restored, and phony, a Disneyland caricature of the Middle Ages. But when I saw the towers of Carcassonne for the first time, I didn't care. It was a dream floating back untouched by time from the Middle Ages, a mirage, a medieval Brigadoon. So what if, in the 1800s, Viollet-le-Duc put northern-style conical caps on these southern turrets or if there were a lot of tourists—and there were. I just didn't want it to disappear. During the few days we stayed in Carcassonne I continually returned to the spot on the Route Saint-Hilaire from which I had first seen the city, and from which it looked like a magical vision brought back to life in the twentieth century. I went at daybreak, at sunset, at night. I had to see it with the sun hitting its walls at every angle. I had to see it on a cloudy day. I had to see it in the moonlight. The sight of this enclosed fortified city, sitting up there on a high cliff, its double walls crowning the steep plateau, the twenty huge towers of the outer wall, the twenty-five towers of the inner wall, the towers of the castle inside, the soaring spires of the cathedral, the battlements running the length of these mighty ramparts, all defying entrance, while at the same time creating—I felt just by looking at it—an impregnable sanctuary for the citizens inside.

The hotel in which Bob and I stayed—the Domaine d'Auriac—is lovely and hospitable, with beautiful rooms, a rock garden with an arrogant swan swimming in an azalea-bordered pond, marvelous food (including a stupendous cassoulet, every morsel of which I devoured, to the amazement of the waiters; only shame prevented me from finishing Bob's as well), but it is outside the fortified city. And I think if I were to visit Carcassonne again, I would stay at the Hôtel la Cité, right inside the citadel. Practically adjacent to the cathedral, it was once the Bishop's Palace, and it has a lovely garden and a swimming pool bordered by the castle ramparts on two sides and the cathedral on another. When I took my swim in the evening, I could look up and see the ramparts around me or, on my return lap, the spires of Saint-Nazaire. I would be living where the bishop once lived. I could read in the wood-paneled library where the bishop once read. But most of all, I would be right in the city when I woke up and when I went to bed.

The first thing Bob and I did when we arrived at the gates of Carcassonne, being sophisticated travelers by this time, was to hop on the little tourist train that was about to leave on its journey around the outside walls. The guide started his little talk by saying, "Carcassonne is a book of stone in which is written the history of feudal military architecture from Gallo-Roman times through the whole history of the Middle Ages." This isn't precisely true—there are a few stages of medieval fortification that are not represented—but it is largely true. If you want to know how a fortified city defended itself against besiegers, believe me, by the time your little train has completed its circuit of the walls, you will know. The tour could have been called "All You Ever Need to Know About Concentric Medieval Defensive Fortifications." And even if you couldn't care less about medieval defensive fortifications, you should take the tour anyway, because the beauty of medieval construction, in direct contrast to classical architecture, which preceded it, and Renaissance architecture, which followed, is the unplanned evolution of its parts in response to changes in warfare—changes that took place over a period of a thousand years.

Since construction began in the first century B.C., with new fortifications being added to old until the end of the thirteenth century, no two views of Carcassonne are the same. Its seeming unity is created by the encircling battlemented walls, which hold the city together. The walls, and the towers they link together, are a joy to behold, and are constantly changing with each different angle and perspective of the train as it moves along the perimeter of the citadel. The shape of the towers and the ramparts changes so dramatically from place to place that taking this train ride is like accompanying Robert Taylor in the opening scenes of *Ivanhoe,* when he travels from castle to castle throughout Europe, singing his troubadour lays, hoping to hear a response from his captured king, Richard the Lion-Hearted, for whom he is searching. Most of the scenes could have been shot at Carcassonne; the photographer would not have had too much trouble making it appear to be different castles. It's not just that the views are constantly changing; it's far more than that. As the little train circles the base of these seemingly endless walls, the towers loom up over you, filling you with awe at their sheer height, their overwhelming massiveness, their awesome impregnability.

Circling Carcassonne on the train, you are circling the history of France from the fall of the Roman Empire to the rise of the French monarchy; you are seeing the evolution of medieval construction, which had its roots in the colonization of the province by Rome in the first century B.C., when the Senate established Carcassonne (Carcaso) as an outpost to guard the trade route (the Via Aquitania) between Narbonne and Toulouse. Carcaso's site, located in a gap between the Montagne Noire to the north and the foothills of the Pyrénées to the south, was selected because of its impregnability. And it was made even more impregnable by massive walls built by the Romans over the next three hundred years. The Visigoths, who occupied Carcassonne during the fifth, sixth, and seventh centuries, maintained and added to these walls and fortifications after they were abandoned by the Romans.

Nothing was built during the eighth century, when the Saracens occupied Carcassonne, and little remains of the Merovingian and Carolingian construction that followed. Construction resumed in the eleventh century, after the first count of the Trencavel dynasty won back the city from rebellious citizens who had taken it by trickery. Back in control after three years of siege, the count built additional walls and a tower to prevent a similar occurrence in the future. In the twelfth century the Trencavels began construction of their castle inside the city walls.

In the thirteenth century, following the Albigensian Crusade, Carcassonne became a royal possession. Construction of the outer wall, or barbican, commenced after the citizens of Carcassonne, still loyal to the Trencavels, revolted in 1262 against royal authority—they thought of the French king and his knights as "those northerners from the Loire." French nationalism was still hundreds of years in the future, and Carcassonne had enjoyed centuries of independence as a feudal state. The king expelled the rebellious citizens from the citadel but allowed them to take up residence on the far side of the Aude River, outside the city walls (where you arrive if you come to Carcassonne by train). After the barbican was built, Carcassonne was deemed so impregnable that the English did not even attempt a siege during the Hundred Years War, in the fourteenth century. This outer wall represents the pinnacle of medieval defensive fortifications.

Some of the walls the Romans built at Carcassonne still remain, so we can see evidence of that Roman insistence on order and precision which has kept Roman walls standing for two thousand years and more. As we chugged past them on the northwest side of the citadel, the guide pointed out walls made of neatly arranged small stones in which were set redbrick lines, or courses, which the Romans used to ensure that the stones were perfectly level. Next we passed a pair of Gallo-Roman towers with the same redbrick courses. These towers are close together, since every spot on the wall between them had to be within range of the principal Roman defensive weapons, the javelin and the catapult bolt; and they are rounded toward the outside because the Romans had learned from the Greeks that a rounded surface was less easily penetrated by battering rams and were efficient in deflecting missiles hurled by catapults. During the Dark Ages rounded towers disappeared from northern France, where Roman occupation had never been as extensive as in the south, and rectangular keeps were built. Then, in the eleventh century, the Crusades brought northern knights to areas bordering the Mediterranean, where the earlier style had never been forgotten. After watching their missiles bounce off the rounded towers, the crusaders went home and rounded off their own.

The wide barbican, or battlemented outer wall, was begun in the thirteenth century by Louis IX and completed by his son Philip the Bold in 1285, and may be the only one in France to encircle an entire city. The top of the wall consists of embrasures (indentations or openings enabling the defending archers to shoot) and merlons (raised portions behind which the defending archer could stand for protection); together, they are called battlements. You will notice that the battlements are only on the wall's outer face, thereby providing protection only for archers facing outward. Therefore, if this outer wall was captured, besiegers would not be shielded from fire from the inner wall. If the barbican was breached, the defenders could fall back to this inner wall.

At Carcassonne this outer wall connects twenty towers, which bulge out beyond the wall. Most are topped with picturesque conical blue- and orange-slate caps of different sizes, but some have crenelated crowns. Each tower would have been a formidable defensive structure in its own right. Some are eighty feet high, and in time of siege were manned by garrisons as large as two hundred men. If a tower was cut off from the rest of the castle, it could rely on its own water source: a cistern for collecting rainwater. On each floor you can see a fireplace, and some of the later towers have latrines, which emptied into the moat below. At each level the towers are pierced by long slits so narrow that it was almost impossible for an attacking archer to shoot inside. From the inside, though, these slits look quite different, fanning out into pie-shaped wedges, with each arrow-slit window making the point of a triangle from which the archer inside was able to defend a wide arc outside; the slits were positioned around the tower so that no area was out of view and range of at least one archer. Above the slits, you can still see the hooks on which the archers hung their crossbows. When built, the towers were spaced farther apart than the Gallo-Roman towers, since the range of the crossbow in use by the thirteenth century was greater than that of Roman or Visigothic weapons. The towers located at the most vulnerable points along the wall have rounded beaked projections. Pierced with additional arrow-slit windows at the upper level, these projections allowed archers from adjacent towers to catch besiegers in a crossfire.

These thirteenth-century towers do not go straight up and down; rather, they were made thicker at the base so that tunneling or mining through them was more difficult. One tower, for example, has walls six feet thick at the top and thirteen feet thick at the base. The slant also prevented movable assault towers from getting close to the wall. If both the outer wall and inner wall were breached, the defenders could still fall back to the wall of the castle itself.

Between the barbican and the inner wall of the city is a wide dry moat, or trench. Attackers who somehow managed to take the outer wall—and, looking at its grim massiveness, it is hard to imagine any attacker actually doing do—would have had to cross this open space, a no-man's-land without a shred of protection from the fire from the towers and battlements of the inner wall. Moreover, the depth of the moat made the high inner wall even higher, so that scaling it would have been all the more difficult. And merely by creating a different level, the moat kept the enemy from bringing wagons, catapults, battering rams, sappers, and siege towers into the city. While there are two gates to the city, there was only one where it was possible to bring in cumbersome machines of war for use against the walls of the castle inside—the Narbonne Gate.

The Narbonne Gate was the single most vulnerable part of the two walls, and consequently it was guarded by a multitude of medieval defensive devices. Flanking the great double gates are a pair of immense towers, eighty-two feet high, their prowlike projections making them look like two mighty sandstone battleships held together by a building constructed directly over the gate. There is a drawbridge, which could be raised in time of attack. Look up and you will see grooves at both the outer and the inner ends of the drawbridge: each one contained a massive iron portcullis. If both were lowered simultaneously, attackers would be trapped between them. Look up higher and you will see machicolations. At Carcassonne the machicolations are covered wooden platforms projecting from the top of the wall, with floor openings through which stones, molten lead, or hot oil or pitch could be dropped on attacking forces. These restorations are the only wooden machicolations I have ever seen; most of them were destroyed by fire and replaced by ones made of stone.

The roadway between the outer gate and the inner gate at the Narbonne towers twists first to the right and then to the left. This is not the result of a drunken engineer but is another deliberate defensive device, used at the gates of most fortified castles to make it more difficult for the enemy to charge the gate with any momentum. (When you visit the museum of medieval warfare at Castelnaud, and see the size and unwieldiness of authentic catapults and siege towers, you will understand the difficulties presented by this wiggling entry road.)

When our little train arrived back at the Narbonne Gate, Bob and I climbed down and, instead of crossing the drawbridge and entering the city, walked along the moat between the two walls. When we returned at sunset, itinerant folk singers and rock groups had set up shop between these great walls; one young man was singing Bob Dylan's "Blowin' in the Wind." I heard "How many times mus' a cannonball fly?" . . . and I thought, for an awful lot of centuries.

As soon as we walked inside the walls of Carcassonne, we were in a city that is almost unique—a fortified city existing in its entirety pretty much as it was in the thirteenth century. This is rare, because most secular construction of the Middle Ages has not been well preserved. Castles and fortified cities were built for military purposes, and, unlike churches, were subjected to constant destruction by fire, battering rams, and sappers. After the invention of the cannon, in 1350, made them obsolete, fortified cities were often abandoned, their walls, from the fourteenth to nineteenth century, quarried for stone. Once we entered Carcassonne's gates, we had the profound sense of being in an enclosed, self-sufficient fortified city, isolated from and safe from the rest of the world. It is a feeling I never experienced while visiting the Roman cities of Provence, which were located, for purposes of transportation, along the banks of rivers. Here, we no longer felt a connection to the rest of the world either by road, by sea, or by river. While from the walls of the citadel the Aude River can be seen far below, it is not an artery flowing through the city and connecting it to the other cities along the Rhône or to foreign cities bordering the Mediterranean, but just another barrier in a series of barriers behind which defenders could continually fall back until, if necessary, they made their last stand in the keep of the castle. This is because Carcassonne was built as a fortified city. It was never a commercial center possessing an economy unrelated to agriculture. It was built by the Romans as a military outpost to protect a trade route. In the early part of the Middle Ages, what made this a city were not trade and commerce but its cathedral, its bishop, and its walls. Cities were places of refuge, sites for the celebration of religious rites, and centers of administration for the agricultural society. Even today Carcassonne has little life of its own outside the tourist trade; most of its merchants disappear with the tourists in the winter months.

After passing through the Narbonne Gate, we hurried over to the Cathedral of Saint-Nazaire because it was almost noon and we had been told that the sun hits the stained-glass windows directly at twelve-thirty. I was glad we hurried, because the reds and blues of these thirteenth- and fourteenth-century windows are truly beautiful with the sun shining through them and illuminating the stories from the Bible. Most fascinating, I think, is "The Tree of Life Window." It usually serves as an example when critics attack Viollet-le-Duc for his restoration of Carcassonne. When he began putting Carcassonne back together again, the bottom panels of this window were missing. They once had shown the four rivers of Paradise, which, if you were knowledgeable in reading stained-glass windows, would have told of the creation of the world as contained in Saint Bonaventure's message of God's love for man. But the artist who restored the window replaced the missing panels with Adam and Eve's ejection from Eden and a depiction of Noah's ark. This mistake changed Saint Bonaventure's message from God's love for man into God's anger at man, and critics have sarcastically labeled it the "Tree of Death Window." In the Middle Ages, when most people were illiterate, stained-glass windows were used to tell them the stories of the Bible, so they could read in pictures what they could not read in books. Had the restorer's mistake been committed in the fourteenth century, when the window was originally created, getting a religious message wrong would have been quite serious. When the window was restored, however, the main concern of the artist lay in getting the colors right. While the mistake makes the window less authentic, it emphasizes the cultural change in concern in the different centuries.

The rose windows, especially the north rose window, which dates from the beginning of the fourteenth century and portrays the Queen of Heaven seated on her throne surrounded by angels, prophets, and saints, is a joy to look at. The windows were added after Carcassonne became a possession of the crown. The simple eleventh- and twelfth-century dark, Romanesque, pointed, barrel-vaulted nave, common to the area, was modeled after the Roman basilica that would have been found in every Roman town.

After the Albigensian Crusade, neither Carcassonne nor the architecture of its cathedral reflected the culture of Languedoc, which was totally destroyed. Instead, the choir and transepts, added in the mid-thirteenth century, show northern architectural influence. The additions were carried out in the Rayonnant Gothic style, with its elegant and elaborate window tracery, which was then evolving on the Île-de-France.* (The name of the style comes from the radial spokes of bar tracery in rose windows such as the north and south windows at Saint-Nazaire. Another characteristic of this style is the replacement of walls by columns so thin that they barely interrupt large areas of stained glass.)

Seeing the cathedral and the former Bishop's Palace right next to it, buildings of such lavish expenditure in a city that was never a center of commercial activity, reminded me of the irrelevance of trade and commerce to the Church's power and wealth. A city of the Middle Ages, unlike one of ancient Rome or of later periods, existed primarily because of its bishop and cathedral. Bishops had not suffered with the cessation of trade; indeed, their prestige, power, and income increased as the economy declined. These fearsome princes of the Church, with their weapon of excommunication, could survive and thrive on economic anarchy. Their power of excommunication rested firmly on the belief of the people that the seven sacraments were necessary for salvation; when a person was excommunicated, he could no longer receive these sacraments—or even enter a church. For example, if a lord had been excommunicated, when he entered

*Sainte-Chapelle in Paris was built at the same time these additions were being added.

Carcassonne the bells would ring (bells were like voices, having a different ring for each occasion, and the people of the Middle Ages understood what they were saying) to tell the people of the city that all religious services and the administration of sacraments had ceased—not only for the excommunicated lord but for the entire town—and would not be resumed until the lord departed, at which time the people would hear the bells ring again, this time in a different tone. You can well imagine how unwelcome the lord's visit would be, since it exposed everyone in the town to the possibility of eternal damnation.

Before entering the cathedral, Bob and I had noticed a sign advertising a tour of the castle to be given in English at two o'clock. To excuse what happened next, I have to say, in my defense, that it was already twelve forty-five and I was starving. Still, I should have known better than to select a restaurant on the basis of convenient location. But I did. We walked into the restaurant nearest to the castle, which happened to be the dining room in the Hôtel la Cité (it had probably once been the bishop's dining room). As soon as I saw the Renaissance décor, the velvet-seated high-backed chairs, the mullioned windows, and the pinched nose of the tuxedo-clad captain, I should have known that this was going to be not just a lunch but a major investment. And given my familiarity with French waiters, with whom civilized, leisurely dining always comes first, I should not have said, "We want to make a two o'clock tour." I think "contempt" may be a pretty good word to describe the expression that came over the captain's face—and "leisurely" is definitely the word to describe the subsequent service. Never has service in any restaurant been slower. At one fifty-five Bob, in desperation, made another mistake. He told the waiter, who had been serving in slow motion, that we no longer had time for dessert and could we please have the check. In response, the waiter and the entire staff disappeared completely. Bob sent me ahead, while he waited for the check, so that at least one of us would make the tour. I scurried out, still chewing on a veal kidney. It was obvious the waiters felt that we were barbarians and that our dining experience should have been far more important than a tour of the castle.

As it turned out, they were right. Our "English-speaking" guide was dressed like a reject from the hippie movement of the sixties. He was wearing a rumpled T-shirt and dungarees, and his blond hair was coiffured in oily shoulder-length curls—a style I'm not particularly fond of in men. But worst of all, he could barely speak English. The only English word he really knew was "okay," with which he began every sentence. As our tour group walked through the castle, he would hurry ahead of us. When we arrived at a tower or rampart or the Court of Love, where troubadours once sang their lyrical songs, he would be hurriedly reading through the tangled mass of papers he was carrying. Then he would close his eyes and raise his head, muttering the English words he had just read in an attempt to memorize them. By the time we gathered, he would have forgotten the end of each newly learned sentence. He would begin the sentence, and the group, in unison, like members of some slapstick comedy skit, would supply the end.

The castle he led us through had once belonged to the Trencavels, rulers of Carcassonne, Béziers, Albi, and the surrounding manors. The remainder of southwest France from Avignon to the Garonne River—in general, the Midi, the land through which we've been traveling since crossing the Rhône and through which we will continue to travel as we visit the Middle Ages—were the domains of the Counts of Toulouse, who tried for centuries, by war and marriage, to absorb the Trencavel domains. Such conflicts had been raging throughout France ever since Charlemagne divided his empire into small counties so that each of his "count officials" could easily cover the district in a single day. But with Charlemagne's death and the decline of any central power or state, the more ambitious lords, like the Count of Toulouse, expanded their holdings. By 1200 much of the south had become the independent little kingdom of the Count of Toulouse. At the beginning of the thirteenth century, marriage rather than war—the Lord of Carcassonne was the nephew of the Count of Toulouse—would soon unite the two families and join the Trencavel domains to the count's.

In general, the area ruled by the Count of Toulouse enjoyed relative peace and prosperity after the expulsion of the Saracens from Narbonne in 759. Although nominally a vassal of the King of France, the count was virtually independent and by the twelfth century had accumulated a vast amount of wealth. At a gathering of princes at Beaucaire in 1174, he gave one of his vassals a hundred thousand gold sous to divide among his knights. At the same gathering, one of the count's vassals, in a medieval game of hide-and-seek, plowed a field with oxen and then hid thirty thousand gold sous in it for men to find. Unfortunately, there were northern lords on hand to witness this display. They saw weakness and effeminacy in the shaved faces of the southern nobles, in their parted hair, in their "locks grown long like women," and in their elegant clothes "whose colors suit each man's mood."

When we arrived at an inner courtyard, we were at the Court of Love once presided over by the wife of Roger Trencavel, Adélaïde de Burlats. As the daughter of the Count of Toulouse, Adélaïde was the heiress of an immense fortune and entertained with opulence and elegance while troubadours sang to her divine and unattainable beauty. The songs of the twelfth-century troubadour usually concerned unrequited love between the troubadour and the lady of the castle. During the Middle Ages, requited love was frowned on in the south, although not as much as it was in the north, where a woman caught in an adulterous liaison might be burned at the stake. Since marriages among the aristocracy were made for political reasons, the love of which the troubadours sang was not between husband and wife. Their songs were primarily about idealized love, but occasionally the troubadour would compose a satire on current political developments or convey news as he traveled from castle to castle. His verses were written in *langue d'oc* (the dialect of the area), and while not terribly good poetry, they make wonderful lyrical love songs.

In 1208 Raymond-Roger Trencavel, Adélaïde's son and a legendary patron of troubadours, welcomed the poets to his court, as had his mother before him. The troubadours had traditionally been knights of noble birth who wrote poetry, and therefore they were acceptable to the aristocracy they entertained, having their assistants, or jongleurs, sing the verses they wrote. Trencavel, however, began admitting troubadours to his court on the basis of their talent, not their social class. This change was indicative of changes taking place in southern society at the beginning of the thirteenth century. The culture was becoming increasingly worldly and skeptical— and the castle at Carcassonne increasingly luxurious in order to accommodate a more elegant lifestyle, one in which the ladies of the castle became famous for the salons they kept. It was a society in which only courtly manners and dress distinguished the aristocracy from the wealthy merchant class. It was a culture in which ideas were freely exchanged, women were treated with respect, toleration was extended to men of differing beliefs and opinions (Jews and Muslims were allowed to live within the protection of city walls rather than outside), and local nobles appointed the clergy so that the bishops owed their position to the aristocracy and not to Rome. It was also a world increasingly antagonistic to the Roman Catholic Church, and to its priests and Pope. One troubadour referred to the clergy in his songs as "high felons ... who sell God." Another man, from Toulouse, called Rome the "head-fount of evil ... arch-cheat and liar!"

The world of Languedoc was quite different from the hierarchical society to the north, where authority was accepted unquestioningly. The people of Languedoc were wealthier, more urban, more literate, more open to ideas, and, oddly, more puritanical in their religious beliefs. That the Church was corrupt at this time cannot be denied; even the Pope denounced its moral decay, warning, "This state of things affords heresy great encouragement." As people in Languedoc questioned the very foundations of the Church's authority, many searched for an explanation for the existence of evil in the world, some turning to the eastern doctrine of Catharism, which espoused the Manichean belief that God, who reigned over the spirit, was in conflict with an evil god, who ruled over matter. The Cathars, or "pure ones," became known as Albigensians because the town of Albi, just north of Carcassonne, was in the center of the movement.

This philosophy was not new; it had been debated in theological circles since the time of Saint Augustine (354–430) but had never been the cause of much concern to the Roman Catholic Church. What did concern the Church now was that the Albigensians also questioned the necessity of the sacraments for salvation. This could not be tolerated, since the unity and income brought by the sacraments were the basis of the Church's power. It is difficult to describe the faith of the Albigensians accurately, because their church documents were destroyed and most of the information about them and about their faith comes from the Catholic Church. We do know they held to an ideal of poverty and nonviolence and that their leaders rejected all worldly luxury and strictly adhered to celibacy and pacifism. The Albigensians denied the necessity of the sacraments and thereby denied the necessity for the Church and its clergy. They denied the miracle of the Mass at a time when great sums of money were left to the Church so that Masses might be said for the souls of the dead. They denied the miraculous powers of saints and their relics at a time when it was common practice for priests to prescribe pilgrimages to special shrines such as Santiago de Compostela, Jerusalem, and Rome as penance for sinners who sought the assistance of a saint in atonement for their sins. This form of penance had become quite lucrative by the twelfth century. Since a large part of the "contributions" received by monasteries along the pilgrimage routes went directly to the Pope, the Albigensian heresy in Languedoc—an area through which most pilgrims passed on their way to Santiago de Compostela—was seriously reducing his income. And by the middle of the twelfth century, the popularity of the Albigensian sect had begun spreading out from Languedoc into Provence and was beginning to gain adherents in Burgundy. Gold was flowing into the coffers in Rome from other sections of France, but it was only trickling in from the wealthiest area.

When local bishops proved unable or unwilling to end the heresy, Pope Innocent III in 1208 dispatched his legates to Languedoc. But the Albigensians felt that the luxury in which the legates traveled proved their point. When one legate asked the reason for the coldness of his reception, he was told that his crimson silk robes belted with rubies were more suitable for a worldly prince than for a prince of the Church. Meeting with the Count of Toulouse, one of the legates, Pierre de Castelnau, a Cistercian monk from the Abbey of Fontfroide, demanded the surrender of all heretics in his domain. The count refused; a bitter argument ensued. When the next day Castelnau was murdered, Raymond of Toulouse was held responsible. Innocent III excommunicated him and declared a crusade against the Albigensians to exterminate heresy in Languedoc.

Although the Pope was throwing a crusade, at first no one came. The King of France, busy with his war against England, declined the invitation; similar heresies existed in every country, he said. The lords of staunchly Catholic northern France apparently felt that while the south of France had always been a great spot for a pilgrimage, it was less of one for a war. Since the extermination of heresy was proving an insufficient incentive to these lords of the north, the Pope offered them an additional lure: each lord could keep any city or fief he captured—together with its income. The northern lords, perhaps remembering southern gold, hurried to battle for the Lord. Baron Simon de Montfort of the Île-de-France, riding a black horse, led the Albigensian Crusade together with the Duke of Burgundy, the Count of Nevers, and other fief-hungry nobles, dividing up the land among themselves before they left. They headed south with a force of twenty thousand men, the number swelled by burghers whose enthusiasm was whetted by another papal promise: the remission of several centuries of Purgatory for each ten thousand heretics slain.

That last promise may account for the extraordinary viciousness of the expedition, although blaming the Pope may be unjust, since Montfort had already proved himself a warrior whose bloodthirstiness was extraordinary even by medieval standards. Whatever the reason, the first siege, at the walled city of Béziers, a town of sixty thousand people whose cathedral spires we saw from the autoroute on the way to Narbonne, set the pattern. The Count of Toulouse, hoping to be accepted back into the Church and to retain his lands, joined this crusade against his own people. When the crusaders left Béziers, not a single person was left alive. Chronicles from the period, quoted in *The Troubadours* by Robert S. Briffault, relate: "They slaughtered clerks, women, and children so thoroughly that not one escaped. Seven thousand persons who had sought sanctuary in the Church of Sainte-Madeleine were butchered there; six thousand were burnt alive in the Church of Saint-Nazaire." When the crusaders asked how to distinguish heretics from faithful believers, Arnaud, Bishop of Cîteaux, replied that the distinction was unimportant. Kill everyone, he said. As the Cistercian monk Céssaire d'Heisterbach was to record, Arnaud said, "Kill, kill. God will know his own."

After the fall of Béziers, the town of Marmande, just west of Toulouse, attempted to resist. "Barons and Ladies, little children and women stripped naked were put to the sword. Limbs and entrails lay strewn about the public places..." At Lavaur, four hundred heretics were burned, and Guiraude, the chatêlaine who had opened her château to the heretics, was dragged through the streets, thrown down a well, and stoned until buried. At Bram, Simon de Montfort blinded a hundred men and lopped off their noses. He had the mutilated men led to Cabaret, which he attacked next. At the cloister of Bécede, where heretics had sought refuge, the deacon and all the friars were burned while the Cistercian monks sang hymns to drown out the shrieks of the victims. After the carnage, the crusaders fought among themselves over the booty and the young girls whom they had driven to the camp like cattle, prodded with pikes.

Before the fall of Béziers, Trencavel was summoned to Montpellier to appear before the Assembly of Crusaders. Although he was not an Albigensian, he was a brave man. When the papal legates demanded that he hand over all Jews and heretics in Carcassonne, the troubadours' patron refused, and added, "I offer a town, a roof, a shelter, bread, and my sword to all the outlaws who will soon be wandering about Provence." He then raced to the fortified city of Béziers to warn the people of the coming attack and to bring back to the safety of Carcassonne all the Jews and best-known heretics of Béziers, men and women he thought most in danger from the crusaders. He was confident that Carcassonne's mighty walls, which had withstood years of siege before, could withstand this onslaught.

In the end, it may have been the young viscount's idealism that allowed these seemingly impregnable walls to be breached. His fortified city was soon surrounded—he had not expected Béziers to fall as quickly as it did. As Carcassonne was placed under siege by Simon de Montfort, jongleurs stood on the walls singing and hurling insults at the besiegers. According to those sympathetic to the crusaders, it was August—August is never a good time to go to Carcassonne—and the fortified city fell in a matter of weeks because of lack of water. That is not the story told by the troubadours who escaped, however. According to them, Montfort, unable to take the city by force, invited Trencavel to negotiate terms under a flag of truce, sacred under the rules of chivalry and honor, but when the young viscount and fifty knights left the safety of the walls, Montfort captured them. One troubadour afterward cried out in anguish, "Lies and injustice have joined battle against truth and right; and lies triumph."

After capturing the weakened and leaderless city, Montfort brought Trencavel back to Carcassonne in chains, threw him in the dungeon, and then murdered him two months later. A troubadour named Guillaume de Béziers, who had escaped the massacre that followed the fall of Carcassonne, wrote the following verse to tell of the tragedy of Carcassonne and the death of his young lord:

> *They have slain him*
> *And never was so great wrong seen*
> *Nor so great a crime*
> *Nor so iniquitous against God and Our Lord as was done*
> *by those traitors of Pilate's sib,*
> *the recreant curs who did him dead.*

Montfort hanged the fifty knights who had accompanied Trencavel. He burned four hundred other prisoners alive and drove the citizens of Carcassonne from the city "carrying nothing but their sins." Some say the inhabitants were driven beyond the walls stark naked.

Languedoc, once so rich in culture and prosperity, never recovered. No court as brilliant as Trencavel's would appear in France for over a hundred years, and then it would be not here in Languedoc but at Blois in the Loire Valley, at the court of Charles d'Orléans. The religion of the Albigensians, however, remained; the practitioners no longer wore black, which identified them to the Inquisitors, but kept concealed little strips of black cloth. By the sixteenth century a puritanical religion had evolved, theology changed, and the people of this area, called Huguenots, would once again be persecuted.

After capturing Carcassonne, Montfort used it as his headquarters to attack the town of Albi, where we shall go next, listening as we go to the song of troubadour Bernard de Marjevois:

> *Ah! Toulouse and Provence and the Land of*
> *Argence, Béziers, and Carcassonne, such I but*
> *late knew you, and such do I behold you now!*
> *. . . the bonds of*
> *law are broke; the troth of oaths is fouled.*

THE FORTIFIED CATHEDRAL OF
Albi

The drive from Carcassonne to the hill town of Albi took a little more than an hour by car. At first I was fascinated by the abrupt change in landscape to lush green as we left the sun-bleached Mediterranean coast and headed north along a twisting mountainous road. It never ceases to amaze me how, when you leave one region of France and enter another, it looks and feels as though you were entering a different country. I dozed off shortly before we arrived in Albi; when I opened my eyes at the fortified Cathedral of Sainte-Cécile, nearly a century had passed. My mind had barely taken leave of the dungeon in which Raymond-Roger Trencavel was murdered by Simon de Montfort when I found myself face-to-face with this cathedral, built a hundred years later—built with money confiscated from the people of Languedoc whom Trencavel had tried to defend. When

the Albigensian Crusade finally came to an end, more than thirty years after the young viscount's death, the world he knew had been destroyed and
along with it the cathedral that once stood where Sainte-Cécile now stands.
The cathedral that rose in its place is a truly amazing structure, totally
unique, resembling nothing I had ever seen before. It is unlike any cathedral in France; and because of the circumstances that led to its construction,
I would conjecture that it is unlike any other cathedral in the world.

Constructed out of brick rather than stone, since it was too dangerous
to transport stone through a countryside still seething with hatred of the
Catholic Church (the brick could be made out of clay from the banks of the
Tarn River, which flows through Albi), Sainte-Cécile's outer walls rise a
hundred feet straight up. There are no graceful flying buttresses supporting walls of stained glass; instead, almost solid walls are supported by a series of cylindrical piers that look like giant cannon barrels concealed in
brick. The original windows, which pierce only the upper reaches of the
walls, too high for any attacker's ladder, are long and narrow, barely wider
than the slender arrow-slit windows of the defensive towers at Carcassonne. Unlike Gothic cathedrals in the north, there is no slanting roof with
overhanging eaves that not only offer protection from the elements but appear to be welcoming the congregation and drawing it in to worship. Instead, a flat roof, hiding a parapet, accentuates the formidable fortresslike
walls, appearing to offer the church protection not from the elements but
from the people. There are several small bell turrets, but to me their se-
verely pointed caps make them look more like modern missiles ready to be
launched than towers whose chiming bells beckon a congregation to services held inside. The massive bell tower—225 feet high—guarding the
cathedral's southern entrance is an enormous stronghold in itself and is
protected from the city by a deep ravine.

Unlike northern cathedrals, which have many entrances, there are only
two entrances to Sainte-Cécile; and one of them—a large ornate porch—
was added centuries later (1515) to soften the austerity of a cathedral no
longer threatened by a hostile congregation. This porch is made of stone,
which by the sixteenth century could safely be transported over roads in
Languedoc. Unlike the rest of the cathedral, it is an example of Flamboyant (flamelike) Gothic architecture, and while the lacy carved stone is quite

beautiful, the entire porch seems tacked on as an afterthought, like lace cuffs added to soften the severity of a black dress.

Bob and I walked slowly around the exterior of the cathedral before having a long lunch at one of the bistros on the plaza of Sainte-Cécile. From the shade of our umbrellaed table we watched the sun play on the rosy bricks out of which the cathedral is built, the sunlight giving depth and texture to the stones and then, as it moved behind a cloud, taking it away, leaving the walls flat and grim. The rosy color of the cathedral's brick saves the cathedral from being ominous, unless you remember the circumstances that led to its construction. I had been told that Sainte-Cécile is beautiful, but beauty is not what I felt when I saw it for the first time. When I stood at the base of its massive walls, I felt dwarfed and insignificant, its soaring height and massive brick walls having the same dehumanizing quality that I had previously felt when entering the Roman Theater of Orange. But Sainte-Cécile isn't Roman. It is stunning, powerful, awesome, overwhelming, and most definitely medieval. The assertion of the Church's domination—both physical and spiritual—is clear. There is no question about the message of the architecture: this is God's Church here on earth, a Church that will not be destroyed.

The Roman Catholic Church that had once stood where Sainte-Cécile now stands had been razed during an uprising during which the townspeople of Albi tried to reinstate the son of Raymond-Roger Trencavel as their lord. The people had slowly realized that the aim of the Albigensian Crusade was the destruction not of heresy but of their local aristocracy. From the very start, Pope Innocent III had intended to replace the southern nobles, over whom the Church had little control, with northern nobles, more submissive to the Church. (These were the nobles who became "soldiers of God" only after the Pope promised they could keep the rich fiefs of the south they captured.) After murdering Trencavel, Simon de Montfort became lord not only of Carcassonne but of Albi as well. During the ten years of his rule, until his death while trying to capture Toulouse, he proved himself both cruel and shortsighted. By systematically destroying the crops, vines, and cattle in the territory he ruled, he wrecked the very economy from which he hoped to enrich himself.

The Albigensian Crusade had begun in 1209 without the participation of the King of France, who was tied down in his war against the English in the north. By the time of Montfort's death in 1218, however, the king had defeated the English. As his gaze turned to the south, he realized that the crusade offered him an opportunity to extend the monarchy's control to France's natural southern border: the Pyrénées. Just as the Count of Toulouse had tried to expand his control over the territories of the Trencavels, now the King of France was ready to expand his control over the territories of the Count of Toulouse, to replace this independent, powerful, and popular lord with a vassal faithful and submissive to the authority of the crown. Theoretically, the count was the king's vassal. In actuality, in the thirteenth century, the count was independent and nearly equal in power to the king. From the moment the king entered the war, the crusade became a war of two opposing cultures: it was the French, supported by the Roman Catholic Church, against the Count of Toulouse, supported by the people of Languedoc, who were fighting to preserve their culture, their religious freedom, their possessions, and their independence. (The people of Languedoc considered the French—whose northern dialect, *langue d'oïl,* was different from *langue d'oc,* spoken in the south—barbarians because they dressed more crudely and bathed less often, and because their lords did not adhere to the gracious, sophisticated code of courtesy of the southern lords.) The Count of Toulouse tried to remain within the Catholic Church, since excommunication meant the confiscation of his lands by the Church. However, in 1212 the Church handed him an ultimatum demanding, among other things, he wear only coarse brown homespun, raze all his châteaux and fortresses, and sail immediately to the Holy Land—where he was to remain indefinitely. These were terms he obviously could not accept.

When the Albigensian Crusade was over and Languedoc was in the invaders' hands, the Inquisition began. It was characterized by spying, denunciation, and torture. Persons accused of heresy were not told the identity of their accusers or the nature of the evidence against them. Theoretically, the accused were allowed legal representation, but the availability of lawyers was somewhat restricted by the Inquisition's practice of regarding them as their clients' accomplices and punishing them along with the accused. The main object of the initial interrogations was to collect names of other people who could be interrogated, names of those suspected of heresy, names of those who might have harbored heretics—names extracted from tortured prisoners. People were denounced for as little as having had dinner with a heretic. Since all that the Church required for forgiveness was a confession, thousands came forward, only to find that a confession was deemed valid if it incriminated others. At first they tried giving the Inquisitors fictitious names; when the Inquisitors were not fooled, they gave names of people who were deceased. To their horror the Inquisitors exhumed and convicted the dead, long interred in their graves, in order to burn the decomposed corpses on funeral pyres. Their property, and the property of their heirs, was then confiscated by the Church. The bitter irony in the words of Jean Tisseye of Toulouse, a simple workingman of the thirteenth century, reveals his feeling that the Albigensians led more virtuous lives than members of the traditional Church, as well as an awareness that the Inquisition's "trials" were more political than religious in nature:

> Listen to me, citizens! I am no heretic: I have a wife and sleep with her, and she has borne me sons, I eat meat, I tell lies and swear, and I am a good Christian. So don't believe it when they say I am an atheist, not a word of it. They'll very likely accuse you too, as they have me: these accursed villains want to put down honest folk and take the town from its lawful master.

He was burned at the stake.

The secret files of names created an atmosphere of suspicion and distrust. They were a source of such terror that the people of Albi repeatedly risked their lives in attempts to destroy them.

When the Inquisition ended, the prosperity that had given rise to the troubadour culture was gone. A person who confessed incurred a penance—generally a heavy monetary fine, followed by a pilgrimage. The pilgrimages and the fines created economic hardship, since they removed a substantial portion of the population from the area for extended periods.

The usual pilgrimage lasted from several months to several years: knights were sent on a crusade to the Holy Land, others on a journey of several months to the pilgrimage sites of Conques, Saint-Gilles, Le Puy, and Santiago de Compostela. (The more troublesome the Church considered the penitent, the longer the Church made the penitent's pilgrimage. The penitent would carry a letter from the Inquisitor which had to be signed by each of the heads of the ecclesiastical institutions he was assigned to visit.)

In 1282, when construction of the Cathedral of Sainte-Cécile began, the Inquisition was still in force. Bernard de Castenet—Inquisitor of Languedoc and Vice Inquisitor of France, the most ruthless Inquisitor in a series of ruthless Inquisitors—was Bishop of Albi. It has been said that he violated not only canon law but all the laws of human decency as well. Enriched by lands confiscated from convicted heretics, he was able to lay the foundations for the Cathedral of Sainte-Cécile. When the money to complete the cathedral ran out, he sent a messenger to the homes of Albi's twenty-five wealthiest families to inform them, politely, that the bishop was considering reviving the Inquisition. Within the week the bishop had enough money to continue construction. (So hated was Bishop Bernard that once when he left the protection of his fortified palace in Albi and traveled to Toulouse, an angry mob forced him to flee for his life to the safety of a nearby convent; he was unable to leave it for several months.) The original church, built in the land of the troubadours to honor Sainte Cécile, the patron saint of music, was gone and in its place rose a fortified cathedral built for the Inquisitor's protection. The architecture of the cathedral's exterior—with its walls of layer upon layer of brick, so massive, so high, crowned with a warlike parapet—is his design, and the word that best describes it for me is "fascistic."

The interior, completed centuries later, when the Church was no longer embattled but merely rich, is as dazzlingly ornate and Byzantine as the exterior is austere. The wide single space, 97 feet high, 318 long, and, if you include the chapels, 97 feet wide, is in the architectural tradition of the single aisleless nave. The magnitude of the inner space is quite exceptional, and the profusion of colors is breathtaking. The red ribs of the transverse arches contrast with the ornate geometric designs and frescoes in vivid blue and gold that cover every inch of the plastered brick walls and vaulted ceiling. Dividing the nave in half is a rood screen delicately chiseled in limestone, its intricate carvings so lacelike and filmy I had to touch it before I could believe it was actually made of stone. The whiteness of the screen's stone, contrasting with the vibrant blues and golds all around, heightens the vividness of the colors on the walls.

I doubt if the congregation who once worshiped here found the lavish decorations, while sensually appealing, culturally or spiritually inspiring. For example, two bays of the vaulting are filled with an enormous fresco of Sainte Cécile executed by Italian Renaissance artists from Bologna around 1508. It is quite poignant to me that the artists didn't know, or care, that the patron saint of the troubadours should have been depicted singing. Another work, *The Last Judgement,* covering the surface of two large interior towers supporting the bell tower, would certainly have been offensive to the Albigensian community. The painting's central panel, which depicted Christ surrounded by the saints the Albigensians abhorred, was destroyed in 1693, but the remaining work still contains a portrait of Blanche of Castile, the French Queen who sent ten thousand soldiers to the stronghold at Montségur, where two hundred Albigensian holy leaders were massacred after a siege lasting nine months.

After leaving the cathedral, we went over to the Berbie Palace (actually, the Bishop's Palace; *berbie* is a corruption of *besbie,* which means "bishop" in *langue d'oc*). It now houses the Toulouse-Lautrec Museum. A low Renaissance palace with large windows has been added to the original fortified château built by Bernard de Castenet. (Seeing the collection of more than two hundred of Toulouse-Lautrec's paintings and more than six hundred lithographs, posters, and sketches is alone worth the trip to Albi.)

While strolling through the Berbie Palace, I walked through a door and found myself outside—on a balcony overlooking a rectangular Renaissance garden of geometrical design. It came as a sudden surprise not only because it was unexpected but because it was so very beautiful. I found my way down to a low parapet surrounding the garden on three sides. The fourth side is where the Inquisitor lived, a windowless medieval dungeon with walls as high as those of the cathedral. Spanning the dungeon's two towers, on the side facing the garden, is a soaring Romanesque arch, made more massive by columns in which cylindrical buttresses are concealed. At first the arch seemed similar to one in Arles built by the emperor Constantine. But unlike that Roman arch, this medieval arch conceals machicolations (a similar arch with hidden machicolations was built into the side of the dungeon that faces the town) to protect the Inquisitor from his flock. Opposite the dungeon is an arcade overlooking the Tarn River far below. When the bishop walked here, he was protected from his worshipers by the steep drop to the river. The walkway ends in a whimsical turreted structure topped with a dunce-cap roof with open views of the Tarn. However, as I walked away from the river, along the short side of the garden, I came upon another turret, adjacent to the dungeon, also windowless but without a bit of whimsy. Inside the barred entrance, I saw cobwebs covering a flight of stairs that led far down into the rock. These were the chambers where the Inquisition tortured suspected heretics until they decided to confess. Many heretics imprisoned here, unable to stand the torture and unable, because of their beliefs, to confess, chose to starve themselves to death.

Although I didn't realize it at first, Albi is one of the cleanest, friendliest, prettiest provincial cities I have ever visited. In the picturesque medieval section, whose narrow streets are closed to cars, you can spend a pleasant afternoon or evening walking along winding, cobbled streets, with hanging gardens, half-timbered tile-roofed buildings dating from the twelfth to the sixteenth century. The upper stories of many of these buildings are open, having been used for drying woad, a plant from which was extracted the dye used in the vibrant blues of the cathedral. Hidden in one narrow alley is an ancient flight of stone steps leading to the cloistered garden of the Romanesque Church of Saint-Salvi, whose cool stone benches have been warmed since the twelfth century by readers escaping the hectic pace of the world outside. As for the Cathedral of Sainte-Cécile, there is a great view of both it and the town from the plaza at the cathedral's base. Bob and I would sit for hours at La Tartine, a bustling, friendly outdoor café whose owner welcomed by name most of the diners, including us by the time we left. As night fell, this bistro and the others around the plaza would fill with townspeople of all ages having a relaxed good time.

. . .

While we were in Albi, the Tour de France came through.

Although in New York I live directly across from the finish line of the New York Marathon in Central Park but have not once walked across the street to watch the runners come in, I waited in the plaza in Albi for hours, absolutely entranced, as I watched the townspeople—very proud of their great cathedral—spruce up the plaza of Sainte-Cécile for its television appearance (all of France is glued to TV sets during the three weeks of the world's most famous bicycle race). All afternoon, pots of flowers arrived by the truckload to decorate the plaza, where the cyclists would finish. As night began to fall, a caravan of tractor-trailer trucks arrived, depositing the small army of men, women, and equipment that travels with the cyclists from town to town: TV crews, race officials, mechanics, masseurs, and doctors—about twenty-five hundred people who prepare for the cyclists' arrival each evening while they race through the French countryside. The racers, who had already sped through Normandy, Brittany, and Bordeaux, had just left the Pyrénées and were now in Languedoc, about to stop in Albi. By the time they raced down the Champs-Élysées and crossed the finish line at the Arc de Triomphe de l'Étoile in Paris, they would have traversed seventy-six mountains and covered over twenty-five hundred miles.

From our table at La Tartine, we had a great view of both the cathedral and the town. We watched as a tent was unloaded from a truck and workmen, now proficient with the experience of eighty-eight previous tours, selected the town's most dramatic site and set up the tent in what seemed like only moments, filling it with flowers, tables, and chairs for the elaborate ceremony at which, each evening during the Tour, an award is presented to the winner of that day's "lap." The sleepy plaza became a sea of motion as groups of people flowed back and forth from café tables to the official's tent to hear the latest news of the cyclists' progress. With each hour that passed, the provincial town became more charged with electricity; every table at every café surrounding the plaza was filled with diners waiting for the spectacle that the French orchestrate so well. We were reminded what a great event it is in the life of France.

THE PILGRIMAGE CHURCHES OF
Conques and Rocamadour

We first saw Rocamadour from the terrace of a little restaurant on the Hospitalet Road. Our terrace jutted out from a cliff overlooking a deep canyon that separated it from the rugged cliff opposite us, to which Rocamadour was somehow miraculously clinging. Sitting there in the hazy light of a beautiful summer morning, above this deep, wide gorge, I realized I had found an ideal place for a twentieth-century skeptic like myself to understand the religious experience of a twelfth-century pilgrim. The monks of Rocamadour had taken one of the greatest cliffs of France and built right into its side not only a church but also a bishop's palace, seven chapels, and an entire turreted and fortified medieval town—and had then crowned the cliff with a castle whose battlements are shaped like crosses. From across the gorge, we could see a steady procession of modern-day tourists making their way up the side of the escarpment, up the 216 steps that twelfth-century pilgrims once climbed. Because of the distance, the tourists were just a line of dots, and it was easy to imagine them as medieval pilgrims in the Age of Faith. Each year hundreds of thousands of them made their way south across France to three main destinations: Jerusalem, Rome, and Santiago de Compostela in Spain. As they made their way south, the pilgrims would stop for the night at monasteries and abbeys possessing relics—the body or some bones of a saint or martyr—places that had become known for miraculous cures and potential salvation. The pilgrims would make "voluntary" contributions for the relics' upkeep, and monasteries came to realize that such objects constituted a potential source of revenue with which to build greater churches for the glory of God.

First, of course, a monastery had to have a relic—and for monasteries in France, this wasn't always easy. The best relics (the ones believed to have the most power for curing and salvation) were those connected to Christ and his apostles—none of whom, unfortunately, had so much as set foot in France.

So French monasteries attempted to remedy this situation by means both subtle and direct. Foulques Nerra, for example, returned from a pilgrimage to Jerusalem with a large chunk of wood. He said that it was a piece of the True Cross which he had bitten off with his teeth, and he enshrined part of the wood in a church that he renamed the Church of Saint-Croix—and over the years it became a regular stop for pilgrims heading for Compostela.

The success story of Conques, which we passed as we drove from Albi to Rocamadour, was illustrative of an age in which pilgrimages were big business. Conques was a popular stop on the famous Pilgrim's Path because of its fabulous treasure: a jewel-encrusted reliquary statue of Sainte Foy, which you can still see today. Saint Bernard could have had this statue in mind when, trying to reform the commercial and corrupt practices associated with pilgrimages, he wrote, "Money brings money . . . [pilgrims'] eyes are feasted with relics cased in gold, and their purse strings are loosed." But Conques had not always been popular. The story of its success—how Conques had obtained the statue and the pilgrims who came to see it—was typical of the age.

Sainte Foy was a twelve-year-old girl who was martyred in A.D. 303 at Agen. Her remains had been encased in a gold statue at a monastery there. As early as the ninth century, word spread that the blind were miraculously cured after visiting her remains; so pilgrims came in great numbers with "purse strings loosened." Conques, on the other hand, was attracting few pilgrims. There seemed to be little reason for them to detour through miles of rugged hills and woods, filled with wild animals, robbers, and imagined demons, to this isolated monastery. In fact, the monks who had settled on this rocky site were threatening to leave. To remedy the situation, in 856 Conques's abbot decided to steal Sainte Foy's relics from the Agen monastery. (The solution to his problem was not unique; over a hundred thefts of relics by rival monasteries were recorded during the Age of Faith. Vézelay, for example, stole the relics of Mary Magdalene from another monastery, and in its turn Vézelay was nearly destroyed when monks from yet another monastery, at nearby Autun, tried to steal those remains, which, as it happened, turned out to be fake.) Conques's abbot selected one of his monks, Ariviscus, for the theft from Agen. Arriving at the Agen monastery, Ariviscus discovered that the relics were guarded night and day by trusted monks. Being in no hurry to return to Conques, he joined the monastery and waited. Ten years later the brotherhood at Agen considered Ariviscus trustworthy enough to allow him to guard the treasure. As soon as he was left alone, he grabbed the statue and escaped back to Conques on horseback, with the Agen monks in pursuit.

The treasure in which the relics of Sainte Foy are encased is a nearly three-foot-high statue put together over several centuries. The face is actually a fifth-century gold mask of a Roman emperor, not of the martyred young girl. Monks of the ninth century joined this mask to a wooden core and covered the wood with thin plaques of Merovingian gold. Monks of the tenth century further embellished it with a crown and earrings of precious stones, then placed it on a gold throne. Its reputation for curing the blind followed it from Agen to Conques, so that by 1031 the monks of Conques had accumulated sufficient funds to start construction of a Romanesque cathedral. But any way they looked at it, the monks realized that blind pilgrims constituted a limited source of income, as well as being a group hardly in a position to appreciate fully the beauty of their newly acquired treasure. As the cathedral rose, the monk in charge of recording miracles noticed that some workmen who had fallen from steeples during construction were recovering. That, the monk realized in a moment of inspiration, could be called a miracle, too. Since at the time cathedrals were being built all over France, the healing of cathedral construction workers constituted a potential growth industry, and it was announced that visits to Sainte Foy would cure not only blindness but injuries incurred by workmen building cathedrals. The resulting Romanesque church at Conques, with its extraordinary polychrome tympanum of the Last Judgment, is considered a model for pilgrimage churches of the period.

While twelfth-century pilgrims were detouring to nearby Conques in great numbers, they were not stopping at Rocamadour. I have to admire the inventiveness, if not the piety, displayed by the monks of Rocamadour to remedy this situation. First, there was the sword. The miraculous nature of swords was a common Celtic belief when this area was still pagan. The evolution of a legend such as Roland and his sword Durendal, or King Arthur and Excalibur, stemmed from the fact that the Druids, the pagan priests of Celtic society, were originally blacksmiths who kept to themselves the secrets of extracting iron ore from stone and turning the iron into swords. Pagans saw taking iron from stone and transforming it into a sword as a magical act, which by the twelfth century gave rise to marvelous tales of chivalry in which God gives the hero a great sword with which to defeat his enemies. (Joan of Arc, the last hero of the Age of Chivalry, would also miraculously find a buried sword.) Rocamadour's sword was supposedly Durendal, whose divine properties enabled Roland, personification of the true and faithful Christian knight, to hold off at Roncesvalles a hundred thousand Saracens long enough for Charlemagne's battered army to retreat back to France. In the *Chanson de Roland,* an eleventh-century heroic poem—a *chanson de geste,* which is available in paperback and which makes as good reading on a modern pilgrimage as it did in the twelfth century when pilgrims recited it as they camped along the road—Roland, wounded and dying, covers Durendal with his body and cries out as he is dying:

O, Holy Mary, said the Count, help me!
. . . For this sword I grieve and sorrow . . .
I should rather die than leave it in pagan hands.
God, our Father, spare France this disgrace!

The monks of Rocamadour made a slight alteration in the story. In their version Roland did not fall on his sword but, rather, flung it into the air with all his might. And, according to Rocamadour's monks, guess where it landed? The twelfth-century pilgrim could see at Rocamadour—as you can see there today—a rusty iron sword embedded in a rock next to the oratory of the Virgin. (Today's tourist office has the good taste to refer to this sword as a replica.)

But the pilgrims still did not come. So in 1166, when a body was discovered near the entrance to the shrine of the Black Virgin, it was announced that it was the body of none other than Zaccheus, a tax collector from Jerusalem who had come to Rocamadour to live as a hermit after his conversion by Christ. According to a contemporary chronicler, the corpse was discovered when an inhabitant of the area, divinely inspired, ordered his family to bury him at the entrance to the Black Virgin's shrine. During the burial Zaccheus's body, miraculously preserved, was uncovered. Zaccheus was renamed Saint Amadour, and the body was placed in the church, close to the altar, for the worship of pilgrims.

Still the pilgrims did not come. In 1188 an ambitious monk produced a list detailing 126 miracles that had occurred at Rocamadour because of the power of its relics. Evidence of the effort to publicize these miracles is found as far north as Mont-Saint-Michel, in Normandy. Still, the pilgrims went to Conques without stopping at Rocamadour.

The monks knew that pilgrims would travel to shrines if they thought important people—medieval celebrities—had also made the trip. So they let it be known that Simon de Montfort had come to Rocamadour to seek forgiveness for his sins. (Actually, Montfort—and his troops—spent the winter of 1212 at Rocamadour not for salvation but for protection: the safety of its fortified location.)

In the thirteenth century pilgrims finally began to come to Rocamadour. They came not to venerate the Black Virgin or Durendal or Saint Amadour's relics but by choice—their choice being that they could come to

Rocamadour or be burned at the stake—for what finally solved Rocamadour's problem was the Inquisition. Rocamadour may not have been the
destination for those pilgrims who had taken to the road for adventure, excitement, or salvation, but it was one of the destinations the Albigensian
"heretics" were forced to visit by the Inquisitors as penance for their "sins."
(Alas, it was not even the Inquisitors' first choice. They had initially sent
the Albigensians on a much more onerous pilgrimage, to the Holy Land,
but found that sending them there was counterproductive, for some of
these supposed converts spread their heretical doctrines in Jerusalem.) The
penitents were required to return to Albi with signed certificates attesting
that they had made the visit. The cult of the Virgin and the worship of
saints were particularly reprehensible to Albigensians. Prostrating themselves before this rather barbaric, soot-blackened statue of the Virgin was
humiliating to a people who had rebelled, even those who had considered
themselves Catholics, against the more "miraculous" aspects of the Church,
which they considered pagan. It was intentional, therefore, that a great
number of the heretics who confessed at Albi were sentenced by the Inquisition to prove their conversion by seeking forgiveness from the Black Virgin and Saint Amadour.

The procedure was quite standardized. On the day of his departure
from Albi, the pilgrim attended a special Mass at which he received an outfit that had been blessed and sprinkled with holy water. The outfit consisted of a tunic whose back was covered with crosses, a knapsack, a wide-
brimmed hat turned up in front, a leather pouch belted around his waist,
and a staff. On his arrival at the base of the great cliff of Rocamadour, the
pilgrim stripped himself of his clothes, allowed heavy chains to be bound
around his arms and neck, and, dragging the chains, climbed on his knees
the 216 steps to the shrine of the Black Virgin, stopping on each step to recite the rosary. There was a symbolic reason for the chains, just as for almost everything the pilgrim did during the Age of Faith. They signified
the weight of the penitent's sins on his soul. The pouch stood for poverty;
the staff, a shepherd's staff, was both protection against the devil and a
beam between heaven and earth. The climb up the steps to the shrine was
a symbolic climb to God; each step climbed was a symbolic step closer to
God. And as he climbed, the pilgrim passed—as the modern tourist does
today—scenes representing the fourteen Stations of the Cross. (You now

see in the caves of Rocamadour, where sixth-century hermits once lived, scenes depicting each of these stations.)

Once the pilgrim arrived at the shrine and the chapel where Saint Amadour was supposedly buried, he prostrated himself before a statue of the Black Virgin and, with appropriate wailing, begged forgiveness for his sins. The priest who recited prayers of purification then unlocked his chains and presented him with the certificate proving that he had come to Rocamadour. The pilgrim could then buy a *sportelle,* his Badge of Rocamadour. The Rocamadour *sportelle,* an oval medal, showed the Virgin seated on her throne holding a scepter topped by a fleur-de-lis. Little rings on the edge of the medal enabled the pilgrim to attach it to his hat. An average pilgrim's hat would be covered with the medals from the shrines he had already visited—the head of John the Baptist from Amiens; an amulet bearing the words "Thomas makes the best doctor for the worthy sick" from Canterbury; the keys of Saint Peter from Rome; the scallop shell of Saint James (Santiago) from Compostela.

I looked at my Michelins, Red and Green, open on the table in front of me and thought the more things change, the more they stay the same. These modern French guidebooks list the best places at which to stay and to eat, and advise the traveler which monuments are worth a detour to visit. The medieval pilgrim, I knew, was guided by the *Codex of Callixtus,* a travel guide for pilgrims that listed the best shrines of martyrs and saints to visit for miracles, the best monasteries at which to stay, which inns along the way were bug-infested, which ones had water that was safe to drink, which ones were free from thieves, where and what to eat, which relics were worth a detour to see. Not surprisingly, the pilgrim, like the tourist today, would find that his accommodations improved with the size of the pouch he wore around his waist (although the fresh hay or the addition of fruit and nuts supplied the generous pilgrim might seem an inadequate improvement to the modern pilgrim). The twelfth-century *Codex* was written by a Cluniac monk to divert the pilgrim and his money from Rome to Compostela; the cathedral there was part of Cluny's expanding empire, which would ultimately include over two thousand Cluniac dependencies, including Conques and Roncesvalles. At Roncesvalles, the next stop listed after Conques, for example, the pilgrim was informed by the *Codex* that he would not only see the relics of Roland's famous battle, which took place at that spot, but would be provided with a bed, a bath, and a dinner including almonds and fruit. In order to give the book authority, its authorship was attributed to Pope Calixtus II—a former Abbot of Cluny who was widely respected in the twelfth century for the reforms he had tried to initiate in the Church. This reform Pope would have had difficulty writing the guide, since he had already been dead for twenty years at the time it was written, but the pilgrims were not aware of that—or of how the *Codex* altered the facts of history to enhance the religious experience of some of the pilgrimage sites along the way. In brief, the altered facts relevant to Rocamadour and Conques concerned Charlemagne, who, in 778, had driven the Saracens out of France, crossed the Pyrénées, and gone as far south as Saragossa in Spain, where the Saracens regrouped and drove him back to France. While retreating across the Pyrénées, in August of that year, Charlemagne's rear guard was cut down in the gorge of Roncesvalles by a small group of Basque mountaineers. This historical event was transformed in the *Codex of Callixtus* to authenticate the relics of Santiago de Compostela. Charlemagne's time in Spain was expanded from months to several years, during which he saw a vision of the martyred Saint James arriving at Compostela in a stone boat. Charlemagne's victories in Spain were thus considered the result of the saint's intervention. By taking advantage of the religious fury against the Saracens aroused by the Crusades, the *Codex* created a religious reason for stopping at Roncesvalles. The Christian Basques became pagan Saracens, and Charlemagne's slaughtered rear guard became a company commanded by Roland.

As I looked across the gorge at the modern pilgrims angling their way up the escarpment, I picked up an American guidebook and read the suggestion that we tourists remain on the Hospitalet side of the gorge and not actually enter Rocamadour, because the town today is overly touristy and commercial. Modern Rocamadour is indeed overly touristy, with booth after booth selling postcards, T-shirts, plastic statues of saints, toy swords, and horns. (The horns on sale at Rocamadour are supposed to represent the Oliphant, the horn Roland blew.) But, of course, Rocamadour was overly touristy in the twelfth century, too. Postcards and T-shirts have just replaced *sportelles* and a rusty sword. So, to see Rocamadour is in a way to see the Age of Faith in a very authentic way.

And whatever else it is, Rocamadour is as dramatic a pilgrimage site as any traveler through time could ever hope to visit. I had never seen anything quite like it. To see that great cliff with a church and a town built right into its side must have been an awe-inspiring experience six hundred years ago. And it is an awe-inspiring experience today.

The Dordogne

AN IMPRESSION OF THE
Hundred Years War

It is less than an hour's drive from the medieval pilgrimage site of Roca-madour to the village of Beynac-et-Cazenac and the medieval wars be-tween France and England known as the Hundred Years War. Beynac, lo-cated in the Dordogne Valley, is a tiny village nestled at the foot of a golden cliff crowned with a battlemented fortress whose golden walls seem to grow out of the cliff like an extension of the rock itself. From the parapet of Beynac's castle can be seen the lovely countryside of the Dordogne Val-ley: a landscape divided into a patchwork quilt of greens and pale golds by breaks of dark green cypress trees and ruffled silvery-green rivers and streams, ornamented with castles, keeps, and stacks of hay. Time seems to have stood still in this pastoral portion of the valley encompassing Beynac, Domme, Castelnaud, and Sarlat, where every meal is a treasured memory and every view a poet's challenge. Although serene and peaceful, it evokes, more than any other part of France, the fierce and brutal Hundred Years War because as you meander along the banks of the Dordogne—a river that once was the bloody border between the French domains and those of the hated English—you come upon not merely fortresses but fortresses in pairs; at every ford, it seems, there is both a French castle and, facing it across the river, a castle of the English enemy—castles such as Beynac, whose barons were faithful vassals of the King of France, and directly across the river, Montfort and mighty Castelnaud, whose lords fought for England. Sprinkled throughout the three-hundred-mile-long valley, moreover, are French and English *bastides* (fortified towns), such as Domme, Bretenoux, Molières, and Monpazier, built by peasants who were coaxed and prodded into constructing them by the promises of rival kings.

The war officially began in 1337, when a French king died without a male heir and successive English kings claimed the double crown of France and England through the female line, and it officially ended in 1453, after Joan of Arc inspired the people of France to victory over the English. It was not a war between two nation states, as one might assume from the use of the names "France" and "England"; rather, it began as a feudal conflict with origins in a tangled two-hundred-year-old maze of hereditary fiefs and family trees. Here, in the Dordogne Valley, I could feel the last gasp of these once-independent feudal lords trying to prevent their independence, their authority—their very lordship, in fact—from being reduced to mere landlordship by the King of France. I could see them switching sides, back and forth, first with the French king, then with the English—wherever their interest at the time dictated.

The towers of the castles that you see at Beynac, Castelnaud, Fayrac, and Montfort were the symbols of feudal authority, independence, and rule of the local lords. From the time of Charlemagne (742–814), only members of the noble warrior class were allowed to build these defensive military towers, and until the French Revolution they remained the affirmation of a privilege reserved for the nobility. However, during the course of the Hundred Years War, the cannon, invented in 1350, slowly came into use as an effective weapon for destroying most medieval fortifications, making these defensive towers obsolete, while at the same time the very purpose for the existence of these lords disappeared. In feudal society they had been vassals of the king, holding their income-producing lands as fiefs in exchange for fighting service each year. These fiefs became hereditary (through the male line: a woman could not inherit a fief except as a dowry). At the beginning of the Hundred Years War, the French king was still dependent on his vassals to make up his armies. By the war's end he relied primarily on mercenaries paid for by the emerging middle class and the Roman Catholic Church. During the course of this war, therefore, the nobility, or warrior class, became as redundant as its defensive towers. In the century following the war, both the towers and the aristocracy would become little more than useless social adornments—adornments that the French Revolution would eventually wipe away.

The best time to wander through the Dordogne Valley is the spring, which was the height of the feudal social season. Both French and English barons disliked fighting during the unpleasant winter months, so it was in the spring that truces were ended and the barons mustered their vassals for war—and as the knights gathered, before the fighting began, hunts and tournaments were held. The sound of oliphants—hunting horns made of ivory and decorated with precious metals—would pierce the quiet of the valley as men on horseback, hooded falcons on their wrists, galloped out of the castles after packs of yelping dogs in search of wild boar and other game. Today, spring is the season before the great invasion of tourists begins, and the silence of the valley is disturbed by the horns of their buses and recreational vehicles struggling along the narrow, winding roads.

If you come to France in August, the month when the entire country goes on vacation, I'm not sure you should visit the Dordogne at all. This heavenly valley is no secret to the rest of France or to the English, whose aristocratic ancestors once fought here, and it is too overrun with English tourists and French campers to be enjoyed. You should come to the Dordogne in order to leave the hectic pace of the twentieth century far behind. You should allow yourself the luxury of letting a sense of feudal society slowly penetrate your consciousness by loafing on a flat-bottomed barque or a kayak (rentable in Beynac), floating down the river looking at reflections of castle turrets shimmering in the water, or by spending aimless hours on a castle battlement looking out at pastoral landscapes where peasants labored for their lords in years long past. You should stay at inexpensive inns, enjoying leisurely midday meals touched with a magic of freshness that somehow allowed me to eat all I wanted and leave France weighing less than when I arrived—and these are not the decorator plates of nouvelle cuisine, designed for people who like to look at rather than eat their food, but course after course of ample portions that make the local farmer happy and content. You should travel through this valley like its meandering river, like time itself in the Middle Ages, when changes took place so slowly that they barely caused a ripple on the surface of daily life, or like its meandering war, which stopped for truces, plagues, and changes of seasons, and in which loyalties were only local and knights enjoyed battles as a game. And as you slowly wander from castle to castle, you realize that each, with its surrounding domain, was a closed and separate little world in which modern concepts of time, war, and nationality had no relevance to the men and women who lived there.

I remember our first trip to the Dordogne: we stayed four weeks; I wanted to stay a lifetime. It was our first trip to France. Bob had just finished his first book, *The Power Broker,* a biography of Robert Moses, which had taken him seven years to write. During those years our travel had been limited to New York State and the projects built there by Moses; and our dining in restaurants outside the Bronx was, because of the size of Bob's advance, all but nonexistent. We had never been to Europe, and when the book began to earn a little money, the very first thing we did was arrange a trip to France. (It is now almost twenty years later, and I have found so much to see in France that I still haven't seen Rome or Madrid.) Bob, knowing that *Mastering the Art of French Cooking* had been my bible during our impoverished years of nonrestaurant eating, had asked Judith Jones, its editor at Knopf, to recommend an area in some remote region of France with wonderful food and a delightful little hotel, and she had suggested, without hesitation, the Dordogne Valley and the Hôtel Bonnet in Beynac.

After spending two weeks in Paris, we rented a car and drove south. We had been told that distances in France were easily covered because of the autoroute. I'm not sure exactly where the autoroute ended then, but it was nowhere near the Dordogne Valley. I remember that after we left it and headed for Beynac, the national road became a winding local road which became narrower and narrower until it became so narrow that at one point we didn't notice we had left it until we arrived at the door of someone's farmhouse.

When we finally arrived at the Hôtel Bonnet, it was after dark—even with the deliciously long summer days of France. The proprietor had kept the kitchen open for us and had saved us the only room in the hotel still vacant—one in the attic. In fact, the room *was* the attic, the whole attic, a long space that ran across the width of the hotel, from one side to the other, with a dormer window at each end. He was apologetic, but after the little room we had just left in Paris, we thought all that space was grand. In the morning Bob staggered out of our featherbed and looked out the window at one end of the room while I staggered over to the window at the other end, and simultaneously we yelled to each other, "You've got to see this castle!" For a moment, as we laughed, we thought we were talking about the same castle, seen from two angles, but then we realized we weren't. There were two massive medieval fortresses—one out each window. We couldn't believe it. I'm not sure, but I don't think either of us had ever seen a castle before, and here, glaring at each other across a broad river, were two of them—the French castle of the Barons of Beynac and, across the river, the enemy castle, the English fortress of Castelnaud.

(As an author I should have gone back to the Hôtel Bonnet and checked those windows to make sure of my castles, because two other castles, Fayrac and Marqueyssac, strongholds of two vassals of the Lord of Castelnaud, are also visible from Beynac. But I haven't and I won't. Places change with time, and so do our perceptions of them, and nothing in the world would ever make me return and perhaps find out that the Hôtel Bonnet is not the most wonderful place on earth.)

Some miles from Beynac, in a farmhouse to which a small wing had just been added and decorated with beautiful Spanish tiles, was a restaurant: Le Souqual. Judith Jones had told us about it, too.

Dinners at Le Souqual were wonderful. The owner and chef was a rigid man, very much a little Napoleon in a big white chef's hat and apron, as spotless and gleaming as if he were overseeing a dining room on the Champs-Élysées. When, that first evening, Bob asked for a Scotch and soda, the owner made it clear that Bob could have the house apéritif—or nothing. But the apéritif, a drink of many colors (and many ingredients: the proprietor once listed them for me, and it was quite a long list; I remember only that the base was Armagnac), was smooth and delicious, and we drank it on a little patio behind the farmhouse facing the great cliff at Beynac, watching the sun set behind the castle on top of it. As the drinks sank in our glasses, the sun sank behind the castle, with the battlements and turrets turning black against the dark red glow behind them.

Sometimes, Monsieur would sip his apéritif standing behind us (he would never sit with us); usually he and his wife, to whom he was obviously devoted, would sip their drinks sitting together on the lawn.

Monsieur and I hit it off, and after we began coming there every night, he would ask me what I would like for dinner the next day. He could drive to Sarlat and get a leg of lamb, he might say, and he could cook it with such and such herbs; or he could go out on the river and catch a *truite*. (So terrible was my comprehension of rapid-fire French then—not that it's much better now—that I thought he had promised to catch me a "treat.") Bob's preferences were never solicited; sometimes, however, he and I would discuss them together during the day, and I would slip them in as though they were my own. Monsieur would make us soup from vegetables he had picked in his garden that very morning (a garden so neat you could see the missing carrots he had picked for dinner), or sauté that newly caught trout; duck confit was his specialty, I still remember, and he used Armagnac not only in the apéritif but in nearly all his sauces.

Monsieur was determined that standards would be maintained, even in this provincial restaurant, and even though the only material available for building a staff was the youth of the countryside. On weekends, when the four or five tables were filled with aristocratic French (or English or Scandinavian) families who lived in grand châteaux in the valley, two plump country girls were the waitresses, and Monsieur, in his big hat and apron, would keep surreptitiously peeking in, big cleaver in hand, to make sure they had done it right—a little field marshal whipping raw troops into shape. And his guests dined, in that room with the tiled floor that had been polished until it gleamed, off gleaming white tablecloths and artistically arranged napkins, off china and crystal and silver that sparkled, while, through the sparkling windowpanes, they watched the last of the sun set behind the fortress on the cliff.

(I remember Le Souqual as fondly as I do the Hôtel Bonnet, and sixteen years later, when we were again in the area, we tried to visit the restaurant—an attempt that told us it's not only home you can't go back to again. We telephoned the restaurant from our hotel and no one answered, so at noon we just drove by. The neat little garden was overgrown, the windowpanes were dirty, and on the locked front gate was a note explaining why. Madame was ill, it said; Monsieur had taken her to the hospital. As Bob and I drove away from that note, and from that little farmhouse, which looked so lonely, there was a very long silence in the car.)

Les Eyzies-de-Tayac

That first visit to the Dordogne region was permeated with a magic I still remember as though it were yesterday. We visited what the French Tourist Bureau calls the "cradle of mankind": Lascaux and the other caves in the Vézère Valley whose walls are covered with thousands of paintings of prehistoric animals because, according to some archaeologists, seventeen thousand years ago Paleolithic hunters, believing that the caves possessed magical powers, felt that if they painted on the caves' walls success in the hunt, they would have success in the hunt itself. By the time Bob and I arrived, Lascaux and many other caves had been closed to tourists because the carbon dioxide in the breath of the visiting hordes was destroying the crystalline deposit that had protected the drawings for tens of thousands of years. We never saw the life-sized drawings and carved reliefs of animals in motion—reindeer drinking, wild goats about to lock horns, and shaggy ponies, for example—that had thrilled so many visitors before us. We saw, by the light of our guide's dim flashlight, only a few tiny drawings on a damp cave wall, and they left me unmoved.

But when, leaving the darkened cave, I stepped outside into the sunlight and saw the pastoral valley of farms and castles quilted on the landscape far below, then I *did* feel a bond with my prehistoric ancestors. Standing on that chalky cliff, where cavemen stood so long ago, I felt as though this was where, as part of mankind, I had begun and where, below in the valley, I had traveled—hunting, taming, farming, warring—until somehow I had reached today. It was one of those moments in life you never forget, when you feel an explosion of inner emotion, or perhaps déjà vu.

I am told the museum, now housed in a restored fortress at Les Eyzies-de-Tayac, about nine miles from Lascaux, provides a wonderful introduction to prehistory, and that the cave drawings have been duplicated at Lascaux II for modern tourists in such a way that it is difficult to tell them from the originals.

On our second visit to the Dordogne, we broke our drive north from Rocamadour by stopping at the Château de Castel Novel, a hotel outside Brive-la-Gaillarde. We had intended to spend only one night and then drive on to the valley. For a number of reasons this became impossible. First was the stuffed and boned rabbit ("lapereau" sounds much tastier), served in a rich red wine sauce, that Bob had for dinner. Bob did not want to leave until he had had the dish at least one more time. Then there was the setting of the tennis court. The Castel Novel's foundations date back to the Roman occupation, and the Romans, of course, strategically located their fortification on a high, steep hill. The crest of this hill was totally occupied by the château-hotel, its rugged old walls crowned with gables, balustraded balconies, and pointed slate-covered turrets. Some distance down the hill, on its first level spot, just above the swimming pool, was the tennis court. It was completely shaded by huge trees growing on the slope above it, so that the court was always cool and we could play tennis even on the hottest days. Our room, in one of the many turrets—I love turrets—was furnished with an antique loveseat and charming breakfast table, and was very quiet, perhaps because of the upholstered walls. Every night we had cocktails on a terrace overlooking the valley below, followed by a dinner, cooked to our taste and served by a warm and friendly staff; I sometimes thought a proclivity for smiling must have been a requirement of employment. In all honesty, the hotel was not on our route to anywhere. But like Colette, who wrote many of her novels here when she was mistress of the château, I loved it, so we stayed.

THE BARONIAL WORLD
of Beynac

We began our second trip to the Dordogne Valley with a visit to the Castle of Beynac. I remembered it as the perfect example of the medieval fortress of a warring feudal lord, but when, after parking a little distance from the town, we were walking toward it along the riverbank, I was worried: had my memory made the castle seem better than it was in reality? Or, if my memory was correct, had the castle somehow been changed during the intervening years? The last time we had been here Bob had just taken up jogging, and a smile came across my face now as we passed the farmhouse where, on that earlier trip, a woman had come running out her door, calling her children to come see the crazy American jogger. Physical exercise was the last thing these farmers needed, and she must have thought it a ridiculous thing for anyone to do on a vacation. When we reached the town and the cobblestoned path leading up the steep slope to the castle, I didn't recognize anything. Sixteen years before, some of the simple little houses huddled at the base of the cliff and along the path had had dirt floors and none had had electricity. They had seemed charming to me, and untouched by time. Now they were all freshly restored, uniformly faced in the same stone, electrified, and probably furnished with minitels. Some had been turned into tourist shops.

But the castle far above them hadn't changed. It was just as I remembered it. Its walls still seemed to grow out of the ocher-colored cliff on which it sits, looming massively 492 feet above the Dordogne. Medieval castles, unlike classical buildings, were evolving structures, with towers and walls added and altered in response to changes in contemporary warfare; this castle, like many others, was not built all at once but over hundreds of years, beginning in the twelfth century. Nonetheless, it has a disheveled architectural harmony. It is a typical medieval fortress, except that unlike most such fortresses it is intact. Most medieval fortresses were destroyed either during a siege or in the centuries after the Hundred Years War, when they were abandoned and their stones carted away by local families building their own houses. It still has turrets, rectangular and rounded donjons, arrow-slit windows, crenelated battlements, and protruding machicolations—all the medieval defensive architectural devices that are so visually romantic to us today.

The major defensive device of this castle, however, lay in its location— its unscalable height. Today that height provides a panoramic view; in the Middle Ages it provided a safeguard against surprise. Sentries could see an enemy approach miles away across the countryside or could spot their boats while they were still far down the river. Moreover, attack was virtually impossible on three sides of the castle because attackers would have had to scale that sheer drop of 492 feet before even reaching the high wall of the castle itself. Only the fourth side, the plateau, had to be defended, and that approach was protected by ditches and two lines of curtain walls built in the twelfth century.

When we entered the curtain walls, we were in a lower courtyard facing a rectangular donjon, or keep. Before the Crusades, this cheerless structure was the residence of the early Barons of Beynac and their men. After the crusaders returned to France, they built fortresses with cylindrical towers like the ones they had seen in Byzantium, without corners whose stones could be dislodged by missiles from catapults.

Our guide turned out to be an unpleasant woman who still seemed angry at the English and their descendants for what had happened some six hundred years ago during the Hundred Years War. Assuming I was English, she seemed to hold me personally responsible. In Beynac, do not make the mistake, as I have done on both my visits, of asking, in English-accented French, whether there is a tour of the castle given in English. At most places in France when you do this, the guides slow down, sometimes even enunciating individual words so that the average English-speaking tourist is able to understand the French, or throwing in a English word or two whenever they are able. The reverse was true at Beynac; the speed of the guide's rapid-fire French increased noticeably. On this second trip I made the additional mistake of letting the guide know I was an American. This appeared to increase her hostility, and my curiosity was piqued. While waiting for the group of French families taking the tour to gather on a castle battlement, I brought up the subject of American tourists and her feelings about them, and she said, "At least the English know what the Hundred Years War was about. American tourists aren't even interested." Thinking about that for a moment, I concluded that her hostility was justified.

We then walked up a steep cobblestoned lane, just wide enough for knights on their armored battle horses to reach the upper courtyard in single file only, not in a massed charge. After twisting and turning up the cliff, we reached the castle's massive wooden gate. Jutting out from the wall above it are machicolations through which Beynac's defenders poured a mixture of heated lime *(poix)* on attackers. The gate was protected from flaming arrows by fresh animal skins soaked with water. If the wood caught fire despite this precaution, water could be poured on it through the machicolations. Entering the castle, we found ourselves in a large, dark, vaulted chamber called the Guard Room. (At least I thought it soon would be dark, because during our visit restorers were removing an anachronistically large window and replacing it with the narrow arrow-slit windows.) It was in this room that during the Middle Ages the entire garrison assembled while the Baron of Beynac, standing in front of the fireplace, issued his orders for the defense of the castle. The door to the room is quite wide and high because the guards entered here with their battle horses, which they then tethered in a room beyond a spiral staircase. The floor of the Guard Room has been restored to its original condition of tooth-shaped stones nailed vertically into a bed of clay and lime. The baron, on his way to a crusade, had seen such a floor in Pisa, admired it, and, as soon as he returned, ordered a similar one laid here. At night the men-at-arms spread straw on this floor and slept on it.

As you walk through the castle, you cannot help but become aware of the meanness of the medieval aristocracy's lifestyle. The early barons did not sleep in what we think of as a bed or even enjoy the privacy of separate sleeping quarters. The post-Crusades castle did have one advance in creature comforts over the pre-Crusades keep. Here at Beynac, in a small adjacent room, you see little niches containing seats with holes in them. These seats project out beyond the wall of the castle and beyond the cliff, too. They are latrines, a medieval luxury. The peasants living at the foot of the cliff were continually being dumped on during the Middle Ages. (Later, during the early Renaissance, when internal wars in France had ended and it was no longer necessary for castles to be built on clifftops, the disposal of human waste posed a problem of another type. Renaissance latrines emptied directly into the surrounding moats. Moats, once needed for defensive purposes, had been retained for their decorative value and were placed close to castle walls to reflect the beauty of the new architecture. But the moats were too close, creating a new problem. King Francis I, for example, was continually moving from castle to castle, leaving when the smell from the moat became too bad.)

In contrast to Carcassonne, where many anachronisms exist, authenticity in restoration is taken seriously at Beynac. The spiral staircase, for example, was restored here only after the solid oak used in its reconstruction had been soaked for years in a solution that aged the wood to a condition similar to that of the existing original stairs. And it was rebuilt as it would have been in the fourteenth century: by one carpenter using a medieval adz.

After climbing the staircase, we found ourselves in the Hall of the Estates General of Périgord, barrel-vaulted like a Romanesque church. This is where Périgord's four barons—Bourdeilles, Biron, Mareuil, and Beynac—used to meet during the Middle Ages, taking great care never to stand in a straight line but only in a circle—thereby symbolically asserting their equality. This tells quite a bit about the seriousness with which these princes took the social pyramid of the feudal hierarchy. Each of these barons, as lord of his manor, held the power of life and death over his serfs, whose forebears had relinquished their freedom, tilling the lord's land in exchange for his protection against Visigoths, Saracens, Vikings, and Franks. In turn, these barons, as part of the feudal system, were vassals of the Count of Périgord, who was a vassal of the Duke of Aquitaine, who was a vassal of the King of France. As vassals, nobles equipped themselves with armor and horses—which only the landed aristocracy could afford—and served as knights for their overlord. (Of course, when you read chronicles written at the time, you find that it never worked quite that way. The chivalric virtues of courage, veracity, and integrity with which romantic literature endows this class of "noble" men, who were thought by the lower class to maintain justice, defend the people from oppression, combat violence and tyranny, and confirm the peace, are invariably contradicted by actual deeds considerably less noble. The Lord of Castelnaud, for example, paid homage to the English king in 1405, but then sold his support to the King of France.)

It was here, in the barrel-vaulted hall, that the great feudal ceremonies took place. It was here that the baron received homage (and payment) from his vassals, who knelt before him, swearing fealty, when he invested them with their fiefs in the ceremony of investiture. It was here that the baron, who had the power of life and death over his vassals and peasants, dispensed justice, or granted a man the right to fish or hunt on his land, or ordered a man's fingers chopped off for fishing without first acquiring the right.

This hall also saw entertainments and feasts, including marriage ceremonies: long tables resting on trestles would be set for one occasion and removed when the purpose of the room was changed.

In this hall, too, jongleurs sang the lyric poetry written by troubadour knights; the troubadour culture in Aquitaine was much the same as in neighboring Languedoc. That culture had gained respectability in this area when William, Count of Aquitaine, on returning from the First Crusade in 1102, "sang before the princes and the great assemblies of the Christians, of the miseries of his captivity among the Saracens, using rhymed verse jovially modulated," according to a contemporary chronicler. Previously, the songs had been preserved primarily through oral tradition. Only the clergy knew how to write, and since the verses were not religious, the clergy considered them beneath notice. But after William, one of the most powerful princes of his day, began singing, the clergy committed his songs and others to their precious parchment. William's granddaughter, Eleanor of Aquitaine, became a patron of the troubadour poets, and one of her sons, Richard the Lion-Hearted, who inherited Beynac when he became Duke of Aquitaine, wrote troubadour poetry in the dialect of *langue d'oc.*

In the early years of her reign Eleanor, like her father before her, had traveled from castle to castle throughout Aquitaine on what were called *chevauchées,* ducal processions, visiting local lords like the Baron of Beynac, who entertained her, her men-at-arms, and her servants with as much lavishness as they could muster. On such travels through the realm, the Duke of Aquitaine collected from his vassals not only their oaths of homage and loyalty but also the produce, a percentage of the harvest, that vassals were required to give their lord each year. Each vassal would feed the duke's entire court, which traveled with him. Transporting agricultural goods without spoilage was difficult, and traveling to the vassal and consuming on-site was a pleasant social method of collection. This practice had been followed ever since Charlemagne divided his empire into counties, areas small enough to be covered in a single day. (I remember my disappointment as a graduate student when I read the "primary documents" of the reign of this great emperor. I was hoping to uncover the mysteries of the cultural renaissance during his reign; instead, I found detailed lists of the number of cows and pigs and the amount of produce that various lords owed and gave to Charlemagne as he and his entourage traveled from fief to fief.)

The flags of the four baronies of Périgord now hang in the Hall of the Estates General at Beynac, flanking the huge fireplace that once provided the only heat. For added warmth, tapestries were hung to keep out drafts during the winter months. In the adjacent oratory, or family chapel, is a fourteenth-century fresco of the Last Supper.

From the hall, we were led out onto the battlements of Beynac. Far below us was the broad Dordogne River, so far away that its silver-gray waters seemed unmoving. And in the distance I could see, as could the sentries who paced here so long ago, the enemy castles: Castelnaud, Fayrac, and Marqueyssac. Below me, on the Beynac side of the river, which in the Middle Ages was part of the fiefs of Beynac, I could see the lands of the manor tilled by the peasants for the baron. I could see the limits of the self-sufficient little world where this petty ruler reigned as lord of the manor, and across the river where the world of another petty prince began. As I stood on that tower, the fractious and divisive nature of the feudal system seemed very clear. Perhaps because of the extreme height from which I was viewing the valley, the plots of land tilled by serfs became geometric partitions more closely resembling the abstract images of fiefs and manors in my mind.

It was at this point that our guide began to explain Beynac's role in the Hundred Years War. She started with Eleanor of Aquitaine's divorcing Louis VII, the French king, taking with her Aquitaine and Gascony—and therefore Beynac—and marrying Henry Plantagenet (Count of Anjou and Maine and Duke of Normandy), who shortly became King Henry II of England. The guide explained how this created a situation in which the English king controlled fiefs comprising most of France, but was nonetheless the vassal of the French king, who controlled very little. When you consider that this was a society in which form and ceremony were taken so seriously that the four Barons of Périgord would not even stand in a straight line lest their symbolic equality in the hierarchy be diminished, you quickly grasp the inflammable implications of having the King of England—treated as a near divinity in his own realm—kneel before and pay homage to a man who in the feudal hierarchy was at best only his symbolic equal.

To our guide, Richard the Lion-Hearted (the son of Eleanor and Henry II) was simply English and therefore cruel. She explained that by the time Coeur-de-Lion became Duke of Aquitaine, the local vassals, spoiled because they had in effect been independent, first during the decades of Eleanor's imprisonment and then because Richard, only a boy, was not yet able to rule as duke, had come to believe that they held their fiefs by hereditary right rather than by their lord's will. Richard replaced the local noble families in Aquitaine with men loyal to him—and killed, maimed, or blinded many of those he removed. At Beynac, for example, when Baron Ademar died, centuries of custom decreed that the fief be inherited by the baron's son. But Richard, in 1195, instead bestowed Beynac on his faithful lieutenant Captain Mercadier. The baron's son threw his allegiance to the King of France. Richard also alienated the local aristocracy when he massacred all but one son of the Fortanier family of Gourdon, whom the Beynacs assisted and hid at the castle at Châlus. This act came back to haunt Richard some years later when he raided Châlus in search of a treasure supposedly hidden there. Châlus was defended by only a few men, but one was young Fortanier. Picking up a heavy, pointed iron bolt that one of Richard's crossbowmen had fired at the castle, he fired it back and hit Richard in the shoulder, inflicting a wound that subsequently caused the king's death. Before he died, Richard asked the young man, "Why did you wish to injure me?" Fortanier replied, "Because you slew my father and my brother. Do with me as you will. I do not repent me of the vengeance I have taken." Richard felt that, according to the code of chivalry, the man had been justified in seeking his death, and ordered him freed. After Richard died, however, Eleanor was beside herself with grief, crying, "I have lost the staff of my age, the light of my eyes." Either she or the grief-stricken Mercadier had Fortanier flayed alive.

While our guide and Robin Hood may have considered Richard English, Richard did not think of himself as such. He considered himself French, and wrote troubadour verse in *langue d'oc;* in fact, he never bothered to learn English. He visited England only twice—once to get crowned and once to collect money for his crusade, preferring his lands in France to those in England.

Soon after Richard's death Mercadier was assassinated, and the Baron of Beynac regained his fief.

My guide was correct in describing Richard as cruel—his massacre of over two thousand Saracen prisoners at Acre during his crusade and countless massacres and maimings during his reign as Duke of Aquitaine attest to that. But life in the Middle Ages was cruel. Certainly, his cruelty did not exceed that of Simon de Montfort, who, a few years later, dismantled the Castle of Beynac during the Albigensian Crusade, calling it "Satan's Ark."

Castelnaud

AND THE JOY OF WAR

Castelnaud, sitting atop an escarpment commanding a view of both the Dordogne and Céou valleys, is the English stronghold that faced Beynac during the Hundred Years War. Our visit to this fortress, now a museum of medieval warfare, helped me understand—as nowhere else I have ever visited—the methods by which men killed one another during the Middle Ages. There is the castle itself, built during the hostilities between England and France and now restored to its original condition— probably to better than its original condition. There are the weapons both of assault and defense that were used during this war. An audiovisual presentation shows the stages of the castle's construction, while another film shows siege tactics in the Middle Ages, and a diorama re-creates one of many sieges the fortress had to endure during the Hundred Years War. We were able to wander about at our own pace, stopping as long as we liked on the battlements.

While a number of tour books list Castelnaud as a ruin, which it was when I had visited it sixteen years earlier, the stones removed from its walls over the centuries have now mostly been restored. Most of its history, however, is still lost. That which is known is more than sufficient to let you enjoy the visit. We know that its lord, an Albigensian, departed in great haste when, in 1214, the army of the Albigensian Crusade, led by the fearsome Simon de Montfort, descended on Castelnaud from the north. This was no small army of thirty or forty knights—the size to which feudal lords of the area were accustomed—but the 40,000- or 500,000-man colossus launched for the crusade against the Albigensians. Estimates of the size of the crusaders' army vary considerably: Catholic chroniclers, wishing to minimize the crusaders' atrocities, offer lower numbers, while anti-Catholic chroniclers, wanting to dramatize the horrors committed in the Church's name, raise the number—sometimes, it seems, according to the degree of their anger at the Church. Simon razed the abandoned fortress of Castelnaud to the ground so that it would no longer be a military threat.

Two hundred years later, rebuilt, it was a scene of repeated sieges during the Hundred Years War. Five times it was captured by the French, five times retaken by the English before they solidified their hold on it and held it for most of the war.

What makes Castelnaud so thrilling, however, is not the specific events that took place here but the visual experience of seeing cause and effect. First, the English fortress itself is obviously a response to the French fortress at Beynac and was built over the two hundred years of hostilities during which the two castles faced each other across the Dordogne. (The contrast between the nastiness of the tour guide at Beynac toward the English-speaking tourists and the overwhelming hospitality that greets them at Castelnaud adds to rather than detracts from the experience.)

Second, you can see the architecture as a direct response to the weapons used at the time. Medieval architecture evolved as a response to changes in weapons, changes that took place over several centuries. Here you see the changes not only in the defensive walls but in the weapons that caused these changes. The early perpendicular walls were altered by the addition of slanting stones that reinforced the base against the sapper, a twelfth-century weapon used to undermine walls. When the corners of the keeps were rounded so there were no corners for the stones of catapults to knock loose, catapults became larger, heaving progressively heavier stones.

You see the progression from catapult to cannon, as well as the response in the growing thickness of the walls. Alongside a twelfth-century wall, you see the twelfth-century *perrière,* a stone-throwing machine able to launch eleven-pound stones. Nearby, beside a fourteenth-century wall, is a *trébuchet,* which weighs twelve tons and could launch stones as large as 110 pounds. Near a fifteenth-century wall is a fifteenth-century *bombarde,* capable of launching stone balls sixteen feet in diameter over a range of several hundred yards.

Seeing the medieval weapons in close juxtaposition to that which they were created to destroy, in a medieval setting, was simply a fantastic experience for me. For years I had read about battering rams, catapults, assault towers, but for the life of me did not really have a sense of medieval warfare. I could not understand why the English longbow was such a major step forward over the crossbow in man killing his brother man until I actually saw these weapons at Castelnaud and realized how heavy a crossbow was, how winding it up to fire the iron bolt (or "quarrel") for each shot required an unwieldy winch; hooks and winches to assist the archer can be seen beside Castelnaud's narrow arrow-slit windows. To fire a longbow, on the other hand, the archer had only to fit an arrow to the string; a man using a longbow could fire as many as a dozen arrows a minute, each of which could pierce the armor of a knight at a distance of 150 yards. Medieval moralists writing chivalric literature considered archers cowards, afraid to face their adversaries in close combat. The Church banned the longbow as an unchivalrous weapon, since it could kill a knight long before he got close enough to use his lance or sword. The English, whose sturdy yeomen were the masters of the longbow (King Edward I of England passed a law making longbow practice obligatory on Sunday), decided to ignore the ban—and English longbowmen slaughtered ten thousand French knights at the Battle of Agincourt in 1415.

The entrance at Castelnaud has the usual medieval defensive devices we had seen at Carcassonne and Beynac for keeping assaulters out. But at

Castelnaud we could tell by entering what these devices were and why they were there. After having zigged and zagged our way up the side of the escarpment, we passed the wooden gate. (The machicolations and hoardings above the gate are of stone. The early ones were made of wood, like those at Carcassonne; the change was obviously a response to the ease with which wood burned.) Then we crossed the drawbridge—protected by a portcullis on each side so that assaulters could be trapped between their iron grates—and finally entered the courtyard, or bailey, where we came face-to-face with what the medieval defenders wanted to keep out: a huge catapult, or "bride," and, beside it, the massive boulders it could hurl. It was immediately apparent how difficult it would have been to have zigged and zagged this primitive war machine up the narrow path we had just climbed, or to get it into the castle's bailey so that it would have a better shot at the inner walls. The guidebook to the castle, citing a text written during the Hundred Years War, informs you that "the town of Sarlat lent a 'bride' and two 'perrières' to knock down the walls. Their balls are not heavy enough to break the walls, but they can burst the roof and knock down the part of the courtine wall between the crenels."

On display at Castelnaud are medieval suits of armor. You can see how short the knights were and how heavy their armor was. Once a knight was dressed, he could barely move and had to be lifted onto his horse. He was totally helpless, a "capsized crab," if his enemy's lance knocked him off. But on his horse—a huge warhorse trained to bite, to kick, and to trample—the knight, armed with sword and lance and protected by a pointed shield, was the medieval equivalent of a modern tank. Prized horses were raised in nearby Gascony, and while they were not as swift as Arabian stallions, they were larger and better able to support the heavily ladened rider. A warhorse cost as much as two hundred pounds. This was an expense the lower classes could not afford, and further separated them from the aristocracy.

As we walked through the rooms of the castle, we passed all the toys these knights used in their games of war: various types of battleaxes, including one with hooks—the weapon with which Richard the Lion-Hearted was fond of slashing his way through the enemy lines—as well as a double-edged slasher, different daggers, a mace, a pike, a lance, a mallet, and even falcon beaks, which were used as weapons at Agincourt.

Although the Hundred Years War went on for a long time, its battles usually lasted only about forty days annually, the length of fighting time a vassal owed his lord each year; the knights would then return home. These short wars were considered fun—at least for the nobility. For France's enormous knighthood, wars and tournaments were a way of life, one that they very much enjoyed.

Bertran de Born (the vassal who referred to Richard not as "the Lion-Hearted" but as "Richard Yea and Nay" because of his duplicity), expressed that love of war in a poem which he wrote:

> *Peace delights me not!*
> *War—be thou my lot!*
> *Law—I do not know*
> *Save a right good blow!*

Another contemporary expressed much the same feeling when he wrote, "It is a joyous thing, is war . . . You love your comrade so in war. When you see that your quarrel is just and your blood is fighting well, tears rise to your eye. A great sweet feeling of loyalty and of pity fill your heart seeing your friend so valiantly exposing his body to execute and accomplish the command of our Creator," adding that it is "such a delectation that he who has not tasted it is not fit to say what a delight it is." This feeling of delight in war was evident at Castelnaud when I saw the weapons of individual combat. I felt as though my childhood toys of castles and silver knights had come to life.

Then I came to the cannon, which ushered in another age.

The Bastides:

DOMME AND MONPAZIER

Domme is not far from Beynac and Castelnaud—perhaps ten minutes from either place. It was one of 260 French and English *bastides* built throughout the southwest of France around the end of the thirteenth century. A *bastide* was a military outpost built in sparsely populated areas, in which the rectangular grid pattern used by the Romans to facilitate the movement of troops and equipment was copied by both French and English kings. Domme, however, was laid out not as a rectangle but as a trapezoid because of the rocky formation of the hill on which it was built. Only at one point in Domme, called the sally port, could troops sally back and forth uninterrupted between the outer walls, as in a perfectly rectangular *bastide*. (According to guidebooks, the English *bastide* of Monpazier is "perfect." Standing in the town square, you can see the outer walls at each end of every street. I hasten to mention that Monpazier is labeled "perfect" not because it is more beautiful or more authentic than Domme—as I thought when I insisted that Bob and I drive a hundred kilometers over a twisting, winding road—but because it is a perfect rectangle. However, if you are near Monpazier, you should visit it, and definitely have lunch at Le Menestel, a tiny restaurant so good I took a picture of the chef and not of the arcaded square.)

The purpose of these *bastides* was the control of the southwest. The Albigensian Crusade and subsequent Inquisition had given Kings of France a foothold in this area, once controlled by powerful independent nobles, and Philip the Bold further strengthened his position against both the English and the local lords by building these outposts. In 1280, for example, he purchased the site on which Domme is now located and where a fortress, razed by Simon de Montfort, had once stood. It was not easy to persuade the peasants to haul the golden stones from the quarry at the bottom of the steep slope—it rises almost vertically for a half mile—to the top and build the walls and defensive buildings that are now there. They complained that they were farmers, not goats. The king promised them a charter granting freedom from taxes and seignorial duties, and made Domme one of the towns in France allowed to mint their own money. The coins minted at Domme were called *obsidinales,* or siege coins, and were made of leather. (The mint can still be seen in Domme's central square.) These leather coins never fostered the confidence inspired by the contemporary Florentine gold florin, known for the consistency of its weight in pure gold, or by the Venetian ducat.

Hardly had the *bastide* been completed when the Hundred Years War burst upon France, and Domme suffered ten sieges. The English won possession of it during the years 1347 and 1348 and again between 1356 and 1369, but in spite of these disasters, the town remained faithful to the King of France.

Domme is exceptionally pretty because of the honey-colored stone from which all its buildings are made. (The stucco that covered these buildings for many years had been removed shortly before we arrived, giving the town an almost too pretty and too uniform look of restoration.) Its entrance is guarded by two huge, cylindrical, rusticated towers projecting from the wall that surrounds the village. We spent a very pleasant hour walking around the ramparts, which overlook an incredibly beautiful countryside. Somewhere in the wall is a secret little door called the "Door of Paradise" because you can't find it easily. I couldn't find it at all. During the Hundred Years War—in 1346, to be exact—traitors opened this door to let English soldiers in. The traitors were captured when the French retook the *bastide.* In the main square, there is a restaurant called the Auberge de la Rode, after the wheel *(rode* in *langue d'oc)* on which these traitors were broken.

We have been following the evolution of French history and architecture by traveling from region to region. Because so much of France's civilization had its origins during the four centuries when it was a Roman province, we began where the influence of Rome was strongest, in Provence, where, in cities like Orange and Nîmes, we saw Roman coliseums, theaters, temples, and triumphal arches.

Then we drove west into Languedoc to watch Rome disintegrate as wave after wave of barbarian invasions plunged France into the Dark Ages. We saw cities like Narbonne, which were abandoned by the Romans to the Visigoths, and caves like Saint-Roman, to which men fled to escape the barbarians. We saw Fontfroide, typical of hundreds of monasteries that sprang up throughout France during the early Middle Ages and provided the only unifying force of the period. Then we headed deeper into Languedoc—and deeper into the Middle Ages, into the approximately four centuries (from 1000 to 1400) during which France, without a strong king, had its political power shattered into a thousand petty fiefdoms, ruled by feudal lords constantly at war with one another to increase their power and their land. We visited a medieval fortified city of Carcassonne and then, as we turned our car north, the medieval fortified Cathedral of Albi. Still farther north we visited typical medieval pilgrimage sites at Conques and Rocamadour. Then, in this section, we drove still farther north, into the Dordogne Valley, the bloody frontier of the Hundred Years War, when France was torn apart by constantly shifting alliances between barons and counts and dukes. And now, as we continue to follow the course of French history, we are going to get into our car and travel north again to another valley, the

Loire Valley, because, just as the architecture of the Dordogne Valley captures the spirit of the Hundred Years War and of its feuding nobles, the Loire Valley is the best setting to see the history and architecture that capture the spirit of the next great age.

This is an age when power shifts from a thousand feudal lords and gradually becomes concentrated in the person of the King of France, until his power is so absolute that he is viewed by the nobility as the sun around which they orbit. The Loire—which, like the Dordogne, has great beauty, although its colors are painted from a dramatically different palette—is two hundred miles north of the Dordogne, and we will head there now. On the way, however, before we arrive at the Valley of Kings, as the Loire Valley is sometimes called, we will make one stop—at the city of Bourges—where we will observe the spirit of a new force emerging at the end of the Hundred Years War, a force that facilitated the eventual rise of the absolute monarch: the rise of the bourgeoisie.

THE CATHEDRAL CITY OF

Bourges

In Bourges is a château built not by a nobleman but by Jacques Coeur (1395–1456), one of France's first merchant princes. Like the château he built, which displays every imaginable architectural style of the age, the story of his life has every imaginable adventure and intrigue; indeed, if his life were made into a movie, no one would believe it.

He was born the son of a furrier in an age when most people accepted the station in life into which they were born. Jacques Coeur, however, believing in the motto he had carved on the wall of his palace—"To a valiant heart nothing is impossible"—and believing in himself, and in his power to shape his own destiny, became one of the richest men of his age. The base of his fortune came from daring voyages to the Levant in which he armed merchant ships and captured eastern Mediterranean markets from the great commercial houses of Italy. By establishing his own trading post there, he reaped the profits that French merchants had been paying to Italian middlemen for over two hundred years.

Shipwrecked while returning to France from his first voyage, Jacques Coeur was captured by natives of Calvi and had to be ransomed to gain his release. When he returned to France, he convinced wealthy merchants in Languedoc to back him on another expedition, and putting together a cargo of silver, honey, linen, cloth, roses, wax, armor, and weapons, he again sailed east. He traded his goods for the pearls, silks, spices, perfumes, incense, rugs, and porcelains that had been brought by caravans from the far reaches of Asia.

In 1441 the dauphin raised him to the peerage, and he became the king's friend and economic adviser. Coeur replaced the debased monetary system with a sound one like the Medicis had established in Florence. In 1446 he received a papal dispensation to carry on trade with the Saracens. His profits from successive voyages were so great that by 1448 he possessed his own small navy of six armed galleys. When a French colony was endangered, he equipped eleven ships for a relief expedition. He created a financial empire, using the rivers of France to connect his network of warehouses in Paris, Tours, Lyon, Marseille, Perpignan, Narbonne, and Beaucaire. With his money this exemplar of the new class purchased the estates of the old, buying more than thirty fiefdoms in the south and center of France from ancient but impoverished noble families. (In one of these domains he activated previously underworked iron, copper, and silver mines. He shipped the ore to Bourges, where it was refined in smelters he had built, and then moved it to his warehouse in Lyon and then to Aigues-Mortes, from whose harbor his merchant fleet sailed to trade with the Orient.)

Jacques Coeur had met Charles in 1422, shortly after the Treaty of Troyes disinherited Charles; that same year the dauphin's mother declared him a bastard and drove him out of Paris, leaving Paris and the entire north of France firmly in English control. For seven years the dauphin wandered back and forth between Bourges and his castles at Chinon and Loches in the Loire, making no attempt to be crowned in the Cathedral of Rheims (held by the English), as had been the custom since A.D. 496. Instead, he had himself crowned Charles VII in Bourges, where he felt safe, and was sneeringly called "the King of Bourges."

The dauphin, a totally self-indulgent man more concerned with his personal pleasures and with money to finance them than with driving the English out of France, relied on Jacques Coeur, who supplied him with all the luxuries he desired and lent him money when he could no longer afford to pay his debts. He also supplied the nobles in the dauphin's court with the luxuries they desired, adding to his princely fortune. After Charles was crowned king, with Joan of Arc standing beside him, it was Jacques Coeur who provided the payroll for the troops who had accompanied Joan of Arc to Orleáns and who freed the monarch from dependence on his vassals by personally lending the king two hundred thousand crowns at one time and sixty thousand at another to pay for a standing army of ten thousand men similar to the one already in place in England. When the dauphin finally drove the English from Normandy, ending the Hundred Years War, a royal cavalcade rode victoriously into Rouen in a scene famous in French history. And among the French lords following the king in the procession was this self-made representative of the new force in France.

In order to endear himself to the aristocratic courtiers, Jacques Coeur lent them money—and continued to lend it as well to the king, the queen, and the king's beautiful mistress, Agnès Sorel, whom he also supplied with richly colored silks and jewels from the Orient. These debtors, already jealous of the rich upstart and his power, were afraid they might be called on to repay their debts and began looking for a pretext to bring him down. When Agnès, whom we shall meet at Loches, died in childbirth, in 1450, Coeur was accused (by an Italian merchant whose trade had suffered because of the Frenchman's success) of poisoning her. There was not a shred of evidence to support the charge, but Charles ordered his arrest. He was then accused of smuggling arms and silver to the infidel Saracens. The men selected to try and judge him, some of the most powerful men of France, were his debtors. They had him tortured until he "confessed," and then found him guilty. The terms of his sentence are also not surprising: Jacques Coeur was to pay the king the colossal sum of four hundred thousand pounds; his property was confiscated and distributed among Charles's friends; and he was to remain in prison indefinitely. Aided by men who had worked for him, men of his own class, Coeur escaped from Beaucaire prison, secretly crossed most of France, and made his way to Rome, where he was given the protection of the Pope. He died while leading a papal fleet to fight the Turks.

Jacques Coeur's career helps us to understand the rise of the merchant class and the transformation taking place in French cities near the end of the Hundred Years War. Out of the war's chaos cities gradually changed from places of refuge, administration, and consumption into centers of trade, production, and commerce. And as commerce revived, a new class of merchants, financiers, lawyers, bankers, and clerks arose. This trend was aided in Bourges after the king purchased the city from its viscount in 1100. The city had shrunk far within the perimeter of walls erected when it was part of the Roman Empire. During the Middle Ages it served as little more than an episcopal see, providing both refuge for the surrounding communities and religious ceremonies for their souls. In general, as with most towns or cities of the period, it consumed more than it produced.

After it was purchased by the monarchy, successive kings allied themselves with the townspeople, undermining the authority of the local lords. It was the king who now saw to the city's defense and the paving of its streets, who granted freedom to serfs as well as tax advantages to merchants in hope of fostering trade and commerce, thus increasing the value of the royal holdings. Eventually, a significant cloth industry developed. By bringing towns and cities directly under royal control and by granting such privileges, the power of the local feudal lords declined and that of the new middle class grew. Its representatives participated in the Estates General along with representatives of the other two estates—the clergy and nobility. It would be from this class that a new class, a nobility of the robe, rather than sword, would develop.

Arriving at Jacques Coeur's palace well before the end of the obligatory French two-hour lunch break, we had ample (more than ample) time to observe the façade before the doors opened. If our lunch had been better, I probably never would have noticed the Gallo-Roman foundations on the palace's west side. There we could see the horizontal lines of brick the Romans used to keep their lines straight, as at Carcassonne. The building's peculiar layout resulted from the architect's use of these Gallo-Roman ramparts in its construction.

I thought the palace was fascinating—a physical manifestation of the royal policy of fostering trade and commerce. (I suggest that you not try to locate the other buildings touted as medieval masterpieces in the local tour book. They are hard to find and not worth the finding.) The palace consists of hexagonal towers, round turrets, a Flamboyant spire, a Flamboyant stained-glass window rich with tracery, Renaissance windows with tiny panes of glass, Romanesque, Gothic, and basket arches, a cornice with gargoyles, two whimsical dummy windows with statues leaning on their carved elbows and looking out, a balustrade decorated with hearts and shells—Jacques Coeur's crest—crenelations, and, inside, a ceiling that looks like the hull of a ship. My first impression was that the architect couldn't make up his mind whether to build a Flamboyant Gothic church, a medieval fortress, or a Renaissance palace, and consequently built a combination of all three. I wondered about the man responsible for this tasteless structure, but I was not being fair to Jacques Coeur, who, imprisoned, sadly never oversaw its completion.

The reliefs throughout the palace are also rather whimsical and good-natured. There are exotic trees, which Jacques Coeur may have seen on his voyages in the East; carvings of the treasures he traded for with the cloth of local craftsmen; a character who may be the master of the mint holding a hammer. On the rim of one of the ornamental panels are the letters "D.I.R.E., F.A.I.R.E., T.A.I.R.E., D.E. M.A.," followed by two hearts, "I.OIE," and, in the corner, "RG." There is no agreement about what these letters mean, and for centuries French historians have argued over their meaning and the meaning of the symbolism throughout the palace.

Bob felt that aesthetically Jacques Coeur's palace was not worth visiting, and perhaps he was right. While it is not breathtakingly beautiful, it does provide insight into the period and illustrates in a very concrete way the desire of the emerging middle class to imitate and be part of the nobility—just as the "trial" of Jacques Coeur illustrates the disdain of the aristocracy toward an "upstart" ennobled by the king (noblesse de robe) but lacking proper bloodlines.

. . .

Within walking distance of the palace is the Cathedral of Saint-Étienne, in which the dauphin was crowned "King of Bourges" in 1422. At the beginning of the thirteenth century, huge Gothic cathedrals began to rise throughout the north of France as its cities and commerce came back to life. The cathedral would have been impossible without mercantile profits and the wealth of the burghers who freely contributed to its construction. They gave for the glorification of God, and they gave for the glorification of their cities. As Bourges grew, its cathedral grew as well: not as a static structure but as an evolving structure, rising without limits, like the class that built it. It was contemporaneous with the Cathedral of Chartres, and it exemplified the new style of architecture emanating from the Île-de-France. This style combined the pointed arch with ribbed vaulting and flying buttresses, with the solid walls of the Romanesque churches giving way to walls of stained glass. Saint-Étienne was the first of these cathedrals to be built south of the Loire.

Before arriving in Bourges, I had read a great deal about its cathedral and expected to see a fabulous jewel in a miraculously preserved medieval setting.

My first feeling was disappointment. I hadn't expected the city to remain unchanged since the time of Caesar, who had described it as the most beautiful of all Celtic cities. After all, Henry James had visited in 1884 and described it as "a *ville de province* in the full force of the term, especially as applied invidiously. The streets, narrow, tortuous, and dirty, have very wide cobblestones, the houses for the most part are shabby without local color. The look of things is neither modern nor antique—a kind of mediocrity of middle age." But I had hoped that in the intervening century the city fathers might have cleaned it up. My hope faded when I got to the cathedral.

Saint-Étienne is one of the great Gothic cathedrals of France, but its façade, with its five great portals, is filthy—gray-black—and faces out on a shabby little plaza. As I looked at the grime covering that immense façade, which overwhelmed the plaza, I thought the cathedral looked like a caged elephant in need of a bath.

Then I stepped inside.

Liturgical organ music lifted my depressed spirits, putting me in a properly religious mood. I had entered through the large center portal, which leads to the nave. The other portals lead to four large side aisles of unequal height, pyramiding toward the center of the great structure. There is no transept. The cathedral is tentlike, and the effect of light filtering from stained-glass windows at three different widths and pyramiding heights is unique and mystical. The central nave soars upward to a ribbed vaulted ceiling that seems to float above. The illusion was intentional. The master builder conceived its design to be an image of the divine order: a heaven floating above earth. The arches, much higher than those at Chartres, seem higher still because the capitals of supporting slender colonnettes are only hinted at, so they seem to continue past the arches to form the ribs of the vaulting overhead. The height and the glass-filled walls are made possible by the ribbed sexpartite vaulting, which is physically lighter than the groined or barrel vaulting of Romanesque churches and therefore exerts less thrust on the lower parts of the outer wall; by graceful flying buttresses supporting the walls outside; and by the four aisles on either side of the nave, which slant out and down as if the cathedral were in some way a pyramid, too. Above these arches, at the uppermost level, lighting the ceiling, are stained-glass windows. The pyramiding structure forces your eye up to the floating church, whose weblike structural supports, on a sunny day, seem to disappear completely.

There is another illusion that the architect created in the Cathedral of Saint-Étienne. As you stand in the central nave looking toward the chevet, the chevet's curve appears not only to sparkle like a jewel but to be dramatically distant and unobtainable. The architect created this illusion of distance by increasing the distance between the arch-supporting columns in the chancel area, so that as you stand at the end of the nave, a trick of perspective makes the chevet seem farther away than it is. (This is possible because the pointed arch—unlike the rounded arch—allows the width between arches to be increased or decreased while keeping the height of the arch constant.) The sparkle is created by the sun filtering through the stained-glass windows of the five radiating chapels.

The miracles of Bourges are the stained-glass windows of the chevet, whose vibrant colors are best seen in the early morning light, when the royal blues and deep reds, accented by purples and greens, glitter like Byzantine glass mosaics. As the people walked from right to left in the five apsidal chapels, they could see depicted the stories of Joseph, Lazarus, the Prodigal Son, the Good Samaritan, the Apocalypse, and the Last Judgment, as well as the story of Saint Étienne. There are also scenes of medieval carpenters, coopers, and wheelwrights—the townspeople who contributed to, and helped with, the construction of the cathedral. These windows, five of which were in place by 1225, encompass the history of the technique and art of glazing stained glass to the seventeenth century. Considering that Bourges's main industry through two world wars was the manufacture of munitions, the survival of these windows is another miracle.

During the twelfth and thirteenth centuries, artisans, merchants, and the new middle class joined together to erect the great cathedral. As the feudal economy became more of a monied economy, the erection of the church moved apace. Henri de Sully, the well-loved and successful Archbishop of Bourges, who increased the land holdings and wealth of his office, conceived the cathedral and saw to its financing. He was in contact with the architects and workmen refurbishing Saint-Denis in Paris and building Chartres. The master masons of the time, along with thirty or so skilled craftsmen, would travel from cathedral to cathedral. (People from the town would contribute their services, hauling the stone and carrying out unskilled work under the direction of the master craftsmen.)

When I left the cathedral, I discovered the archbishop's garden and palace on its southeast side. Sitting on a bench, I looked across a geometrically patterned garden designed by André Le Nôtre—France's greatest garden designer—at the cathedral, encased in a long line of airy flying buttresses. Grassy squares, rising in gentle tiers, were trimmed with shaded alleys and red and yellow flower beds, which seemed wonderfully delicate and beautiful against the massive gray stone structure rising behind them. In the sunlight the gray stone of the cathedral melted into white, and somehow the grime disappeared. The cathedral no longer reminded me of an elephant but looked quite beautiful, perhaps as its thirteenth-century archbishop had hoped it would.

The Loire Valley

LE CHATEAU D' AZAY-LE-RIDEAU ~ XV° siècle

The Valley of Kings

The first book my mother read to me was a collection of fairy tales, filled with castles and captive princesses who were always saved by chivalrous knights in shining armor. Fairy tales do not generally come true. If you marry a frog, he stays a frog. And Sleeping Beauty, we all know after reading Freud, was just waiting for puberty, and magic is merely the explanation given for phenomena we cannot explain empirically. However, as with irregular Latin verbs, there are exceptions to most rules. For example, thirty years after my mother stopped reading to me, I was completely bewitched when I discovered an enchanted valley called the Loire, where kings and princes and princesses lived in castles more wonderful than I had ever imagined as I fell asleep each night listening to my mother's voice. I even found the Castle of Sleeping Beauty, or at least I found the Castle of Ussé at the edge of the dark and mysterious Forest of Chinon, through which Prince Charming fought his way to wake Aurora, the sleeping princess, with a kiss. It is the romantic castle, with poetically Flamboyant Gothic towers and turrets, which inspired Charles Perrault to write "Sleeping Beauty."

Ussé is only one of a thousand fantasy castles in this enchanted valley, which is like a necklace containing a thousand Renaissance jewels. Most of them were built from a stone that whitens with age, so instead of becoming grim and sober with the passing centuries, they have become more and more beautiful. And as mysterious and romantic as Ussé is, it is not even my favorite château. Chenonceau is.

While it is true that you can enjoy viewing these castles for the sheer aesthetic delight they provide, knowing the historically significant, often pivotal, scenes that took place within their walls, as every Frenchman does, will immensely increase your pleasure and understanding. If, in fact, on your first trip to the Loire Valley you visit a limited number of castles, and visit them in the order in which they were built, you will be able to journey through several centuries of French history and sense the changes that took place as a divided feudal world was slowly absorbed by the monarchy, as the King of France evolved from an elected first among equals to an absolute, hereditary monarch. Touring this way, of course, is not necessary if you have all your Merovingians, Carolingians, Capetians, Valois, Bourbons, Angevins, Plantagenets, Burgundians, Armagnacs, Henrys, Francises, Charleses, as well as the terms feudal, manorial, seignorial, Gothic, medieval, Renaissance, Reformation, classical, and Baroque, firmly arranged by century in your mind, and if you know which should be remembered and which should be put aside as extraneous to your enjoyment of the castle you are visiting. However, if you, like a group of friends who accompanied me to a production of Shakespeare's *Henry V,* have no idea that Agincourt had anything to do with the Hundred Years War or with Joan of Arc, I suggest you begin as my husband and I did on our last visit to the Loire, at the medieval city of Montrichard, and watch the history of France unfold as you travel from one royal château to another—watch the austere military fortresses of feudal France (Chinon, Loches, and Langeais) blossom in the Renaissance (Amboise, Blois, Chenonceau, and Chambord) as, at the same time, the power of the aristocracy declined and royal authority increased.*

*There are a number of centrally located and charming towns in which to stay while visiting the Loire. Montrichard is perhaps one of the loveliest, filled as it is with a variety of hotels, charcuteries for exquisite picnic supplies, and a riverbank with a public park complete with tennis courts and an indoor swimming pool. Traveling in chronological order may add a few miles to your tour, but distances in the Loire Valley are relatively short—all of France is smaller than the state of Texas, and from Angers at one end of the valley to Orléans at the other is less than two hundred miles (a distance I once traveled in Texas for a good barbecue). Most of the châteaux you will want to visit are in a far smaller area surrounding Tours.

THE FEUDAL KEEP OF
Montrichard

We discovered Montrichard quite by accident. We had overslept and were on our way to Loches when we noticed that it was getting close to the hour of twelve, the hour in provincial France when all the charcuteries, pâtisseries, and boulangeries close for a very long lunch, and we had not yet purchased our food for the day's picnic. Luckily, at just that moment we entered the wonderful town of Montrichard. My first observation on getting out of the car was that the entire town just smelled good. I then proceeded to make a grave mistake by buying most of our lunch at the first charcuterie we found; and while the salads and pâtés turned out to be terrific, we later observed, as we hunted down the boulangerie for our loaf of bread, that we were passing one shop after another which could have supplied us with a variety of other regional delicacies we had never tasted.

As we leisurely walked down the street on our way to the town's leading tourist attraction, a medieval donjon, the pace of the townspeople picked up momentum—everyone was speeding from charcuterie to boulangerie to pâtisserie—and we realized that the lunchtime curfew was about to descend on the town and us. Soon everything would be closed for two hours, not only boulangeries and charcuteries but the donjon as well. Moments later we saw the heavy door of the donjon-museum slam shut, so we loaded our picnic purchases into the car and set out once again for Loches.

We made it as far as the other side of the River Cher, which flows through Montrichard and is certainly a factor in its being among the most charming towns I have ever visited. As we crossed the bridge, we noticed a delightful park along the banks of the river. Since it was twelve o'clock, and all historic buildings, not just the one at Montrichard, would be closed until two, we decided to have our picnic and view the medieval section of Montrichard from what turned out to be the best vantage point: a picnic blanket strategically placed along the water's edge. Now we could view the feudal world of Montrichard during those two magical hours in which the modern world of France fades behind closed doors. (When traveling, you have to look on the bright side of everything, including oversleeping.)

From across the river I saw one of the many keeps, or towers, I had noticed everywhere since I began to tour this valley. Understanding this one helped me understand them all. This grim square tower, with its curtain wall and ramparts built on the highest hill in the area, looms ominously over the medieval cluster of buildings below. The dark, gray-plated spire of the Romanesque Church of Saint-Croix pierces the silhouette of the fortress above like a giant medieval lance, adding to, rather than diminishing, the overall martial severity of the scene, transforming this peaceful section of France into what it had been a thousand years ago—Touraine, a battleground divided and fought over by two powerful counts, the Count of Anjou and the Count of Blois. Each had more land and more power than their contemporary, the first Capetian king—Hugh Capet, whose dynasty was barely an infant in the year 1010, when Montrichard came into being. Both Counts wanted to expand the land they controlled because land in the eleventh century was the only source of wealth and power in this moneyless, tradeless time. And both wanted domination of all this land, which tourists now call the Loire Valley.

In fact, the conflicts of expansion that took place in the small area between Montrichard and Loches were not so very different from feudal conflicts taking place in Burgundy, Aquitaine, Champagne—or, for that matter, throughout all of what would someday be France. Charlemagne, two centuries before, had divided the state into three hundred counties, roughly corresponding to the ancient Roman *civitae*, but with the decline of any central power, the more ambitious counts expanded what had become their hereditary domains. And no one was more ambitious, more greedy, criminally violent, unscrupulous, and pious, than the wily Count of Anjou, Foulques Nerra, the Black Falcon.

Foulques Nerra (970–1040) became Count of Anjou at the age of seventeen, and the keep at Montrichard was his creation. Nearly a thousand years have passed since he built this windowless fortress with walls so thick—nine feet—that they withstood not only the attacks of hostile knights but the ravages of time as well. Built in 1010 on the highest hill in order to oversee the surrounding countryside, it is just one of twenty-three keeps he built, only an outpost in his battles of defense and conquest with successive Counts of Blois. The keeps were one day's march from each other, so that whenever he and his knights left his military headquarters at Loches, they never had to spend a night unprotected by thick walls; it is one day's march from Loches to Montrésor, another day's march to Montbazon, another day's march to the ruins of his keep at Langeais. In fact, Foulques Nerra could march all the way to Pouancé, the farthest spot in his huge realm, without staying at any fortress but his own.

The first keep he built was the model for all of them, and its method of construction reveals his wiliness. Sometime between 991 and 994, Foulques asked Eudes, Count of Blois, for permission to build a shelter for his hunting dogs on Eudes's land, where Langeais now is. The permission was granted. Foulques, as Count Eudes expected, erected a large wooden shelter. Then, as Eudes did not expect, Foulques had a large trench dug around the shelter. Next he moved in a garrison of soldiers, under whose protection his workmen dug a large hole behind the wooden walls and then lined with stone what would become the foundation of the keep. Inside the wooden structure, the stone structure grew taller. When it was finished, it was just like the keep here at Montrichard: a tall, square structure with narrow openings that became progressively narrower toward the outside so that the archers inside had a wider range of attack with their arrows than those shooting into the keep.

Each of Foulques's keeps consisted of three basic levels: a dungeon below ground, a hunting lodge, and a guard room. Like the one at Montrichard, the keep at Langeais was built on a point high enough to dominate the Loire; when it was completed, Foulques had command of the vital river artery at that point. His immediate objective, which he achieved, was to cut off communications between the Count of Blois to the east and the count's vassal and ally, Gelduin of Saumur, to the west. His ultimate objective was the capture of the town of Tours, held by the Count of Blois. Before attacking Gelduin, Foulques built the keep here at Montrichard, on Gelduin's land, overlooking and controlling the Cher, and cutting off Gelduin from his other lands at Chaumont; then he built another at Montboyan, across from Tours and overlooking the Loire at a point closer to Blois.

This method of construction not only allowed the Black Falcon the stealthy encirclement of his enemies and the domination of areas that had not previously belonged to him, but also made the land itself more valuable. Large areas of the forests surrounding the keeps were cleared, providing both wood for the barricade, which protected the workmen while they constructed the stone keep, and visual clearings for the sentries manning the completed towers. When all twenty-three towers were built, Foulques had achieved effective surveillance of all the area's rivers, the main arteries of transportation, as well as of the surrounding countryside. This clearing of the forests not only deprived his enemies of cover but also created new farmland for the peasants.

In each keep, Foulques placed a man faithful to him who was invested with the land and became his vassal (his knight, his soldier) in his wars with successive Counts of Blois. And just as he, as Count of Anjou, held his fief from the King of France, and was obligated to come with thirty-four knights when the king summoned him, this vassal held his land as a hereditary fief from *his* lord, the Count of Anjou. His vassal became the lord of the manor and of the serfs who farmed the land now cleared of forests; he dispensed their justice and received a part of whatever they produced. Foulques Nerra would move from one of his vassal's keeps to another, accompanied by his entire entourage (his chancellor, his marshal, his seneschal, his cup bearer, pages). These tours of his domains were conducted for a number of reasons, one of which was to inspect the keeps and ensure that his vassals did not become too independent. Another was to obtain that percentage of the agricultural produce which was owed to him— produce difficult to transport without spoilage but easy to consume on the spot. Foulques Nerra was also instrumental in establishing vineyards within his domain, whose produce he would also consume when he made his tour of fiefs.

Close to Montrichard is Gelduin's town of Pontlevoy. It was here that one of the bloodiest battles of the eleventh century took place when Foulques Nerra crushed the combined forces of the Count of Blois and Gelduin of Saumur, leaving between six thousand and ten thousand dead. (I don't know if these figures refer only to the knights killed in battle or also include the peasants who always died during these bloody battles, and whose homes and crops were always burned; often, their deaths were not considered worthy of reporting.) With the dénouement of the Battle of Pontlevoy, the borders of the Angevin domain expanded to include the Castle of Saumur.

Bloody battles, like the one at Pontlevoy, were not the way Foulques preferred to expand his realm. Like many great military strategists, he preferred avoiding actual battle, and since he was a wily opponent, he fought relatively few. Instead, he expanded his realm the way France's feudal lords had been expanding their domains during the past two hundred years—by marriage. Foulques married his children to the heirs of the realms he coveted. An example of the cold-blooded nature of marriage—perhaps a rather extreme example, but an example nonetheless—was Foulques Nerra's own marriage to Élisabeth of Vendôme, by which he acquired the independent county of Vendôme, her dowry. Unfortunately for Élisabeth, Foulques Nerra wanted to create not only an empire but a dynasty (his descendants would ultimately include Richard the Lion-Hearted, all the Plantagenets of England, and the legendary Kings of Jerusalem), and a dynasty requires a son. Élisabeth, after giving birth to a girl, was sterile. Since divorce was not an option in medieval Catholic France, and a son was necessary to Foulques Nerra's plans, he got rid of his twenty-year-old wife. Publicly accusing her of adultery, he had her tried at an ecclesiastical court in Angers by judges he knew would convict her; then he had her dressed in her gaiest clothes and personally led her out to be burned at the stake in the square in front of the cathedral.* Foulques Nerra's second wife, Hildegarde, didn't make Élisabeth's mistake; although she had three daughters, she had the foresight also to have a son, Geoffrey Martel. The father-son relationship, however, seems to have left something to be desired. At one point Geoffrey, tired of waiting for his father to die—Foulques lived to the age of seventy, a rare feat in the eleventh century—tried to assert his independence. Foulques, in a fit of anger, had the son bridled and saddled like a horse. It is said that while Foulques stood over his rebellious son, he repeatedly shouted "You are conquered, you are conquered" as the son crawled at his feet, begging to be pardoned.

One of the most prolific builders of his age, Foulques Nerra built the twenty-three keeps and many churches and monasteries. He also built the first bridge that crossed the River Cher, here at Montrichard, now replaced by the medieval bridge we had just crossed. Its Gothic arches are now all made of stone, but in the insecurity of Foulques's day the last arch was made of wood so that it could easily be destroyed when the enemy attacked. Gone also are the city gates, locked to keep enemies out or opened to let pilgrims pass on their way south. Montrichard was on the route to Santiago de Compostela, the most popular pilgrimage destination after Jerusalem and Rome, and so many pilgrims passed through these gates on their way to Spain that they were called the Porte d'Espagne.

Montrichard was on the pilgrimage route because of what Foulques Nerra had done. Not only had he built the church here and the monastery of Beaulieu outside Loches, but he had also presented both towns with relics that made them worthy of a detour in the *Codex of Callixtus*. This was the Age of Faith, and Foulques Nerra was worried (justifiably, in my opinion) about his salvation. As was the custom, he expiated his sins as violently

*This is the account given in *La Chronique de Sait Aubin d'Angers*. In the *Chronique de Saint-Florent*, Foulques Nerra merely stabs Élisabeth to death as she is escaping from a room in a tower in which he held her prisoner.

as he committed them. He built the monastery at Beaulieu to atone for the murder of the Count of Maine; he frequently had himself flagellated naked upon a wicker board for deeds of which I am unaware, but he certainly had plenty to choose from; and he also made at least four pilgrimages across the Mediterranean to Jerusalem—an astounding number considering the difficulties of travel at this time. On one of these pilgrimages he returned with a large chunk of wood. He said that it was a piece of the True Cross which he had bitten off with his teeth. (The chronicle used at Beaulieu contends that it was a large stone from the tomb of Christ that Foulques bit off with his teeth, rather than part of the True Cross. While I would like to have seen his dental records before accepting either story, no one at the time stepped forward to ask the count for documentation.) The wood was divided between the Church of Saint-Croix (Cross) at Montrichard and the monastery of Beaulieu, where he himself would be buried. Foulques Nerra felt that salvation required his burial near a truly miraculous relic, and knowing even the little I do about his life, I think he was right. Whether the legend was true or not, pilgrims believed the relic worthy of a visit and came through Montrichard to pray at Saint-Croix and then proceeded on to Loches—as I recommend you do after visiting Chinon.

THE ROMANESQUE ABBEY OF
Fontevraud

If you have not visited an abbey or monastery in Burgundy, Languedoc, or the Dordogne, provinces where the monasteries are far more exciting than those here in the Loire Valley, or if you have not stopped at the Romanesque church at Vézelay—if, in fact, you are visiting only the Loire Valley and nowhere else—I advise you to visit the Romanesque Abbey of Fontevraud near Chinon. Since monasteries were such an important part of life in France during the Middle Ages, you should see at least one.

Although the construction of Fontevraud was begun in 1099 by a hermit, its head was always a woman. Generally, it was a place for the educated woman who had no husband. In the twelfth century its walls enclosed a Benedictine monastery, a convent for nuns, a general hospital, a leper hospital, and a house for educated ladies "who chose to retire from the world." I think the word "chose" requires a bit of explanation. Since a woman was deemed incapable of bearing arms and defending a fief, she was therefore deemed unable to inherit a fief. But when she was married, she carried off part of her father's land as her dowry. Feudal lords therefore not infrequently insisted on their daughters' "choosing" to retire from the world so that they need not reduce the size of their domaine. In fact, it became commonplace for only one daughter to be married off, usually the youngest, and for the elder sisters to enter a convent. Feudal lords could, in this way, personally enjoy the rights and privileges of the daughter's dowry for as long as possible. By the late Middle Ages, wedding ceremonies had become increasingly more lavish; the degree of lavishness was a barometer of a lord's rank in society. That made daughters even more of an economic liability. Accordingly, the number of young ladies choosing to retire from society increased. It is no wonder that, with customs like these, the birth of a son was more welcome than that of a daughter.

While most of Fontevraud's occupants were women without husbands, the abbey is most famous for a queen who had two, both of them kings. Eleanor of Aquitaine, like her mother before her, spent her last years within its walls. She had educated most of her children, including Richard the Lion-Hearted and John Lackland, here. And it was to Fontevraud that her second husband, Henry Plantagenet, King of England and Count of Anjou, had unsuccessfully tried to make her "choose" to retire. Since Fontevraud was within his realm, generously supported and protected by him as Count of Anjou, he wanted Eleanor to renounce her provinces in France and retire here as abbess. He would not seek an annulment, as Louis VII had done, and thereby lose her dowry, which was most of southwest France. But at fifty-three Eleanor wasn't willing to retire from the world. In fact, she wasn't willing to do so for almost another thirty years. Finally, she came at eighty, and was buried here beside Henry and her beloved son Richard.

I first visited Fontevraud on a rainy day, and while I would like to be upbeat, I have to admit I found it gloomy and depressing rather than beautiful. I thought at the time that the abbey's long use as a prison by Napoleon may have left its mark on the structures. However, others find it quite beautiful, noting its "purity of style," its restored Romanesque kitchen, and, unlike me, don't seem to mind that it has been stripped of everything except the marvelous Plantagenet tombs of Eleanor, Henry, and Richard. So I suggest that if you choose to visit it, you visit it only on a sunny day.

There is another reason for visiting Fontevraud in the sun. Perhaps the most enjoyable aspect of the abbey is its four medieval gardens, where every effort has been made to re-create them as they were during the time of Eleanor of Aquitaine. The Jardin Bouquetier exists now, as it did then, to provide flowers for the altar in the abbey church. The flower beds are separated with anachronistic sixteenth-century tiles, alas, twelfth-century tiles being too rare to leave outdoors. Two flowers of historical significance can be found here, the *planta genista,* the plant which Henry Plantagenet's father wore in his cap, and which provided the family sobriquet, and the fleur-de-lis, the three-petaled iris. According to legend, Clovis, the first Christian King of France, won one of his great victories in a field of these three-petaled flowers. He chose it as a symbol for his banner. Seven centuries later, Louis VII, wanting to emphasize his descent from Clovis, made it the symbol of France. (His followers called it "fleur-de-Louis," which evolved into fleur-de-lis.)

The Jardin Médicinal et Condimentaire next to the one-time leper hospital contains herbs, such as pennyroyal, rue, agrimony, wormwood, feverfew, and squill, which were used in medieval medicine. There is an orchard of fruit and nut trees. The largest garden, however, is the vegetable garden, which in addition to vegetables grows flax for linen, hemp for rope and canvas, soapwort for soap, and teasel for carding wool. Since drinking water presented a problem in medieval times, most monastic kitchens brewed beer and made wine, so hops and grapes are here as well.

Walking around the four gardens, you have a sense of a self-contained, self-sufficient world producing just about everything it needed for daily life. And if you look up from the garden at the abbey itself, you can easily see why the abbeys and monasteries of this period were called "fortresses of God." Fontevraud, large, solid, and as massive as the strongholds and castles of the period, was constructed to provide safety as well as services. The church, so big, so monumental, is as awe-inspiring now as it was intended to be then. The simple rectangular floor plan of the early Christian church has been expanded to form a cross. A series of domes, familiar in Eleanor's southern provinces but rare in this area, forms its roof. The supporting rounded arches are low, wide, and everywhere. The architect of the twelfth century was still having trouble supporting such a roof—not being as adept as his Roman predecessor in the execution of a barrel vault. Consequently, he cut few windows for fear of weakening the walls supporting the domes. Flying buttresses outside also help keep the building upright.

I apologize for my overall lack of enthusiasm for the place, which I found touristy and grim. I promised myself to return on a sunny day (on which I would make a stop at its noted restaurant, La Licorne).

Medieval Chinon

From Montrichard to Loches is an easy drive, only twenty-one miles. And Loches continues architecturally and historically the story begun at Montrichard, so it isn't necessary to visit the château at Chinon, which is in ruins and definitely out of the way. It isn't necessary for any reason except for the sheer pleasure of sitting at one of Chinon's charming cafés or tearooms overlooking the River Vienne and enjoying delicious pastries and ices, or having lunch at what may be my favorite restaurant in the valley, Au Plaisir Gourmand—or, perhaps, to touch the spirit of Joan of Arc. For while the Loire Valley is a valley of kings and princes, it is also the valley of the seventeen-year-old peasant girl, who, in 1429, in her little village of Domrémy, 350 miles away in the northeast of France, heard the voices of her beloved saints telling her to go to Chinon, where the dauphin (the uncrowned heir to the French throne) was in residence, to bring him to Rheims to be crowned, and to drive the English from Orléans.

The country between Domrémy and Chinon was so thickly covered with English armies and with brigands that it seemed impossible to cross it safely. Fourteen years before, taking advantage of civil wars, Henry V of England had invaded France and decisively beaten the French at Agincourt. Ever since, he had been systematically devastating northern France, capturing castles and towns, ousting French lords, killing their vassals, installing English vassals in their place, pillaging the villages in the surrounding countryside to sustain his troops during the sieges, stripping towns of everything worth taking, slaughtering the inhabitants, hanging beheaded townsmen from trees, and then, because Henry V felt war without fire was like "sausage without mustard," burning everything in his path. This war had been going on ever since Joan was born—in fact, intermittently, ever since 1337, when a French king had died without a male heir and successive English kings had claimed the double crown of France and England through the female line. And this devastation was taking place in and around Domrémy, where Joan of Arc was born. All through her childhood, churchbells had tolled to warn her and the other townspeople to flee into the woods—"like wandering beasts," in the words of one peasant—where they hid until the bells told them it was safe to return.

English troops had reached as far south as the Loire Valley, with Orléans itself under siege, when Joan of Arc heard the voices of her saints in the chiming of her churchbells, and set out for Chinon to end this endless war. The journey of this young woman dressed in white, who said she was a virgin and whose demeanor awed even her rough companions on the trip so that they did not think of making sexual advances, was in itself viewed in 1429 as somewhat of a miracle, not only because brigands and hostile English soldiers were everywhere in northern France, and she had come 350 miles without encountering a hostile soldier or brigand, but because it had long been believed in France that a virgin dressed in white would come from the Bois Chenu, a wood near Domrémy, to save France. And France, when Joan of Arc set out on her journey, was in dire need of saving. In fact, if ever a miracle was needed, it was then.

The scenes of Joan of Arc's legend were enacted throughout the Loire

Valley—at Blois, where she and her soldiers celebrated communion at the Church of Saint-Sauveur and received the royal fleur-de-lis standard from the Archbishop of Rheims before marching on Orléans; at Orléans, where her victory over the English in 1429 turned the tide of the Hundred Years War (and moved the French to call her "the Maid of Orléans"); and at Loches, where, after her victory at Orléans, she begged the dauphin to come with her to Rheims and receive his crown from God as all French kings had done in the past—and where a copy of her trial is kept on view to record for posterity the purity of her heroism and her betrayal by her king. But it is at Chinon that you feel her presence most.

Strolling along the narrow cobbled lanes of this delightful medieval town nestled at the base of the escarpment on which the fortress stands, walking along streets that sparkle with reflections from mullioned windows whose tiny panes of colored glass catch the sun, past houses whose bricks are cut into diamond patterns by ancient beams, past buildings with romantic turrets, past doorways with elaborately carved wooden archways, I felt a sense of another time, another place.

Though on our previous trips to the Loire I was always urging Bob to drive to Chinon for lunch or tea, I admit I only partly felt the history that had captured Bob's imagination from the very first moment we visited this town. I therefore decided to return alone and stay the night in the medieval part of town. By sheer luck, a parking space appeared, not at the hotel at which I had a reservation but in front of the Hostellerie Gargantua, where Rabelais's father once practiced law. Carrying my bags up the winding staircase, I knew, as soon as I stopped to catch my breath at the first landing, that I had chosen the perfect place to stay. Standing on that landing, I found that I was looking out an open Gothic window at the fortress I had come to see. The Flamboyant carved stonework provided a perfect frame for the ruins of Chinon outside. From my room, located in a little Gothic turret, I looked out over the Vienne River and the medieval rooftops of Chinon. That evening, I dined on the hotel's terrace, next to an arch of roses, and listened to the peal of churchbells every half hour. My view from the table was of the steeply rising cliff, topped by the château's curtain wall, sharp and clear against the sky. But nothing, I thought, was as beautiful as—very late that night—the sight of the fortress of Chinon in the moonlight, framed in the Gothic window on the staircase of my fifteenth-century hotel.

Very early the next morning I went in search of Joan of Arc. With the cobbled streets deserted, I came to the Grand Carroi, once the heart and crossroads of this medieval town. I saw the very well on which the little Maid stood to mount and dismount from her horse. I walked on the very streets where Joan once walked, past the very house in which she once waited, fasting and praying, hoping that the dauphin, residing in the fortress so high above the little town, would grant her, a peasant, an interview at the royal court. Standing in this town where the commoners had worked and lived, looking up at the château high above, where the aristocracy had spent their time, I experienced an understanding I had never felt before. I had read that Joan waited in Chinon while her companion, a nobleman and a relative of the dauphin, tried to obtain an interview for her. As I looked up at the château from the town below, Joan's place in feudal society became clear to me. Phrases my eye had skimmed—"of noble blood," "of peasant stock"—took on an importance I had not previously given them. Just being in Chinon, a town so unlike any place in America, I was able to understand the events of Joan of Arc's life in a way I never had before. When I first encountered her, on a junior high school stage, and I spoke the lines Shaw gave Saint Joan, I imagined her a female George Washington, driving the English from her America-like nation. But Joan's fifteenth-century France was not eighteenth-century Revolutionary America. Nor did Joan of Arc, and the people who believed in her, look at life in the cynical way we do now. It is difficult for us, a people whose heroes seem to fight only for themselves rather than for a greater cause, to comprehend a fifteenth-century Joan of Arc and the people who believed in her. Books today try to explain away the miraculous events of Joan of Arc's life empirically. The moldy rye bread she ate and the lightheadedness brought on by fasting are cited to explain why this religious peasant girl saw visions of Catherine and Margaret dressed as queens and heard these saints command her to raise the siege at Orléans and lead the dauphin to his coronation at Rheims. Coincidence and luck are cited to explain her safe journey from Domrémy through bands of hostile soldiers and flooding rivers as she made her way to Chinon. Knowledge of the buried sword, miraculously found at the Church of Saint Catherine, is explained not by divine visions, but by the fact that Joan and her companions stopped at the church on their way to Chinon. But in Chinon I realized that the facts and legend of her life are among those phenomena of history in which legend and fact are intermingled to such a degree that neither is true without the other. What the people of fifteenth-century France believed to be true had a truth real in the consequences it produced: a faith strong enough to replace despair, to bind the fragments of a feudal country into a nation with a messianic patriotism strong enough to finally drive the English out of France.

Later that morning I drove into the countryside so that I could see the château from across the Vienne. I tried to imagine how the fortress must have looked to Joan as she approached it on horseback in that March of 1429: a massive château, virtually a manmade cliff of walls and towers rising out of an enormous natural escarpment, a manmade fortress rising out of a natural one, a series of martial keeps—rectangular, cylindrical, and square—connected by a curtain wall, towers that must have seemed in the distance similar to all the keeps of Foulques Nerra she had passed throughout the region, but which, as she came closer, actually reflected, in their differences, the slow changes that had been taking place over four hundred years, during which such offensive structures had evolved into defensive strongholds. As I looked at the distant château, the curtain wall seemed to join together a collection of keeps, but actually, that wall, as it circles the rectangular escarpment, joins together three distinct fortresses, separated by dry moats: the Château du Coudray, to the east, the oldest section with remains of tenth-century walls begun by the Counts of Blois; the Château de Saint-Georges, to the west, with its Angevin cylindrical keeps and curtain wall built when the Kings of England held Chinon in the eleventh and twelfth centuries; the Château du Milieu, with the thirteenth- and fourteenth-century Royal Loge, palace, and apartments built by successive Kings of France.

It was following in her footsteps at the ruins of the château that I felt closest to Joan. I don't know why this was true, because only the steepness of the hill approaching the château is the same today as it was when Joan of Arc went for her audience with the dauphin. The château is in ruins now, but when Joan arrived in 1429, Chinon was at the height of its grandeur. Its formal gardens were filled with flowers. There were two chapels—the Romanesque Chapel of Saint George, built by the King of England when Chinon was his fief and favorite château, which a thirteenth-century chronicler called "one of the most beautiful in the world," famous for its carved relief of the patron saint of England slaying the dragon; and another chapel, similar to the Romanesque church in Vézelay. Only fragments of them remain, including a capital now on view that vividly depicts the devil in the midst of the flames of hell and reminds us that these deeply carved capitals related different religious stories for the illiterate, like Joan, who could not read the printed word, to see when they came to pray.

The royal apartments were many and connected to the Great Hall, where Charles held court, by a gallery of ornately carved and painted wood, with mullioned windows opening on gardens. In fact, enclosed within the walls of Chinon there existed a lovely self-sufficient little state capable of withstanding months of siege. The mill tower was filled with stores; the cisterns were filled with drinking water; the courtyards were filled with cows, horses, and pigs; and the air was filled with a variety of smells. It was here that the dauphin had fled the English and Burgundians two years before.

Joan of Arc had never seen Charles until she arrived at Chinon. Charles was not eager to grant her an audience; he finally did so only to prove her a fake. It was a time when many religious fanatics claimed to have direct communication with God, as well as a time when an increasingly cynical aristocracy considered such claims to be nonsense. The dauphin finally agreed to see her because he thought it might liven up the evening to expose a fanatical virgin as the fraud he believed her to be.

As you follow Joan of Arc up the steep path from the town to the château, it becomes easier to comprehend why the people of France believed in her. Her identification with the legendary virgin, dressed in white, who would save France had already begun to take hold with her ride from Domrémy. The chaos that had existed for so long had produced a climate in which a miracle seemed the only solution. Her legend was embellished with an incident related by Vita Sackville-West in her biography *Saint Joan of Arc.* As she crossed the drawbridge to enter the château, right at the entrance through the Tour de l'Horloge (Clock Tower), she was accosted by a knight who insulted her by saying, "In God's name! Is that not the Virgin? If I could have her for one night, I would not return her in like condition," she replied, "In God's name, you deny Him, and you so near to your death."

And when, less than an hour later, the knight fell from his horse and, weighed down by his armor, drowned, the story of the encounter was spread by Joan's companions. However coincidental the knight's death may have been, the people of France began to believe in her and in the visions she saw.

When Joan of Arc entered the fortress at Chinon that evening, it must have been one of the most dramatic scenes in French history. The Great Hall, seventy feet in length, was lit by fifty torches; the monumental hooded fireplace, which remains today, was then attached to a roof; the cold stone walls were hung with luxurious tapestries; and the room itself was filled with three hundred noblemen attired in the colorful dress of the period—their rank indicated by the length of their sleeves.

The dauphin, in order to expose her as a fraud, had exchanged his clothes with a nobleman of lesser rank and shorter sleeves, and had made himself inconspicuous among the crowd. But although another nobleman wore Charles's robes, and Joan had never seen the dauphin, she immediately recognized Charles and marched straight to him, through a crowded room and said: "Gentle Dauphin, my name is Joan the Maid. The King of Heaven sends word by me that you will be anointed and crowned in the city of Rheims." The Lord, she said, had sent her to lead him to Rheims "and to raise the siege of the good city of Orléans held by the English."

When the dauphin demanded proof that she had been sent by God, Joan related an incident that she could have known only by miraculous means: she told Charles she knew that one night "in the château at Loches, he had risen from his bed and, in the privacy of his chamber, prayed on his knees that if he were not the true son of Charles VI, he might be allowed to leave France, seek refuge in Scotland or Spain, and give up the kingdom to the English to survive in peace." She then told him: "I tell you in the name of Our Lord Christ that you are the heir of France and the true son of the King." Since the basis of royal power in France was hereditary and thought to be divine, direct descent from the king (and thus from Charlemagne) was therefore essential to establishing a legitimate claim to the crown.

But the dauphin was still not convinced that the voices Joan heard were divine. At the time of his birth his father, Charles VI, was insane (the king sometimes ran through palace corridors howling like a wolf, or cringed in corners saying he was made of glass and his courtiers were trying to shatter him, and murdered hunting companions for no apparent reason). His mother, the scandalous Queen Isabella, was conducting a not so secret affair with the king's younger brother, the dashing Louis d'Orléans, regent of France, and had implied Charles was a bastard in the Treaty of Troyes. Charles—like most people at court—was convinced that he was indeed a bastard. Therefore, Joan of Arc's revelation that he was the true son of Charles VI was heard with a great deal of skepticism. The dauphin demanded proof of her virginity, and she was kept on the first floor of the Château du Coudray while her virginity was verified. Only then did he give her soldiers—and then only a token force—to relieve the siege of Orléans.

Why troops were contingent on Joan's virginity—in fact, the importance of Joan's virginity and its continual verification during her short life—is an aspect of fifteenth-century culture that may be hard for the twentieth century to comprehend. Joan's virginity was very important to the growth of her legend, in part because of the long-reported prophecy—given by Merlin among others—about the virgin dressed in white from the Bois Chenu. This legend had circulated throughout France long before the official outbreak of the Hundred Years War. Eleanor of Aquitaine knew of it two centuries earlier, and had tried to capture the imagination of the French by dressing herself in white to lead the Second Crusade to Jerusalem. But whereas Eleanor never touched the hearts of the French—perhaps because it was well known that she was no virgin—Joan of Arc succeeded. She herself helped the legend along by dressing in white, and then there were the circumstances in which her sword was found.

The discovery of the sword followed the verification of Joan's virginity. The townspeople of Chinon purchased her a suit of armor to wear to Orléans. She graciously accepted each item of attire until they offered her a common sword. She would have no sword, she said, but a sword to be found at the church of her blessed Saint Catherine in Fierbois (where, as it happened, she had stopped briefly on her way to Chinon). Swords have been a part of French legends from earliest times; while in Provence we saw that the early Celts believed their Druid priests (originally blacksmiths) magically turned rock into swords. Magic became sacred as pagans became Christians. A sword became part of the legend of Roland, France's most Christian knight, and a sword became part of the legend of Joan of Arc when she told her followers to go to the Church of Saint Catherine. There, she said, they would find a sword buried behind the altar. A rusty sword was indeed found there, and according to the legend the rust miraculously fell away to reveal the sword that Charles Martel, Charlemagne's grandfather, had used to defeat the infidels at the Battle of Tours in 732.

Even before the Battle of Orléans, therefore, the story of Joan the Maid had begun to spread throughout France. But it wasn't until her victory there that the people came truly to believe in her, because—although there are rational explanations for her victory there—at the time some of the circumstances seemed miraculous.

The officers assigned by the dauphin's courtiers to assist Joan deliberately misdirected her, and when she arrived at Orléans, which the English had been besieging for six months, she found herself on the wrong side of the river. Since the English controlled the bridge across the Loire, her guides expected that she would have to return upriver to Beaugency to cross, which would have made her look like a fool. There seemed no other choice: transporting troops across the river by boat seemed impossible because the boats would have had to be brought upriver from another town, and the prevailing wind was howling in the wrong direction at that moment. When the guides told her that she would have to return to Beaugency, she calmly told them to wait awhile and all would be well. Then, suddenly—the soldiers believed it to be a sign from heaven—the wind changed its direction, and Joan of Arc was able to cross the river and relieve Orléans. She rode into town dressed all in white on a great black charger. The people, who had heard that she and her troops were coming, greeted her as a saint. They followed her through the streets, trying to kiss her sword or touch her horse.

What happened next shows how the power of legend can affect the events of history. While she was at Orléans, the French attacked the English without informing her, and were already falling back in retreat by the time she arrived at the battle, but when the already-legendary Maid met the retreating French soldiers, she was such an inspiration to them that, like the wind, they changed direction and drove back the English. And as the news of her victory spread, her legend became real to the people of France.

After Orléans, Joan followed her dauphin to Loches, in order to persuade him to be crowned at Rheims. But before you leave Chinon, take a look at the model of the castle on display in the guard room, see the poignant words carved into the dungeon wall in the room where the great noblemen of the Order of the Knights Templars—who had been robbed of their inheritance by King Philip the Fair (1308)—were held prisoner until burned at the stake in Paris. Walk through the narrow streets of medieval Chinon, especially along the Rue Voltaire and the Grand Carroi. Climb the escarpment to the troglodyte Chapel of Saint Radegund, where on the wall of the cave there is a wonderful fresco of Eleanor of Aquitaine riding with a falcon on her arm. Or, if you are in Chinon in August, enjoy the medieval fair that takes place there the first week of that month. See if you can find the secret door leading to the subterranean passage that connected the château to the house of Roberdeau, where Agnès Sorel, Charles VII's beautiful mistress, lived. He was hopelessly in love with Agnès, who was as extravagant as she was beautiful. He could not tolerate a single word said against her, and after she died, he could not bear to be at Chinon, where he had spent his only happy years, as her lover. He never returned, and the château, so long a favored royal court, was left to fall into the ruin and decay we see today. Charles moved his court permanently to Loches, where we will continue our tour.

However, I would never abandon Chinon until I had enjoyed my lunch. I hope you will stay long enough not only for lunch but also for a late-afternoon pastry and coffee at a café along the river. Chinon is a wonderful town in which to spend a long, leisurely day, and having come here, you should not rush away.

THE ROYAL CHÂTEAU AT
Loches

After the victory at Orléans, Joan of Arc followed Charles to Loches, where he had set up court. Sensing that her time was short, she wanted the dauphin to accompany her immediately to Rheims for his coronation. His counselors, on the other hand, felt he should wait until his position was stronger, until he had won back Normandy or, at the very least, the rest of the Loire Valley before leaving the safety of his castles. He himself preferred the comfort of his castles to army camps or to traveling through the English lines. As the fifth of five royal princes, he had been reared to be a pampered prince of the realm, not a king, and he was content in the former role. He had come to Loches to escape Joan's importunings, but she had doggedly followed him, and listened to him talk of fêtes while she talked of battles, crowns, and war.

Perhaps even more than at Chinon, here at Loches you have a sense of entering the courtly world of the aristocracy that Joan confronted. In fact, if you were too lazy to drive all the way to Chinon, or didn't have enough time, don't feel too bad, because if you take away Chinon's charm, the romantic atmosphere evoked by its massive ruins, and its unforgettable restaurants, there was no need to go there: Loches has a wonderful medieval château sitting high on a rocky spur that rises up from the Indre River and dominates the valley and river below, just as a proper medieval castle is supposed to do. And most of the people who had been whoring and warring at Montrichard and Chinon were doing much the same thing here.

While you never have the sense of entering a fortress that could withstand months of siege, as you do at Beynac, Castelnaud, or Chinon—and while at Loches you don't (or at least I don't) feel the heroism of Joan of Arc—you do find yourself in a self-contained walled city where you see the end of the Hundred Years War through the eyes of the dauphin, and you do get a sense of why he wasn't particularly eager to trudge through mud and live in tents in order to obtain his crown. If Chinon is the spirit of Joan of Arc, what I felt at Loches was the dauphin's effete nature.

Chinon is historically a little confusing—having been so ravaged by time that it is sometimes difficult to tell a room from a garden, let alone what was built in the tenth century and what was built in the fourteenth. But Loches is not confusing at all. It has two distinctive medieval castles separated not only by centuries but by a lovely garden walk. When Joan arrived at Loches with her companions, Dunois, Gilles de Rais, and Masson, the tenth-century fortress built by Foulques Nerra was already being used as a prison and was separate, as it is today, from the Royal Loge, where Charles stayed.

In fact, much of today's Loches is similar to the Loches where Joan again confronted her dauphin. A wall—a mile long—still circles the entire medieval city, isolating it from the modern world as effectively as it once protected the city from its fifteenth-century besiegers. Loches was once enclosed by two outer walls, and the ruins of the second are still there. In the fifteenth century the space between the two walls was an open field that besiegers had to cross without protection from the arrows of defenders standing on the inner wall. Enough remains of this ruined outer wall, or barbican, to protect Joan's fifteenth-century world from your twentieth-century car, because it is here, in this no-man's-land of yore, that you park your car and enter feudal France on foot.

You enter the city through the arched gate of the Porte Royale—flanked by two thirteenth-century towers—which once guarded the entrance. (The anachronistically large window was cut at a much later date.) If you climb, as I did, to the top of one of the two towers, you can literally turn your back on the modern world and see a thousand years of French history encircled within these walls. To the left is the Church of Saint-Ours, where people have been worshiping since the Celts became Christians in the fifth century; to the right is the rectangular fortress Foulques Nerra began in the eleventh century. The rounded towers were added by his heirs—the later Counts of Anjou; beyond the church is the Royal Loge of the Kings of France, begun during the Hundred Years War and completed when that war was over. As you look around the area within the walls you cannot help feeling the self-contained nature of the place that Joan of Arc saw when she arrived.

If you have just begun this tour of France, go to the donjon first and review the three hundred years of history before Joan of Arc arrived at Loches—three hundred years of feudal France. And then go to the Royal Loge and watch the monarchy begin to consolidate its power. Walk along the Mail du Donjon to Foulques Nerra's fortress, cross the bridge that once spanned a moat, making this massive fortress even more impregnable, and take a look inside the keep.

It is very depressing. There are no windows, just solid walls 100 feet high, 170 feet long, and 9 feet thick. This was a structure built solely for defense and war. The cruelty of its builder, or, perhaps, its subsequent use as a prison, is chilling even centuries later on a hot day. Even though the floors are gone, you can make out that there were once three of them, since three sets of fireplaces decorate the wall to tell you so. This is an incredibly dank, dark, and dreary place, and I couldn't wait to leave. If, before entering this fortress, I had been amazed to learn that Foulques Nerra had made at least four pilgrimages to sunny Jerusalem, now, seeing one of his best châteaux,

I was amazed that he didn't go more often. I could also understand how Il Moro, the Duke of Milan, held prisoner here in a windowless cell from 1500 to 1508, died at the very moment he was released, supposedly from excitement at seeing the sun once more.

You are, however, overwhelmed with a feeling of this donjon's impregnability and cannot help being awed at the incredible feat of Foulques Nerra's descendant Richard the Lion-Hearted, when he and his followers scaled its walls and recaptured the fortress in the space of three hours. This fortress at Loches (as well as those at Chinon and elsewhere) had been Richard's, because he was the heir of both Foulques and William the Conqueror, Duke of Normandy—not to mention his mother, Eleanor of Aquitaine. Richard was therefore not only King of England but also held Anjou, Normandy, and a large portion of southwest France when he set off on the Third Crusade.

As we all know from reading *Ivanhoe,* Philip Augustus returned from Jerusalem before Richard and plotted against him with Richard's brother John Lackland, who was ruling England in Richard's absence. In exchange for arranging Richard's capture and imprisonment on his return, John gave this fortress at Loches to Philip Augustus, and Richard was then secretly held prisoner at the Castle of Trifels for an outrageously high ransom (150,000 marks), which his brother, of course, refused to pay. Richard was finally found by his faithful troubadour Blondel, who had traveled from castle to castle in Austria, singing outside the walls until at one castle his song was answered by Richard. When Richard was finally ransomed, he learned that his brother had traded Loches away, and he scaled these unscalable walls with a band of faithful followers to get it back.

Go now to the Royal Loge and watch France become a nation in quite an agreeably restored château. From the outside you can easily see that its construction took place at two distinctly different periods, between which circumstances had been greatly altered. The first part of the château was completed when Charles VII was dauphin, before the Hundred Years War had come to an end. It is austere, devoid of architectural decoration, and consists of one small turret on the most easily defended side and four small turrets and a huge one on the more vulnerable side. Four of the five turrets, with arrow-slit windows, are positioned for defensive reasons. They do not balance the corners of the château, as do the turrets of early French Renaissance châteaux, where these basically defensive elements have been transformed into whimsical components of rather romantic design. The second portion of the loge is quite different, since it was built thirty years later, during the peaceful reign of Charles VIII and Anne of Britanny. It is a typically Gothic château or hunting lodge. Its walls and roof are not as high as the earlier section. Dormer windows on the sculptured façades are topped with carved hounds to show that this was now a hunting lodge, hunting being the favorite pastime of the nobility. And the turrets are gone, as was the need to keep watch over the countryside.

As you enter the Royal Loge, you find yourself facing a portrait of the dauphin on the wall of the antechamber, or Charles VII's Room. Close by is a painting of Joan of Arc and a case containing a manuscript of her trial.

The next room, the Great Hall, served many functions in the fifteenth century. It was where the dauphin feasted, danced, received his vassals, and, then, at night, opened his traveling chest and spread his sleeping mat. This is also the room in which the Maid of Orléans begged him to come with her to be crowned; it was here, according to Vita Sackville-West, that she knelt before him, clasping him round the knees, and said, "Gentle Dauphin, do not hold such long and wordy councils, but come to your coronation at Rheims. I am most eager you should go there." And when, thinking of his comfort and safety, he hesitated, Joan said, "In God's name, I know what you are thinking and what you would like to know about the voice I have heard, as concerns your coronation, and I will tell you that I entered into prayer after my usual manner. When I complained that no one would believe what I said, the voice replied, 'Daughter of God, go, go, go, I will aid you, go.' "

You may wonder why it was necessary to take the dauphin north, through English-controlled lines, to be anointed and crowned in the Cathedral of Rheims rather than at the perfectly lovely Gothic cathedral we visited at Bourges, which the dauphin's forces controlled and where he had already been crowned. The answer would have been quite simple had you been living in France during the Middle Ages: the King of France had to be crowned at Rheims and nowhere else. That was where all Christian Kings of France had been crowned since 496, when, according to legend, a white dove flew down from heaven with a phial of oil in his beak to consecrate Clovis, the first Christian King of the Franks.

In the eleventh century Hugh Capet had made good use of this legend when he had himself and, later, his son crowned there. Hugh Capet's military position was so weak that he literally could not travel through his own lands without being robbed by bandits, but his acceptance as God's anointed king, and his son's acceptance as his successor, were important precedents in establishing the hereditary nature of kingship in France. And although, on July 17, 1429, when the dauphin was crowned King Charles VII of France, the oil in the phial had long since dried up, the belief in it was still fresh in the hearts of the French peasants.

Once Joan had led the dauphin to his coronation, however, it was not in his best interest to allow the continued existence of this charismatic figure. She had to be destroyed, and her legend along with her. And so the King of France made no effort to ransom her when she was captured by the Burgundians; he made no effort to stop the Burgundians from selling her to the English, who had from the beginning declared that they would burn her at the stake if they captured her; he made no effort to influence the judges at the trial the English conducted to destroy her reputation before killing her, and he made no effort to save her from being burned at the stake as a witch.

In the next room of the Royal Loge is Agnès Sorel's tomb. The life-sized carving of Charles's mistress looks so virtuous that during the Revolution she was mistaken for a saint and her tomb, then in the Church of Saint-Ours, was partially destroyed. But she was no saint. She was merely a beautiful, and notorious, seductress, as her portrait on the wall reveals. For ten years following the end of the Hundred Years War, she seduced, enchanted, and drained him of everything, including the tax revenues he raised from a suffering people. The clothes she wore were said to be finer than the clothes of any princess in all Christendom. (Her dresses were made of silk imported from the Orient by her close friend Jacques Coeur, and the collars of the dresses were adorned with gold and precious gems.) Diamonds and other jewels were squandered on her in a way that shocked a country long overtaxed to support a war and now overtaxed to satisfy her every whim. She had become Charles's lover when she was eighteen and remained his mistress until her death, a decade later. While Charles would not raise a cent to ransom Joan of Arc, he would squeeze a nation to satisfy Agnès's insatiable craving for clothes and jewels. The French, who were loathe to disparage a king, generally blamed her and the sexual spell she cast upon Charles for his exorbitant lifestyle.

When Agnès died, her tomb was placed in the Church of Saint-Ours, on which she had bestowed rich gifts during her lifetime. After Charles's death, the canons of the church objected to the remains of this immoral woman being buried within such sacred precincts, and the new king, wily Louis XI, agreed that her body could be removed—but only if the Church of Saint-Ours returned her generous gifts. The tomb remained in the church until the early nineteenth century.

The last part of the château contains the rooms of Charles VIII (1470–1498) and Anne of Brittany, built when the region was secure from attack and Loches had become just a royal hunting lodge. I have to admit that this is not the best place to visit this royal couple. Langeais is. But don't plan to spend too much time at Langeais, since it is not a pleasant town like Montrichard, Chinon, and Loches.

THE CASTLE OF
Langeais

L angeais was built in only four years during the 1460s, resulting in a perfect example of fifteenth-century military architecture, with a unity of
style not evident in most medieval castles. Everything appropriate for a fifteenth-century fortress is here: the high walls; the massive towers (rounded
rather than square), the water-filled moat; walls slanted at the base for ex-
tra thickness against mining and missiles. The entrance to the castle, designed in best medieval fashion, has narrow passages with several turns,
called a bent entrance, accommodating no more than one or two people at
a time and making it almost impossible to bring in large supply wagons. It
has a drawbridge, a portcullis, and projecting stone machicolations,
through whose many openings the usual molten lead, pitch, stones, burning hoops, or boiling water could be dropped on attackers. Ironically, these

machicolations are the only decorative relief in the castle's overall, depressing severity. There are the usual arrow-slit windows. (By the fifteenth century, archers, once considered unchivalrous because they could kill without coming close enough to be killed, were an accepted component of a military operation in a society that cared less and less about chivalry.) There are the usual crenelated sentry walks. There is the inner courtyard, or bailey.

However, while the outside of Langeais is feudal and military, the inner courtyard shows the first signs of the influence of the Italian Renaissance, which had begun in Italy in the fourteenth century. And the interior rooms have been restored and well decorated with fifteenth-century antiques and reproductions. Even the tile floors have been completely restored with an attempt at authenticity. Since the castle was constructed for the King of France, the materials used, especially the chestnut woodwork, are of the highest quality.

The reason that the outside looks feudal and militaristic while the interior reflects the Italian Renaissance is quite simple. The outside was completed by Louis XI when he feared an invasion of France by Brittany. And the inside was completed after the fear of a Breton invasion had been ended in best feudal fashion—by the marriage between Anne of Brittany and Charles VIII of France. With the threat of internal war ended, Charles VIII went off to Italy to war.

Although I can see the advantages of enlivening historical fact to make tours more entertaining, the account of the union between Anne and Charles given by the guide on my last visit exceeded the limits I am willing to endure. While standing in front of life-sized wax figures, my guide tried to turn this marriage into a fairy-tale love story in which the beautiful lame princess falls in love with the ugly frog of a prince. The true story is somewhat less romantic. Brittany had long been one of the most autonomous duchies and self-contained provinces of France. Its duke had always chosen his own allies, maintained his own parliament, established his own university, and, by special treaty with the Pope, selected Brittany's own bishops and clergy—a concession the King of France had not yet been able to wring from Rome. (In fact, when you visit Brittany today, you will find it still preserves its own identity.) When the Duke of Brittany died in 1488 without a son, leaving only eleven-year-old Anne of Brittany as heiress, his duchy became her dowry—and she proved equally determined to preserve its independence. Charles VIII, although not insane as his great-grandfather had been, was dull-witted, so when his father, Louis XI, realized he was dying, he left his daughter in charge of affairs of state. When the Duke of Brittany died, Anne of Brittany, fearing marriage to a French king meant that Brittany would be absorbed by France, arranged for her own marriage—to Maximilian of Austria. Charles VIII's sister, also named Anne, seeing the danger to France in such a marriage, promptly sent a force of French soldiers to blockade Anne of Brittany's capital at Nantes and bring her to Langeais, where she was forcibly married to Charles. A further humiliation was a provision added to her marriage contract: if Charles should die before she did, she would be married to the next French king (so that Brittany would stay part of France). The young duchess arrived with as much dignity as she could muster under the circumstances, in a traveling dress of cloth and crimson velvet, trimmed with 139 sable skins. Medieval chroniclers tell us that Anne limped because one leg was shorter than the other but that the defect in no way marred her beauty. I have a feeling beauty had a lot to do with dowry in the medieval eye.

Charles VIII may or may not have been in love with Anne, but he was certainly in love with Italy. He is said to have exclaimed, on being shown the Duke of Milan's palace, that he "would give a lifetime as King of France for a year as Duke of Milan." Charles spent a lot of time waging war in Italy—and the grounds and interior of Langeais show the influence of his years there.

Langeais is reluctantly included on our journey because its château shows the transition from the severe military architecture of the Middle Ages to that of the Renaissance. But while the château is perfect for the architectural purposes of this tour, I have never enjoyed visiting it, and I have tried four times. Each time, the guide—you have to go on a guided tour—has embodied all those traits which Americans who hate France identify with France. All were rude and arrogant, and one, learning I was American, spoke French at an increased speed. The guidebook in English is carelessly written; it reads as if a non-English-speaking person had quickly translated it, with infrequent glances at a dictionary, and a cheap one at that.

Instead of dominating the river below as a medieval castle should, the Castle of Langeais dominates and oppresses the poor little town out of which it rises like a gloomy medieval monster. The crowds, even in May, are horrendous. I also defy you—if you are an American—to have an enjoyable or hospitable meal, even though the Michelin gives one of its restaurants a star. While sitting in my car in a parking lot—I never found a café in Langeais where I could leisurely sip a cup of coffee—I concluded that Chinon and Loches are not only more pleasant but better, if less conveniently located, places to experience the end of the Middle Ages before entering the French Renaissance at Blois, Amboise, Chenonceau, and Chambord. In fact, Charles VIII didn't like Langeais any more than I do. Shortly after his marriage he moved to the royal château at Amboise, to which he brought back a colony of artists from Italy. Charles's life was a short one. He waged war for four years in Naples. But it was not in knightly combat that he lost his life. He returned to Amboise and was killed in a duel with a doorway, when, on his way to a tennis match, he forgot to look where he was going. He died unexpectedly from a bump on his head at the age of twenty-eight, without a son.

THE GARDENS OF
Villandry

*It is a commendable and seemly thing to behold out
of a window many acres of ground . . . [of] comely
proportions, handsome and pleasant arbors, and, as
it were, Closets, delightful borders of Lavender,
Rosemarie, Box, and other such like.*

—CHARLES ESTIENNE

After leaving Langeais, drive as quickly as possible to the gardens of
Villandry, only eight miles away. You will need the mental refresh-
ment Villandry provides after what you have just endured at Langeais. You
might think of the experience with a little historical perspective: having just
endured the Hundred Years War, you, like the early Renaissance Kings of

France—Charles VIII, Louis XII, and Francis I—are ready to think of comfort, pleasure, and gardens. The first thing they did when they found they were no longer threatened by war at home was to wage war abroad in Italy; the second thing they did was to clear away the feudal fortifications of their respective châteaux and replace them with terraced gardens of geometric and labyrinthine designs similar to those now seen at Villandry. In fact, the same architects and engineers who had during wartime constructed military fortifications now applied their engineering and hydraulic skills to retaining walls and terraces instead of protective walls and watchtowers, to fountains and reflecting pools instead of moats.

When these three Kings of France went off to conquer Italy, they were conquered instead by the Renaissance, which had been taking place during all those dismal years France was being consumed by internal wars and plagues. Among the first captives the kings brought back to France were Italian landscape designers, who would create formal gardens of harmony and symmetry at their royal residences (at Amboise and Blois) similar to those surrounding the lavish palaces of the Italian princes. Although these royal gardens no longer exist, the gardens here at Villandry are said to be faithful reproductions of gardens created during the first part of the sixteenth century in France and are based on contemporary manuscripts detailing the landscape designs at Blois. Landscape architects today have even tried to duplicate the aroma sniffed by Renaissance courtiers by planting the same herbs and flowers that existed then. There are differences—some gardening books complain that Villandry has a more unified and controlled design than did gardens of the sixteenth century. At that time, the beds were laid out to depict coats of arms and were decorated with animals carved of wood; today they depict varying shapes of hearts with curving geometric designs, possessing more of an Art Deco feel than would have existed then. More serious, however, are the charges gardening fanatics have made against individual flowers and vegetables. For example, when the potato was found in the vegetable garden at Villandry, gardening fanatics charged that it did not arrive in France until the eighteenth century and therefore found it guilty of being anachronistic. (My sympathies, however, are with the poor potato, which I feel has been much maligned throughout the ages, not only in France but in Russia as well. In tsarist Russia, the potato, the main staple of the peasant, was formally excommunicated by the Greek Orthodox Church for its sexual deviances—the potato reproduces without need of a partner. Its planting was forbidden, and peasants were allowed to starve until Tsarina Catherine forgave its sins.)

Personally, I like to think that the aroma rising from the ancient herbs and flowers is much the same as it might have been when the members of the sixteenth-century court ambled in the gardens of Villandry. And I feel the sense of peace and harmony that was sought then when I look out over the three terraces of orderly floral beds or see the crenelations of the keep reflected in the pool and hear the splashing water from the fountains. I confess that, anachronistic though they may be in some respects, I heartily approve of the gardens at Villandry, which are like no others I have seen.

THE ROYAL CHÂTEAU OF
Amboise

I drove along the left bank of the Loire from Villandry to Amboise, passing towns that are cheeses and wines, wishing as I passed the caves of
Vouvray that it was not quite so early in the morning. After about twenty
minutes I caught my first glimpse of the Château of Amboise. By the time
I arrived at the bridge crossing the Loire to Amboise, the view was so stupendous I had to get out and take a picture of it. I parked my car, with my
purse inside, intending to take one photograph and leave. But I was absolutely captivated by the airiness of the château, the result of the graceful
wrought-iron balcony and the Flamboyant design rising from the six up-
per-story windows, which seemed to be tugging the building skyward, so
that the empty spaces of the six arches at the château's base appeared to be
created by their pull, with the château itself barely holding on to the cliff by

the columns of its arches. In fact, in the morning mist, it seemed that the building was kept from floating away only by one of its two huge round plain towers, which help make the château's appearance so unique. Because of the mist and the angle of my view from across the river, the château seemed to have already pulled away from the second outsized tower, to which it is connected tenuously by a long, inadequate wall, like a kite on a string. I began walking across the bridge snapping one picture after another. Finally, when the château would no longer fit within the viewfinder of my camera, I stopped clicking and for the first time looked at this feudal fortress dressed up in Renaissance clothes. It looked so beautiful sitting there on its triangular plateau sculpted by the Loire and Amasse rivers and overlooking the two rolling valleys these rivers also left behind. All trace of the Amasse River has now disappeared under the town, along with the remains of Gauls, Roman legions, and a long line of feudal lords who for a thousand years fled to the safety of the escarpment and farmed the fertile valleys.

All that is now left is the royal château created during the time three French kings brought the Renaissance to France. Two of those kings, Charles VIII and Francis I, spent their childhood at Amboise. Once each became king, he put his energy—and his subjects' money—into making it more like the palaces he had seen while waging war in Italy. Charles VIII had entered Naples dressed as a Roman emperor and brought back Italian artists to plan the alterations to the feudal structure. He had built those two huge towers which make the castle's appearance so unique, not for defensive reasons but so that Anne of Brittany's carriage would have convenient entrances by which she could be driven up to the castle grounds, without her being jolted around the long perimeter of the escarpment to the single entrance that had sufficed throughout feudal times. Anne became pregnant almost immediately after her forced marriage to Charles, and Charles, elated at the prospect of an heir, did everything for her health and comfort. In a way the towers could be considered a defensive architectural device; after all, I had only recently left Chinon, where the failure of a king to produce a male heir had begun a hundred years of war. When I thought of things in that light, the expenditure for these towers—indeed, almost any other expenditure—that would ensure Anne's health and comfort seemed a reasonable precaution.

Despite all the precautions, however, this child—and three others—did not survive, and Charles died without an heir. In accordance with the terms of her marriage contract, Anne was then married to his successor, Louis XII, to try again to produce a future king. Her new husband removed the royal court from Amboise, preferring the château at Blois, where he had spent *his* childhood. Called "the Father of His People," Louis XII was an astute politician and a generous man under whose reign France prospered and became more centralized, at the expense of the feudal lords. Stationing a garrison of troops at Amboise in case of emergency, he gave the royal palace there to his brother's widow, Louise of Savoy, because her son, Francis, his nephew, was next in line for the throne of France if he and Anne did not produce an heir. Louis felt that Francis needed to be close to him to observe how the country was governed. Louis loved Francis and made sure he had the best of tutors and the best of companions; and whenever Francis visited him at Blois, the parks were stocked with deer and other game for the hunts the boy loved from the time he was able to ride.

The night before I arrived in Amboise, I had, while browsing in a secondhand bookstore in Tours, come across a book containing a journal written by Louise of Savoy, who was mistress of Amboise for almost the entire period the transformations to the castle were taking place. As I read this journal, it became apparent that one of the most interesting aspects of Amboise was the rivalry between Louise and Anne of Brittany. In fact, the most interesting stories of all the Loire châteaux usually concern the intrigues of the powerful women of the court. And there is a valid reason for this: it was the women who ran the châteaux while their kings and lords were off fighting. While Anne was married to Charles VIII, she spent more time at Amboise than Charles did. Louise, who succeeded Anne as mistress of Amboise, brought up her children here, Francis and his brilliant sister Marguerite of Navarre. Later, when Francis was king, Louise lived here during the first half of his reign; it was here, as queen mother, that she acted as regent while Francis was held captive by Emperor Charles V of Spain.

In 1499 both Anne and Louise were in their early twenties, but they could not have been more different. Anne was a stern and rigid Catholic, so given to praying that two fireplaces were built in the tiny jewel of a chapel at Amboise to keep her warm. Usually churches of the period had none; penitents were supposed to suffer. Louise, on the other hand, was a well-educated, free-thinking, violently ambitious woman, whose ambitions revolved around her son, whom she called "my Caesar" from the moment he was born.

Perhaps the tensest moment between the two women occurred on October 13, 1499. Anne, pregnant with Louis XII's child, spent her confinement with her sister-in-law Louise, awaiting the arrival of what everyone but Louise hoped was a son. If the child was a daughter, then Louise's five-year-old son, Francis, would remain the heir apparent. But a daughter, according to another clause in Anne's marriage contract, would inherit Brittany. The child was a girl, Claude of France, and from the moment Anne gave birth, Louise was determined that the baby princess would marry her son, and not some foreign prince who might interfere with her son's succession to the throne. Anne, still plotting a Brittany independent of France, was just as determined that such a marriage not take place. There would be two other eligible bachelors available—King Henry VIII of England (1491–1547), then eight years old, and Charles V (1500–1558), who became king of Spain at sixteen and Holy Roman Emperor at nineteen. Anne's aim was that her daughter marry Henry. One of the aggravations of Anne's life was that Francis was an utterly charming and precocious child, whom Louis loved and treated like a son. When his daughter, Claude, turned eight, Louise, who had been lobbying for years, had her way and the little princess was promised to Francis. As Francis grew older, Louis began to find him too frivolous and his passion for beautiful women a serious flaw; widowed at the ancient age of fifty-two, Louis tried again to produce an heir by marrying the teenage sister of Henry VIII. Not long after, realizing he was about to die, he turned to his young wife and said, "I give you my death for a New Year's gift."

Suddenly I stopped thinking about the stupidity of the sixteenth-century French "electoral" system and began thinking about how stupid I had been to leave my purse, containing my passport and all my money, on the seat of a locked car. As I started back across the bridge, I remembered reading how easy it had become for car thieves to open cars (although thieves in France were evidently outclassed by the thieves in Italy; Hertz had rented me the Mercedes only after I signed an agreement, required of all Mercedes renters, never to take it into Italy). Walking back, I realized for the first time that I had crossed *two* bridges while snapping my pictures; there is an island in the middle of a very wide Loire at this point. I stopped looking at views of the river, which was hard to do because the Loire, with its floating islands of trees reflected in the still water and its banks of golden sand, looked so peaceful and beautiful from the bridge, and hurried on to my car. As I left the bridge, I happily noted that the car was still there. Then I saw where I had parked—illegally in front of a police station—and the saying "God protects angels and idiots" passed through my mind as I noted the absence of a ticket.

All that worrying, however, had made me quite hungry, so I stopped at a tea shop before checking into my hotel. Amboise, I should mention, is one of those marvelous French towns of perfect size—big enough to have excellent restaurants and pastry shops, and small enough so that you can park anywhere and walk to wherever you are going. In fact, if you park in the shade along the river, you can easily walk to tea shops, restaurants, and the château, as well as to Le Clos-Lucé, the Renaissance home Francis gave to Leonardo da Vinci. I advise walking rather than driving, because on foot, when you turn a corner of one of the narrow cobblestoned streets, you may suddenly come face-to-face with an enormous tower or a Flamboyantly decorated door, or see a portion of the château through the arch of the medieval clock tower.

Walking here in Amboise felt different from walking the medieval streets of Chinon. When I looked up from the streets of Chinon at the ruins of the defensive fortress above, I intuitively felt the difference in station between the lord living in the castle and the townspeople below. There was also a sense of marketplace, a sense of vertical connection between the farms spreading over the hills surrounding the town, the tradespeople of the town, and the lords of the manor above. And if at Langeais the castle seemed menacing as it loomed over me in the street, here at Amboise the château was inviting, a giant wrapped present delighting the eye and waiting for me to enter and find a magic land inside. It was as though in driving from Chinon to Amboise I had driven from the crumbling feudal world to the very dawn of the Renaissance. If Chinon is a charming fifteenth-century medieval village, Amboise is a delightful sixteenth-century Renaissance town, where everything pleases the eye.

The pastry shops in particular delight the eye, and there is such a profusion of them that any sweet tooth can find heaven. Along the little street leading from the foot of the château through the clock tower that was once the gate to the city, shop windows are filled with displays of fresh lemon, raspberry, and strawberry tarts and candies, and pastries made from chocolate and from every combination of fresh fruits and nuts. I selected an elegant little shop for my coffee and cake and, after quite a few tense moments of indecision, finally chose a marvelous concoction of nuts and chocolate on a thin pastry. I tried to convince myself that I was actually getting into the spirit of the Renaissance by eating this delicious praline-like morsel, and that for the purposes of traveling through history it was necessary to indulge myself with sweets and other physical pleasures as I entered the Renaissance of France, a period when restraint of any kind had disappeared.

One of these pleasures turned out to be my hotel, Le Choiseul, located beside the Loire at the base of the escarpment on which the Château of Amboise was built. When I arrived and saw that the cliff behind the hotel was filled with caves boarded with wooden gratings, I confess my first thought was that it could use some landscaping. The next morning, however, while having coffee on my terrace overlooking this cliff filled with caves, I noticed that a group of French tourists had gathered at the entrance of one of them and that the wooden grating had been removed. I hurried out of my room and joined the group.

I had expected a gloomy, low-ceilinged cave, but the top of the cave was exceedingly high—three times my height, in fact—and where the ceiling met the wall, there was a carved lintel, Roman in feeling. The cave was quite wide, very long, and very Roman. This large cave led to two smaller caves at the far end. They contained silos, which looked like tiny spaceships, and had holes in the floor, connecting with other caves at lower levels. The Granaries of Caesar, as these caves are called, were first used by a Gallic tribe, the Tourones, which gave the area of Touraine its name, and then were enlarged by Julius Caesar's legions, which conquered the tribe when Caesar conquered Gaul. If you have read Caesar's *Gallic Wars,* you will remember that the major tactic the Gauls had used to try to defeat the Romans was to burn their own villages, towns, and provisions in an attempt to starve the Romans. I was fascinated to learn that the legionnaires had countered by hiding stores of wheat in these caves. I was also fascinated to learn that these caves were known to Louise of Savoy. I wondered whether it was the caves or her reading of Caesar that had inspired her; for when Louis and Anne returned to Amboise for their first visit after being married, she entertained the royal couple with a play based not on the life of a saint (as had been the custom at Amboise when Anne was married to Charles) but on the Roman conquest of Amboise and Caesar's arrival down the Loire on a flotilla of small ships. And when Francis won his first victory as king, defeating Swiss mercenaries at Milan, she called him "my son, glorious and triumphant Caesar, subjugator of the Helvetians." Helvetians was the name Julius Caesar had given the Swiss.

After leaving the caves, I realized that the cliff was part of the escarpment on which the château was later built. I realized this when I turned a corner and came face-to-face with the base of the Minimes Tower Charles VIII had built to make life easier for Anne. Walking to the château's entrance, I passed the Church of Saint Florentine, which Louis XI built in 1470, the year Charles, his heir, was born. Previously, pilgrims passing through Amboise on their way to Compostela had been allowed to pray at the chapel inside the château. Fearing that they might infect his only heir, a sickly, malformed baby, with plague, Louis XI built this church outside the château's walls. As it turned out, every precaution Charles's father had taken to protect his dynasty and realm was thwarted by Charles himself, who signed away portions of the realm in disastrous treaties and died at twenty-eight without an heir. (I should mention that my low opinion of Charles VIII was not shared by the tour guides who took me through the various châteaux in which he dwelled, or by Philippe Tourault, whose biography of Anne of Brittany they quoted. It was Charles's youth and not his stupidity that caused his father, Louis XI, to hand the government of France over to his older sister, whom a number of other historians say was a female version of the cunning old king.)

After Charles's death, the crown went to Louis XII, the son of the poet Charles d'Orléans. The poet had been blessed with an heir when he was seventy, which must have infuriated Louis XI. The poet's son was everything the king's son was not. He was tall, handsome, athletic, and brilliant, while Charles was so ugly that even in a time when royalty was always described in the best of terms, Charles's bulbous nose, his enormous head, his marked shortness, his splindly legs, the whiteness of his large heavy-lidded eyes, and the foolishness of his appearance when he entered Naples dressed as a Roman Emperor did not go unmentioned. Louis XI, known for his cunning, had tried to prevent the crown from going to the Orléans' branch—a branch that had caused a great deal of trouble for the crown in the past—by a method that I think gives new meaning to the words "sly" and "cunning": by forcing his handsome, brilliant nephew to marry his ugly and crippled daughter Jeanne in the hope that she would be so repugnant to him there would be no heirs from the marriage. Jeanne was apparently so unpleasing to behold that Louis d'Orléans's mother fainted when she saw the princess that her brilliant son either had to marry or face the loss of his lands for disobedience to the crown.

Arriving at the château, I learned it would not be open for an hour. So I walked over to the Church of Saint-Denis, where, after Charles's death, Louis d'Orléans, as Louis XII, annulled his marriage to Jeanne.

The view of the château and town from the steps of this church is quite wonderful, but if you have no time to spare, save your climbing for the walk to Le Clos-Lucé, the Renaissance house that Francis gave to Leonardo da Vinci, who spent his last two years here. A wooden handrail once connected this house of rose-colored brick and white tufa stone to the château so that the royal children could come here and play. In its charming garden Francis played ball with his sister Marguerite and practiced archery and games of war with other boys of the nobility. Years later it was here in this pleasant garden that Francis would spend afternoons with the greatest artist of the Renaissance, discussing plans for the palace he wanted to build at Chambord, as well as for the magnificent decorations for the balls, tournaments, and masquerades that Francis provided twice weekly to entertain his courtiers and that dazzled the courts of all Europe. His mother liked this comfortable house and often lived here instead of at the cold, formal château.

Le Clos-Lucé itself has nicely decorated Renaissance rooms and a basement filled with the inventions Leonardo put his mind to after he felt his hand was no longer steady enough to paint. I hadn't expected to be interested in them, but I was thrilled when I saw how his genius soared from his generation into ours; there were models of everything from suspension bridges to helicopters and armored tanks. After touring the house and eating a sugared crêpe in the garden, I watched a movie of Leonardo's life.

The house was once owned by a former cook named Étienne, who had made his way out of his kitchen and his class because of the quickness of his wit. One day Louis XI, wearing a rather shabby hat, had come into his kitchen and asked Étienne what he earned. Not recognizing Louis, Étienne replied that he made as much as the king. "What does the king earn then?" asked Louis XI. "As much as he spends, the same as I do," replied the cook. Happily for Étienne, the king liked the answer and made him first majordomo of the château and, later, warden of the forests of Amboise and Montrichard. Étienne could just as easily have lost his life.

At nine o'clock, when the château was opened to tourists, I walked up the cobblestoned ramp to the entrance, paid my admission, and asked if there was a guided tour in English. The woman at the cashier's booth told me there was and that I should wait in front of the Chapel of Saint-Hubert in the courtyard. I walked up another stone ramp lined with flowers, and found the tour guide waiting for a group to gather. Again I asked if there was a tour in English, and realized my lack of communication with the cashier when I was handed a sheet of paper enclosed in plastic. I was disappointed. I had hoped the cashier's *"oui"* meant that there would be an English-speaking guide.

Like most things enclosed in plastic, the paper contained the facts but missed the little human touches. For example, when I entered the guard room, the plastic told me I was looking at a high-backed Renaissance chair. But the French-speaking guide—after pointing out that by the time of the Renaissance, furniture was no longer made of native oak but of exotic woods—added that the back of the chair was made so high and thick to protect the person seated in it from being stabbed, a fact that certainly enlivened the tour and illuminated an aspect of sixteenth-century life I had not previously zeroed in on. However, unlike Chinon, which schedules hourly tours in English—perhaps because the English Plantagenet kings occupied the castle for so many centuries—most châteaux have no tours in any language other than French. Most do provide a plastic-enclosed fact sheet in any of several languages. However, I have learned that bookstores located at the entrance to most châteaux sell little booklets in English; and if you read the booklet *before* going on the guided tour, you will have read almost everything the group will be told in French.

While touring Langeais I had, I admit, become annoyed at not being given anything to hear or read in my native language. I had assumed it was perversity on the part of a nasty French town. After becoming friendly with one of the guides at Amboise, though, I learned that she was spending her evenings listening to a tape of a stilted English version of the tour she gave in French so that she would be able to give her talk in English. I realized then what should have been obvious to me from the first, that there were just not that many trained guides fluent in languages other than French. When she told me of an incident that had occurred just a few days earlier, I understood that I had no right to expect English-speaking guides—and also how deep our feelings about language are. She had asked a group of tourists gathered in front of the Chapel of Saint-Hubert whether they all spoke French. She learned that all but one spoke German. Being bilingual in French and German, she good-naturedly said she would give the tour in German. The reaction was not quite what she expected. The single non-German-speaking tourist burst into tears, saying that her entire family had been killed in Germany during the last war and she could not bear to hear the language spoken.

This guide also told me that a group of Americans was expected to arrive at nine forty-five and that a tour would then be given in English. I was quite happy to wait. One of the pleasures of touring by yourself is being able to leisurely enjoy the settings of various châteaux, and in the case of Chinon, Loches, Villandry, Amboise, Chenonceau, Blois, and Chambord, these settings—the parks surrounding them—should be experienced at length. There are so many châteaux in the Valley of the Loire that it is quite tempting to see five or six in a single day. But if you do that, you fail to become acquainted with their differences and miss the sensual experience of just being there. It is somewhat like falling deeply in love; it takes time. For example, if you walk along the wall of Amboise that overlooks the Amasse Valley—something that few tourists seem to do—you can see how the château was built on a strategically located promontory created by the meeting of two valleys. As you walk farther away from the château, you can escape the clatter of the modern world under the branches of a huge tree and look out over the two valleys as the Druids must have done while watching for the approach of the Roman legions, or as the Gallo-Romans must have done as they waited for the Viking ships that used the Loire as an artery of terror centuries later. You can see, as Foulques Nerra did when he built a tower here, how no invader could approach undetected, not Roman, Viking, Saracen, or dreaded tour bus. The shaded walks that stretch away from Amboise were once gardens planned by Pacello da Mercogliano, an Italian Renaissance landscape artist Charles brought back from his wars, who used his hydraulic skills to bring water up from the Loire. They were once much like the gardens at Villandry, only these were filled with exotic animals. But the gardens are gone. (We are, in fact, lucky to have any of Amboise at all. A nineteenth-century owner, short of funds, used the site as a quarry, selling off the buildings stone by stone, so that the Queen's House of Seven Virtues, as well as the church where Leonardo da Vinci requested to be buried are now dispersed in houses throughout the town.)

If you walk to the rear of the park, you will find a moss-covered bridge crossing a weed-filled moat leading to a stone gateway that once was the Porte des Lions, the château's only entrance until the two towers were built for Anne of Brittany. Actually, the gate was called Porte sur les Lions, and the difference in prepositions is significant: this bridge was above (*sur*) a moat filled not with water but with lions. Here you can appreciate the lengths to which Charles went to keep his stern queen amused. Her favorite entertainment, I learned on this trip, was to have her servants throw a live donkey into the moat so she could watch the lions tear it to shreds. I don't know if the lions were the same lions grown old, or whether Francis's ferocious hunting dogs were too much of a match, but when Francis became king and had three of his dogs placed in the moat so that he could watch them fight the lions, he had to order the dogs removed because they were on the verge of killing the lions.

I walked back to the Chapel of Saint-Hubert to await my tour. I love this little Flamboyant Gothic chapel because it is so up-front and to the point. If you consider that hunting was the favorite pastime of the nobility at this time, and then look at the chapel's steeple, you will see antlers sticking out all over. Then look at the frieze on the tympanum. There is Saint Hubert kneeling before a giant stag with Christ between its antlers. Hubert became the hunters' saint, so the story goes, when he went off hunting on a Sabbath. Just as he was about to kill his stag, a vision of Christ appeared before him, preventing him from sinning. The moral was clear to the residents of the château: they should not hunt on Sunday. Above Saint Hubert, Anne and Charles are carved praying on either side of Saint Christopher.

The tour of the château includes rooms decorated with Renaissance furniture and tapestries. (I apologize, but furniture does not excite me.) There is, however, a room that may interest the historical necrophiliac— the fifteenth-century Hall of States—if the events that took place there, and on the balcony outside it, are known. If Amboise was the site of the dawn of the Renaissance, it was also the site of the end as well. All during the reign of Francis I, from 1515 to 1547, the Reformation had been kept in check in France. Mainly because Francis's attitude toward religion was pragmatic, he burned only a few of the growing number of Huguenots (French Protestants)—just enough to satisfy the Catholic Church, the institution on which the legitimacy of his reign was based and the source of a large portion of his funds. In fact, had he taken seriously the issues involved, he probably would have had to burn his sister, Marguerite, whom he truly loved, and who, when she was not writing novels to entertain her brother, was giving refuge to the free-thinkers (Protestants) of Europe at her court in Navarre. However, he was followed on the throne by several very weak kings—the husband and sons of Catherine de' Medici—who lost control of the country to an aristocracy that used the Reformation as a pretext to break up the growing centralization of power in the person of the king.

The Amboise Conspiracy, as it became known, was an ill-planned and abortive venture "doomed," as Irene Mahoney says in *Madame Catherine,* "from the beginning by its lack of competent leadership" on the part of the Huguenots. Shortly before it took place, Catherine, trying to avert civil war, had persuaded her son, King Francis II, to grant clemency to "religious Huguenots" as opposed to "seditious Huguenots." The Duc de Guise, the leader of the Catholic League, whom we shall meet shortly at Blois, was opposed to granting clemency of any kind. What the Huguenot conspirators hoped to accomplish is vague: some wanted to ask the young king for permission to practice their religion; others wanted to murder the Duc de Guise. The royal court was at Blois in March of 1560 when it was informed of the conspiracy. During a long period of peace, most of the feudal fortifications at Blois had been removed, as the castle turned into a beautiful— but vulnerable—Renaissance château. Catherine, her son Francis II, and their courtiers and troops hurriedly rode to Amboise, where the fortress had been adorned with decorations but not destroyed, and was still impregnable.

If you stand either on the balcony of the long Hall of States or by the walls overlooking the Amasse Valley, you can see even today that any advance on the château could have been detected. Even so, a hundred Huguenot horsemen were able to ride right onto the château's grounds, crossing the bridge by the Porte des Lions. The attackers, once there, seemed as surprised at being able to enter the courtyard as the royal guards were at finding them there: neither group had a plan of action prepared. When the king's guard detected them, at first everything was confusion. "There was such alarm and running up and down in the court and crying 'To Horse! To Horse!' " reported the English Ambassador. The Huguenots were easily captured. Catherine de' Medici, who felt betrayed by the conspiracy, showed no mercy. The conspirators were tried and found guilty in the Hall of States, and then they were slaughtered. As Irene Mahoney relates, some were hanged from the balcony outside this room. Some were tied into sacks and thrown into the Loire far below, where they drowned. Some were decapitated, and their heads impaled on poles around the château grounds. Others were tortured to death on the rack. Travelers along the Loire the following week could look up at the Château of Amboise and see rows of corpses still hanging from the château. The smell of death so permeated Amboise that the royal family, fearing the onset of the plague, quickly left for Blois, as we do now.

THE ROYAL COURT AT
Blois

I can't explain what happens to the quality of light in the Loire Valley between Amboise and Blois. Perhaps the sand beneath the river is more
golden or the slopes along the edge are a different green or the sun reflects
off the water at a different angle. I do know that if I were a landscape
painter, this is where I would set up my easel. It's almost as though the river
itself knew that the towers and turrets along its edge were no longer in-
habited just by counts and countesses, and dukes and duchesses, but that it
was now suddenly running through the Valley of Kings, and had accordingly turned itself into a river of shimmering gold appropriate for the royal
family.

More than the quality of the light changes after you pass Amboise on
the way to Blois. In fact, if you have come directly from Langeais without

stopping at Amboise, you will find Blois so welcoming a town you might wonder if you were still in the same country. After the irritation of touring in Langeais, it is pleasant to relax and just meander through the marvelous old section of Blois, where you can sit in a friendly café and drink in the splendid Renaissance château resting on the highest hill of Blois. From the town below, the château seems at first to echo the Renaissance design of the Vatican Palace in Rome, but as you walk around the town, it mysteriously changes shape to echo different stages of the early Renaissance in France.

Wandering through the old section of Blois is a delight that I heartily recommend. There are tiny parks containing Gothic and Renaissance statues. Friendly shops, medieval houses, and Renaissance mansions hug lanes that wiggle their way up toward the château and then, finding the slope too steep, finally give up and turn into a staircase.

This elegant, friendly town has been known for its hospitality ever since the fifteenth century, when the owner of the château, the poet Charles d'Orléans, returned from England, where he had been held hostage for twenty-five years. It has been said that the gracious hospitality he displayed upon his return to the Château of Blois set an example that was followed in the area over which he was lord. I find that a very interesting concept, especially since the word that best describes both his poetry and the town is "charming." Dining in Blois one evening, at Bocca d'Or, a romantic restaurant located in a fifteenth-century vaulted cellar and run by a young couple of mixed marriage (American and French; luckily for the restaurant, the wife-hostess is California friendly and the husband-chef is French), I was given a menu written in both English and French, and was reminded of the tradition of hospitality established so long ago in Blois by Charles d'Orléans, who wrote his charming verses in both languages. I wondered if it could possibly be true that the example he set for his domain was the cause of the pleasant, hospitable atmosphere that pervades the entire town today.

I also wondered why the Château of Blois was the domain of Charles d'Orléans, a royal prince, rather than the Count of Blois. Researching that not so interesting question led to an intriguing possible answer: because Charles's father was a great lover. His father, Louis, Duke of Orléans, you may remember from our visits to Chinon and Loches, was mad King Charles VI's younger brother. In the early 1400s, as regent of France, he was caught raiding more than the French treasury, creating concern over the legitimacy of the dauphin. I refer again to his affair with the scandalous Queen Isabella of France merely because she was not the only woman he seduced—the last Countess of Blois appears also to have had that honor. Apparently he charmed the young countess not only out of her "honor" but out of her husband's money as well. By pleading poverty, Louis d'Orléans was able to deceive the pretty young wife into obtaining so much money from her cuckolded husband that this once immensely wealthy count became impoverished and was forced to sell the Château of Blois for two hundred thousand livres. He sold it to Louis d'Orléans, who was of course quite able to pay for it—with the cash he had obtained by charming the young countess or had put aside from his raids on the royal treasury.

Shortly after his purchase—in 1407, to be exact—Louis was murdered by the Duke of Burgundy, so he was unable to spend any time at his newly acquired château. But his wife and sixteen-year-old son, Charles, lived there. Despite Louis's various mistresses, his wife appears to have been desperately in love with him. She was Valentina Visconti, daughter of the Duke of Milan, and so in love with Louis that she died of despair shortly after his death—having carved on a wall of the château words that your tour guide will undoubtedly point out to you: *"Plus ne m'est rien, rien ne m'est plus,"* which translates poorly into "Nothing means anything to me anymore."

Louis's son, Charles d'Orléans, must have been quite fond of him as well—so much so that he spent his entire inheritance passionately seeking revenge for his father's murder. By 1415, when Charles, as leader of the Armagnac forces at Agincourt, was captured, he had no money left to pay the English his ransom; the sum had been set outrageously high at the instigation of the Duke of Burgundy so that Charles would be unable to return to France. He spent the next twenty-five years either writing poetry in the cold, damp Tower of London or, according to an English account, hunting and socializing with the English nobility. In either case, after a quarter century an heiress was found in France with a dowry large enough to pay his ransom, and he was able to return to Blois and his bride, the thirteen-year-old Marie of Cleves.

Until recently it was thought that Charles d'Orléans poured what money he had into building the modest arcaded wing of the château, mis-named the Charles d'Orléans Gallery. However, it was actually built by his son, Louis XII; Charles would not have had the necessary funds. What he did with his money when he finally returned to Blois was give it to impov-erished poets and men of letters whom he welcomed to his court in the style of an Italian Renaissance patron of the arts. His reception of men was based on their intellectual genius or accomplishments, regardless of how ill-bred they might be, rather than on their bloodlines, a break with the traditions of the French medieval court, which accepted stupidity as long as lineage was good. This lack of concern for noble blood is more revolutionary than Americans, coming to France with so little hereditary baggage, may fully appreciate.

So while Charles didn't imitate the Italian Renaissance architecturally, he did imitate the classical world in perhaps a more typically French way: he provided artists with hospitality and stipends, and used the Hall of the Estates General at the château, where the medieval French Parlement in-termittently met, to conduct intellectual competitions. The aging Charles, by then bearded and hoary, always dressed in a long furred gown of black velvet, presided in the barrel-vaulted room as groups of poets vied with one another to create verses on a given theme, echoing the ancient Greek competition in which poets vied at the Feast of Dionysus by writing plays on the same myth. At his court at Blois each of the assembled poets would complete a poem using a first line written by Charles. It was during one of these competitions that François Villon (a convicted thief, who for a short period of his life left the grimy taverns, in which he was most com-fortable, to enjoy Charles's patronage—and, some say, friendship) com-pleted Charles's line "I die of thirst by the fountain's edge." That became the poem known as "Ballade du Concurs de Blois," one of Villon's very worst poems.

That evening, over dinner at La Péniche, a restaurant on a barge moored to a quay in Blois,* I pondered the question of which of the stories of Charles's imprisonment was true: cold dank cell in the Tower of London

---

*La Péniche is a restaurant whose food is very much to my taste. I have been told it has one of the best wine cellars in the area, and while I can neither confirm nor deny this, I can say that watching the sunset, even drinking only Per-rier water, is one of the most relaxing ways to end a day of touring Blois.

or sunny afternoons hunting with the English nobility. I decided, while watching the sun play with the colors of the Loire and shade the stone arches of the bridge visible through a porthole, that he had spent his captivity enjoying sunny afternoons hunting, because when he returned to Blois, he was in good enough health to sire a daughter at sixty-four, and, at the age of seventy-one, when people of the fifteenth century had a hard time just living that long, a son, who would one day be Louis XII, King of France. However, his lack of bitterness and lively amorous spirit may have stemmed simply from having a thirteen-year-old bride.

The château at Blois is difficult to understand, but like a good book, it is easy to enjoy and actually becomes more pleasurable with each succeeding visit. Like all the feudal châteaux we have visited so far, it is perched on a promontory high above the town. The first time I climbed the stairs to the top of the escarpment, I noticed that, though the château was indeed up there, it was not dominating and guarding the river in the same way as the feudal fortresses built by Foulques Nerra and his descendants did. In fact, the château did not even face the river. I concluded, erroneously, that whatever reason possessed the Counts of Blois to place their primary fortress in such a poor military position derived from the same poor military strategy that lost them Touraine to the Counts of Anjou.

I later found out that I had been unfair to Thibaut the Tricky and his descendants, for it was not the Counts of Blois who turned their backs on the river, but rather Charles d'Orléans's son, Louis XII, who cleared away most of Blois's feudal architecture at the beginning of the sixteenth century, after he became King of France. When his cousin Charles VIII unexpectedly died without an heir, the crown of France and Anne of Brittany became his. Louis d'Orléans was born and had spent his happy childhood at Blois, and now, as Louis XII, he made Blois the royal residence. The first thing he did as king was to divorce, with the Pope's blessing, the daughter of Louis XI, whom he had been forced to marry, and send her off to a nunnery. The second thing he did was to marry the widowed twenty-two-year-old Anne of Brittany so that he could continue to rule France without threat (at least from Brittany) of internal wars. (He didn't have to worry about the Duke of Orléans because he *was* the Duke of Orléans.) The next thing he did as king was to level most of the walls, ramparts, and keeps that the Counts of Blois had been building for centuries and replace them with Renaissance gardens, which had enchanted him ever since he was a child visiting his grandparents in Milan—which he would later conquer and then lose. He built his Gothic loge so that it opened up on and was facing not the river, from which there was no longer a military threat, but three-dimensional labyrinthine and geometric gardens (similar to those we saw at Villandry), filled with porcupines, parrots, peacocks, and other exotic birds and animals that walked freely among the plants and statues. These gardens, designed by the Neapolitan landscape designer Pacello da Mercogliano, were connected to the royal loge by an arcaded stone bridge decorated with stag heads, now gone.

Some say Louis cleared away the feudal fortifications to show he was absolute monarch and had no need of them. Others say he did so because he liked the openness and luxury of the palaces he had seen while in Milan and Naples. But it should be mentioned that though he tore down the defensive walls and keeps at Blois, where he held court and received foreign ambassadors, he always kept a full garrison of 5,000 soldiers and 1,180 lancers at easily defended and quickly reached Amboise, to which he could retreat in case of any danger.

Louis's château at Chambord, also quickly reached, was staffed as well, but not with soldiers—it was kept ready as a hunting lodge, hunting being the favorite pastime of the nobility and the king. And since the Loire Valley was where the king and his court liked to hunt, in the sixteenth century the valley was (as the Île-de-France would become in the seventeenth century under Louis XIV) the center of the kingdom; Blois, during the reign of Louis XII, was the center of the court. When Louis XII went hunting at Chambord, his personal servants at Blois, all 322 of them (a number that considerably increased when Francis I became king), as well as chests containing hundreds of tapestries he had inherited when he ascended to the crown, came to Chambord as well. (The mobility of the court was not appreciated by all, as we learn from Benvenuto Cellini, the great Italian Renaissance goldsmith and sculptor who was brought to France by Francis I. He wrote:

We followed the Court with the weariest trouble and fatigue. The reason for this was that the train of the king drags itself along with never less than 12,000 horse behind it; this calculation being the very lowest; for when the Court is complete in times of peace, there are some 18,000. Consequently, we had to journey after it through places where sometimes there were scarcely two houses to be found and then we set up canvas tents . . . and suffered, at times, very great discomfort.

At least one fellow traveler shared Cellini's distaste for these trips, as is evidenced by his prayer, recorded for posterity:

O Lord Almighty, turn and convert the heart of the King from this pestilent habit of journeying, that he may know himself to be but man and that he may show a royal mercy and human compassion to those who are driven after him not by ambition but by necessity.

Louis XII may have thought he was turning his back on the river because gardens pleased him more, but he was—and this probably would have come as a surprise to him—actually being carried by the tides of history when he turned his back on the feudal past and did his renovations. He was the first King of France to be unchallenged by any feudal lord. The absence of internal threat of war, as well as a diminishing dependency on the nobility for arms and money, produced this shift, a shift in the political spectrum that would continue as the monarchy relied increasingly on other classes for support. This shift in power (and a growing royal debt) had been set in motion in the latter part of the fifteenth century when the king stopped relying on the nobility's feudal obligation to supply men and arms and began instead to borrow money to maintain a standing army. During the early sixteenth century the king turned to the middle class, instituting the custom of borrowing money that would (in theory) be repaid out of future taxes. During the reign of Francis I (1515–1547) the brilliance of the monarchy was enhanced by gold from the vast riches of the

French Catholic Church, whose revenues then began to flow into the French king's treasury rather than the Roman Pope's.

According to French art historian Michel Melot, these political and economic shifts were reflected in the architecture of Blois. At the very moment in history when the balance of power shifted from the regional princes of France to the person of the monarch, around whom the regional princes of France orbited, Blois ceased to be the residence of feudal princes and became the residence of the king. The feudal structure became a royal structure with national political functions and was surrounded by châteaux that sprang up like satellites throughout the Loire Valley. In the sixteenth century many châteaux in the valley were no longer possessions of minor, independent lords protecting their independent fiefs but appendages revolving around the royal court. The château of Villandry belonged to Francis I's financial secretary. When he was given the job of overseeing the construction of Chambord, he found Villandry too far to travel to each day, so he quickly built Villesavin close to Chambord, using the materials and craftsmen Francis had collected to construct Chambord. Magical Azay-le-Rideau was given to the captain of the king's guard; Sleeping Beauty's enchanted Ussé was the château of an ennobled bourgeois family that supplied cup bearers and chamberlains to the court; the exquisite château at Chenonceau was given by the king (along with the crown jewels) to his mistress; Talcy was purchased by a Florentine cousin of the queen; Vendôme was given to an illegitimate son of the king; Troussay was the manor of the squire of the king; Champigny was built by a member of the court who had accompanied the king on his war in Naples; Gué-Péan was a fashionable hunting lodge belonging to a member of the court and was where the King of France hatched one of history's most intriguing plots against England.

When we enter the Château of Blois, we see that the defensive architecture seen at Langeais, built at a time of transition from a feudal age to a royal one, is gone (there are no moats, drawbridges, portcullises, ramparts, keeps, machicolations, crenelations, arrow-slit windows), since Blois was redesigned after the transition was complete. The defensive architecture has been replaced with a new architecture, one reflecting the artistic changes that had been taking place in Italy for over three centuries, as well as Blois's change from a residence of a warring feudal lord to that of a king with national power and international interests. The growing need for comfort, for luxury, for entertaining and impressing the nobility and binding them to the court, for conducting diplomacy, is expressed in the architectural innovations. The function of the nobility as warriors had virtually come to an end; they now served as members of a social hunting party, guests at a banquet (no longer providing food but eating it), and participants in tournaments and games. They amused themselves by jousting, hunting, or attending social and diplomatic functions. For example, the Archduke of Austria, with whom Louis XII was "contesting" various territories, was invited to spend a week at Blois, which he did. This type of diplomacy, revolutionary at the time, consisted of a series of balls and dinners—the menus of which became known throughout the courts of Europe.

The architecture of the courtyard of Blois, with its three wings, is in effect a reflecting mirror not only of the personalities of the kings who built the different wings but also of the age in which these wings were built, when awareness of the Italian Renaissance burst upon a France no longer consumed with, and isolated by, internal war and plagues.

I felt like an Ebenezer Scrooge of history seeing the ghosts of architecture past, present, and future as I stood in the courtyard at Blois, surrounded by three separate and distinct wings, which illustrate the evolution of the sixteenth century with architectural masterpieces, feeling the changes in society that were taking place as these wings were built.

If you let your eyes move first to the Romanesque Hall of the Estates General, then to the Flamboyant Gothic wing of Louis XII and to the early Renaissance wing of Francis I, and then to the French classical wing of Gaston d'Orléans, you can literally see the changes taking place artistically, architecturally, and historically. You can see the French architects move from the feudal structures of the early Middle Ages to the Flamboyant Gothic ones of the late Middle Ages, and then place Italian Renaissance designs on top of their own Gothic architecture. And finally you can see the architects move on by adapting and assimilating the Italian Renaissance in a purely French classicism.

First, note briefly the only vestige of feudal France that remains in the courtyard, a portion of the thirteenth-century Hall of the Estates General, built by the early Counts of Blois. While the barrel-vaulted Romanesque interior is magnificent, the feudal façade of rubble stone is grim. It originally had no windows at all; the two windows you see were added in more recent centuries. The once impenetrable structure is barely visible in the courtyard, which is probably why the courtyard is such an aesthetically overwhelming experience. Although not so intended, the structure becomes symbolic, falling into the background, as did the Estates General during the reigns of the two strong kings, Louis XII and Francis I, who governed without it, relying instead on their own counselors, who were increasingly from the bourgeoisie. While the nobility continued for some time to maintain the virtually nonfunctional feudal architecture in their own domains as an indication of their rank in society—in the eyes of the people, fortifications symbolized their lord's seignorial and judicial powers—the king, on the other hand, cleared away the defensive architecture at Blois to show his.

Note the difference between the feudal structure and the Flamboyant Gothic architecture of the Louis XII wing, which for the most part obscures it—the grimness of the older building, the openness of the newer one. When a sixteenth-century nobleman entered the courtyard of this palace or the Italianate gardens that existed then, a statement was being made by the surroundings through which he walked. The gracious luxury of the architecture, and the enchantment of the gardens, implied that this was the residence of a king who felt secure from attack, able to devote himself to his own pleasure and comfort. There is a certain unity and harmony of style. But the architecture is still Gothic (or Flamboyant Gothic, because of the flamelike decorations), especially at the entrance to the courtyard, which frames a reproduction of a statue of Louis XII, and around the attic windows. The decorations are lacy, flickering, flaming designs, curving, emerging, and disappearing lines of tracery.*

The architecture of the Middle Ages permeates the Louis XII wing. The high roof is steeply sloped slate. The use of the patterned red and blue brick combined with stone that I find so charming throughout the vicinity of Blois is still used in this wing. You will also find marvelous deeply cut storytelling carvings of fantasy animals, gargoyles, dolphins, angels, and

---

*The best example of Flamboyant Gothic architecture in the area is the façade of the cathedral at Vendôme, where you can best see the curving, emerging, and disappearing lines of the tracery.

monks similar to those found in French Gothic cathedrals of the period. But there is a difference: at Blois the underlying metaphysical message of the carvings found on ecclesiastical buildings has been replaced by a feeling of whimsy. And the only real symbolism is political, not religious—seen in the emblems of royal authority: the fleur-de-lis pattern covering two of the four columns, the porcupines and ermines, symbols identifying, respectively, Louis XII and Anne of Brittany.

While this wing has a certain unity of style, is open to light and air through its many windows, and emphasizes luxury and comfort in its interior, the Renaissance philosophy has not really taken hold. Neither the entrance to the wing nor the entrance to the tower is centered or balanced. Decorative devices used in Italian Renaissance architecture are present— for example, the columns supporting the arched arcade are decorated with lacy fleurs-de-lis and other delicate foliage designs—but they seem important only for overall effect rather than as sequential narrative components. Unlike the Gothic carvings, the patterns here are repeated and are not deeply cut, as in French medieval style; nor do the carvings have the metaphysical and symbolic significance common to Gothic art. However, the most important aspect of the Louis XII wing is the perceptible change to an architecture concerned with comfort rather than defense.

Louis XII was somewhat frugal, and his wing at Blois still has the feel of a modest manor house. His successors were not.* At right angles is the Francis I wing, created by Louis XII's nephew, son-in-law, and successor. While it was built less than twelve years later, the change is striking. The manor house has become a palace. There is a monumentality, a brilliance, a feeling of luxury and exquisite taste, about the wing that does not exist in the Louis XII wing. The increased lavishness of expenditure poured into this wing at Blois becomes overwhelming at Chambord. Francis I never liked Blois, whose existing buildings and surrounding town restricted him and didn't correspond to his taste. He concentrated his efforts on Chambord,

---

*The size of the royal court, fifteen thousand under Louis XII, continued to grow, as did the royal budget. The change in spending is illustrated by a single figure. Two hundred thousand livres was the purchase price of the Château of Blois itself, two hundred thousand was also the amount spent by Francis I on a single purchase of fabric. By the end of the reign of Francis I, the royal debt had reached the astounding figure of forty million livres.

which presented a clean canvas for the picture of royal magnificence he intended to paint.

Nonetheless, though the Francis I wing is still a Gothic structure overlaid with Renaissance design, French architects created a masterpiece by completely assimilating the new designs to the old structure. Just as Louis XII cleared away the feudal fortifications when he became king, Francis I remodeled as much of Blois as he could when *he* became king. The first difference you notice when you shift your eyes from one wing to the other is that, except for the chimneys, the medieval patterned red and blue brick has been replaced by the carved stone blocks used by the Florentines. The roof, while still sloped in medieval fashion, is not so steeply sloped as Gothic structures had been. There are no pointed towers. Here, you feel the playfulness of the French artist toying with the art he has seen in Italy; he tries to embellish, but not abandon, his beloved Gothic structure. The flaming dormers have turned into scallop shells containing statues of ancient Greeks or Romans. All the windows of the wing's lower story are framed with pilasters topped with the Corinthian capitals that the Romans once loved so well and that the French will come to adore. Each of the stories is divided by a double molding, so the pilasters are crossed with the strong horizontal lines, a feature of Renaissance design. The columns at the entrance are fluted in the style of the ancient world, and windows, while open and airy, are still not symmetrical.

The most dominant feature of the Francis I wing is a structure standing outside in the courtyard: the three-dimensional wedding-cake staircase crowned with scallop shells. The difference between the rather simple and typically Gothic spiral staircase encased in the rectangular tower of the Louis XII wing and this projecting polygonal openwork staircase, enriched with medallions of the salamander (Francis's symbol), is striking. Francis chose the salamander because it can spit fire and cross fire without burning; since it could not be touched by fire, it was considered the symbol of power.

Also in the courtyard is the Gaston d'Orléans wing, built between 1635 and 1638, after the Wars of Religion, which interrupted Renaissance construction. It was designed by François Mansart, who had completely assimilated the philosophy of the Florentine Renaissance and the architecture of ancient Rome and Greece, and would have leveled the other structures in the courtyard had Gaston d'Orléans become king. Gaston, the brother of Louis XIII, would have been king had Louis died without a son. He was therefore supplied with construction funds for his palace in order to divert him from plotting against his brother. These funds came to an abrupt halt when Louis XIV was born.

This staircase was later the scene of one of the most infamous murders in the history of France: the assassination of the gallant Duc de Guise by Catherine de' Medici's bizarre son, Henry III, the transvestite King of France. In fact, the murder that took place here on December 23, 1588, is so richly evoked on the guided tour of the château that you can almost smell Henry's perfume and feel his presence, his earlobes drooping with jewels, as you walk through the darkly wallpapered rooms.

The wallpaper itself is, of course, as anachronistic as the Villandry potato: there was no wallpaper in sixteenth-century châteaux. In 1588 opulent silk tapestries and velvet hangings embroidered with precious stones covered natural stone walls; they were transported, along with the king's bed, when the nomadic court became a traveling city and moved from château to château. But don't let the wallpaper and other nineteenth-century restorations interfere with the drama of the murder, which the well-versed tour guides describe quite authentically while pointing out sufficient remaining sixteenth-century decorations for you to imagine the luxury and good taste of the period. The rest of the interior can be enjoyed as an entertaining stage set for the murder.

There is, however, one further obstacle to the American tourist's full appreciation of the drama. This murder took place not during the first part of the sixteenth century, a period of lavish construction by two strong French kings, but during the latter part of the century, when a series of weak kings, overburdened with the debts of self-indulgence, plunged France once again into civil war—the so-called "Wars of Religion." The problem in understanding the drama is that it involves so many leading characters—and they all seem to be named Henry. In fact, one phase of the Wars of Religion is sometimes facetiously called "the War of the Three

Henrys"—not that three adequately summarizes the problem. There are other Henrys: King Henry II, a contemporary of King Henry VIII of England, and Henry II's third son, Henry III, who assassinated Henry, the Duc de Guise, the leader of the Catholic League, because Henry the duke was plotting to replace Henry the king on the throne of France and, some believe, become Henry IV. And then there is the man who actually was to become Henry IV—a man who was at the time head of the Huguenot faction, and his name was (you guessed it) Henry: Henry of Navarre (whose grandfather was also a Henry). The French aristocracy's lack of originality in the matter of names is also apparent in the princesses of the time—they all seem to be named Marguerite. The lover of Henry, the Duc de Guise, was Princess Marguerite, granddaughter of Francis I. She is not to be confused with Princess Marguerite, wife of Henry of Navarre and sister of Francis I—or Princess Marguerite, daughter of Francis I. We should, I suppose, be grateful that this is the War of the Three Henrys and not the War of the Three Vercingetorixes, Thibauts, or Enguerrands, names that luckily never became popular with the aristocracy.

The murder occurred in 1588. Henry III, the third of Catherine de' Medici's weak and sickly sons, was on the throne of France. He had just summoned the Estates General to meet at Blois in the hope that the representative body would support his faltering reign. However, only someone as out of touch with the temper of his subjects as Henry III could have entertained such a hope; he was not the charismatic king his grandfather, Francis I, had been. Francis never called a meeting of the Estates General. He bound together the diverse provinces of France by the force of his personality, cementing bonds between the crown and the feudal lords with his chivalric quest for glory and empire in his Italian wars. Nor did Henry III understand—as had his melancholy, taciturn father, Henry II—the value of the pomp and pageantry of war. Aristocratic participation in tournaments had grown in importance in direct proportion to the waning military function of the feudal knight, tournaments becoming symbolic decorations for political occasions. Rather, Henry III wore the pomp and pageantry upon his person, and not as a symbol but as an embellishment. According to Sister Irene Mahoney, on one occasion he dressed himself in a gown of pink and silver damask, its "enormous sleeves embroidered with emeralds and pearls." On another, the premiere of a play being presented at Blois by a troupe of traveling Italian actors, Henry "appeared powdered and rouged, with beauty spots on his cheeks, his wide collar open, his neck bent beneath ten strings of precious pearls, while his small black toque glittered with diamonds 'heavy as pieces of ice.' He dazzled more than he knew for as he walked through the ballroom the little gold and silver chains ornamenting his dress jangled until the king seemed like some giant music box that someone had set playing—but that in a short time would wear itself out."

Wear itself out it did. To the people of sixteenth-century France, who idolized chivalry and the noble warrior, this king, who dressed in women's clothes and overburdened them with taxes to pay for the extravagances he lavished on his *mignons* (pretty young "boykins," as Ronsard called them, who wore long elaborate coiffeurs, ornamented with jewels, topped with the little velvet caps Parisian whores were fond of wearing), was a travesty of a monarch, and he was openly mocked throughout France.

Moreover, the necessity for a king to produce a male heir, since the alternative method of succession was not elections but war, was particularly important now because of the Wars of Religion, which, by 1588, had been in progress for twenty-six years. If Henry III did not produce a son, the next in line to succeed him on the Catholic throne of France was the Protestant Henry of Navarre, leader of the Huguenots. Thus, Parisians watched the brothels of Paris, hoping to find their king in attendance there, hoping for some indication that, despite Henry's abhorrence of tournaments, his extremities of mood, his passion for little boys, and his penchant for painting his face and dressing in women's clothing, he would produce a male heir. Henry boasted that he would do so. His heirs would "piss on the graves" of those plotting against him, he promised. But when Henry's younger brother, the Duke of Anjou, the fourth of Catherine de' Medici's sons, died, all France knew that Henry III was likely to be the last of the Valois dynasty.

The leader of the Catholic League, Henry, Duc de Guise, was as much a man of the times as Henry III was not. The duke's father had been one of France's greatest heroes; in 1552 he had defeated the fifty thousand-man army of the Emperor Charles V with only ten thousand knights, and so fiercely did he seek combat that his admiring contemporaries likened him to Saint George in search of a dragon. His handsome young son was also the model of the gallant warrior and charming lover his century admired. When the young duke's Catholic forces were attacked at Poitiers by the Huguenots, he saw the battle—his first—as an opportunity to show the world that he possessed the military genius of his murdered father. The young duke routed the Huguenots by skillfully directing the hurling of burning hoops, as well as the pouring of the usual boiling oil and hot pitch, on Huguenots scaling the walls of the besieged city, and, at night, secretly damming the Clain River so that it flooded and drowned the besieging soldiers encamped along its banks. He was hailed in Paris for killing two thousand Huguenots while losing only three or four hundred men. In another battle, refusing to retire from the field despite having received a sword wound that slashed his cheek and nearly cost him both his eye and his life, he won another victory—and, from his admiring men, an affectionate nickname, "Le Balafré" (The Scarred One).

Guise's entrance into Paris, after a victory over the Huguenots, resembled a Roman triumph, with more than thirty thousand people shouting "Long live Henry, Duc de Guise" as they struggled in the narrow streets to get a glimpse of their champion. King Henry, on the other hand, was openly mocked by Parisians, who posted placards all over their city declaring, in that derisive, sneering manner at which Parisians are so adept, "Henry by the grace of his mother, uncertain King of France, imaginary King of Poland, janitor of the Louvre . . ." When the duke and his soldiers arrived in Paris, the king sent his mother, Catherine de' Medici, to divert the duke's attention while he fled to his castles in the Loire. The Pope and Queen Elizabeth of England were astonished at his cowardice; Elizabeth is said to have "marveled that a prince . . . should take so weak and strange a course." The Pope cried out in astonishment, "Fled, but why? For fear of being killed? But if he were to die thus, he would at least die as a king."

Henry and Henry were different in every way. The duke's shoulders were as broad as the king's were narrow. He stood erect where Henry stooped. The duke was glorious in battle and, reputedly, in bed, and he dressed the part of the charismatic hero, usually in white satin, with a black cape nonchalantly swung across one shoulder.

Moreover, not only was Guise the epitome of the chivalric ideal, the noble warrior, the embodiment of the perfect past of Charlemagne and Roland to which the aristocracy harkened back with romanticized memories, but in addition, as a priest in the town of Toul "discovered" from "evidence," he was a descendant of none other than Charlemagne himself (and therefore worthier of the crown he was ambitious to wear than was the Valois king). All of France was in love with him. Even the King's sister, Princess Marguerite, was in love with him. Dancing with him at a ball held at Blois, she was so obviously smitten with him that later that night, her mother, Catherine de' Medici, and her brother, the King—who were in the process of planning a marriage between Marguerite and Henry of Navarre, which they hoped would end the religious wars—had literally torn her clothes from her back in their rage at her for endangering so pivotal a political union. According to the Spanish ambassador, who was present at the ball, "Mother and son pounced on Marguerite and struck her roughly. When they finished with her, her clothes were so torn and her hair in such disarray that the queen mother, fearful that someone would see her, spent an hour in rearranging her dress." Marguerite was notably uncooperative with her mother's marriage plans for her. At the ceremony by which she was finally married off to Henry of Navarre, the only way her brother could get her to signify "I do" was to actually push her head forward in a nod of agreement. Even after she was married to Henry of Navarre, she continued to call Guise "my Hercules," "my Alexander."

As you walk through the Château of Blois, you will see portraits of the brave and handsome duke dressed in the white he often wore (as did Joan of Arc) as symbolic evidence of virtue. Obviously, this leader of the Catholic League had no intention of letting the Protestant Henry of Navarre follow Henry III to the throne. Although the Estates General had been summoned into session by the king, who spared no expense on the lavish reception with which he hoped to woo the delegates, its heart was not with him but with the duke. It was Guise's intention to force Henry's abdication at this assemblage, and he, along with his brother, the Cardinal of Lorraine, had taken the politically astute precaution of seeing to it that a majority of the delegates were faithful to him and not to the king. But Henry, while much maligned and deviant as a potato, was not a fool; he had adroitly countered in this human chess game by linking both of the Guise brothers to a traitorous plot against the crown.

When your guide takes you into the Hall of the Estates General, try to remember the rich costumes depicted in the narrative paintings of the Duc de Guise and of his murder and the aftermath. In fact, try to summon to your mind all the noblemen pictured around him. Try to replace your denim- and polyester-clad tour group with feudal noblemen robed in lush velvet trimmed with fur, with lacy ruffs about their necks, plumed hats, sword hilts embellished with precious stones, orders of chivalry on golden chains sparkling on tunics of silk and satin brocade, who filled the hall on the autumn day in 1588 on which the Estates General convened. Try to feel the pageantry—religious and political—that took place as a procession of five hundred delegates from the three classes of French society, the clergy dressed in episcopal purple, the velvet-robed nobility, and the soberly clad bourgeoisie convened. Imagine the scent of burning incense that filled your nostrils as you toured the Cathedral of Bourges; the same scent filled this hall when the delegates met. Try to hear the Latin hymns that the delegates sang as they marched, four abreast, into the hall.

Look up as you enter this Romanesque hall and see the flower Clovis found on his fifth-century battlefield, the flower that Louis VII made the royal symbol of France—for above you here is a vaulted sky of golden fleurs-de-lis painted on a field of blue. As you walk between the richly painted timbered arches, picture the violet velvet banners embroidered with heraldic golden fleurs-de-lis that hung from the massive wooden columns. Imagine the pageantry of that sixteenth-century October day.

Leading the religious procession that marched from the courtyard into the hall was none other than the Duc de Guise, dressed almost as though he had stepped out of the painting in the room you just left, in Irene Mahoney's words, "entirely in white satin, with the jeweled orders of chivalry hung around his neck; his sword hilt was also studded with jewels, and in his hand a baton embroidered with golden fleurs-de-lis." Behind him followed the delegates from the nobility in their ceremonial robes.

Henry III, dressed on this occasion not in a gown but in the robes of a king, brought up the rear of the procession. Courtiers dressed in violet velvet emblazoned with silver fleurs-de-lis held a satin canopy above him as he walked. On the first day of the convocation, Henry III spoke, and he spoke well, in a last-ditch attempt to win back the delegates' loyalty. But when he finished, the clergy, whose land he wanted to confiscate to pay his enormous debts; the nobility, whose power and rights the monarchy had usurped; and the bourgeoisie, whom he did not provide with the economic stability which had made commerce possible and which had allied them to former kings—all voted to strike from the record of the king's remarks every word he had uttered criticizing the Duc de Guise. During the long months the Estates General met, as autumn changed into winter, it became increasingly obvious to all that the king would be deposed and replaced by his great enemy. Wrote one delegate, "By each act [the king] really lost power and put them [the Duc de Guise and his brother, the cardinal] in greater arrogance." When the assembled body openly mocked him, Henry III decided that the Duc de Guise had to die.

While paintings depicting the murder and its aftermath hang in the château and provide the tourist with the drama of the event, the *son et lumière* at Blois, presented in both English and French on warm summer nights, is delightful theater (once you adjust to the fact that there are no actors and the role of the gallant Duc de Guise is played by a flashlight) and should not be missed. As you sit in the courtyard at Blois, surrounded by Gothic, early Renaissance, and classical wings, a ghostly voice retells the story that partisans and enemies of Guise alike have never tired of relating (albeit with different details): how the gallant duke met his death. And your eye follows the flickering light from the duke's quarters in the château's west wing . . .

He is sitting in his room while his servant lights a fire to warm his master on that dark, drizzling December morning. The king's messenger arrives with word that the king wants to see Guise immediately in his private chambers. (There is actually a difference of opinion as to what exactly the duke was doing when the messenger arrived. My favorite version, provided by a Frenchman, Jehanne d'Orliac, has the gallant duke in bed with a seventeen-year-old girl when the king requests his immediate attendance. The duke, according to this version, does not have time to say his usual prayers before rushing off to meet his death. Although Guise has recently been warned by the Spanish ambassador that his life is in danger, he has replied that he knows the cowardly king to the very core. "He wouldn't dare."

As you sit watching, the light flickers from Guise's quarters as he fearlessly goes to meet the king. It flickers across the courtyard, where the duke makes his way through sleet and rain, alone and unafraid. Meanwhile, the king has one of the two entrances to his antechamber barricaded so that, once the duke is inside, there will be only one way out. The light moves to the base of the wedding-cake staircase, where the commanding officer of the royal guard of archers is standing. As Guise glances up, he sees the steps lined with archers, but the officer explains that the guards have come to ask the king for back wages, lest they have to sell their horses. The duke believes the officer; the light circles up the staircase as Guise climbs to the second floor, his black cloak about his left arm, his gloves in his hand. He enters the royal antechamber by the one remaining narrow doorway. The door shuts behind him—and as he pulls aside the velvet curtain to enter the room, eight of the king's men, hidden behind the heavy drapery, attack him. Confident that he can fight them off alone and escape through the second door, the great warrior draws his sword, but that doorway and his escape have been cut off. Impeded by his cloak, he fights with his assassins all across the room before finally falling, gasping out, "My God, I have been killed." Henry, remaining hidden until he is absolutely certain the duke is dead, finally emerges. "I did not know he was so tall," he sneers. Then he kicks the corpse in the face. The duke's brother, the Cardinal of Lorraine, who is waiting outside in the council chamber, has heard the noise and sprung to his feet crying, "They are killing my brother." Instantly, the marshal at his side draws his sword. The cardinal is then taken prisoner and thrown down a hole you'll be shown during your tour of the château. (It connects a room outside Catherine de' Medici's study to a dungeon below, and was said to have been used by the Sinister Queen to get rid of the bodies of her discarded lovers.) Spies report to the king that they have overheard the imprisoned cardinal say, "I hope that I may not die before I shall hold the head of that tyrant between my knees, and make a crown with the point of a dagger." Whether uttered or not, these words seal the cardinal's fate.

While the body of the Duc de Guise lies on the floor of the king's bed-chamber, Henry makes his way to a secret staircase, hidden in the wall in a corner of his room, and descends to the room where his mother, then seventy years old, lies dying of pneumonia. He tells her what he has done, proclaiming "I am king now!" and expecting her approval. Catherine, so much shrewder than her son, expresses doubt that he will be king for long, but the elated Henry ignores her. Despite her warnings, he orders the murder of the imprisoned cardinal.

Even his sinister mother is horrified to learn her son has killed the cardinal. Now she fears not only for his life but for his soul as well . . .

Hanging on the wall of the château is a poignant painting of Madame de Guise, requesting the bodies of her murdered sons so that she may bury them. But there were no bodies to be found. Some say they were destroyed by fire, others by quicklime. King Henry was determined that there should be no martyrs' bones to be worshiped.

The result of the king's actions was less than he had hoped for and very much what Catherine expected. He was murdered just eight months later by a fanatical priest. And Henry of Navarre, who, we all know, felt Paris was well worth a Mass, gave up his Huguenot practices and became King Henry IV.

I should warn you that the nature of your tour and of the ghosts summoned up from the past will depend a great deal upon your guide. I took the tour of Blois twice. The first time, in 1974, was with a guide whose description of events corresponded to what was then found in history books. The second time was in 1990. The revolution—not the French but the feminist—had intervened, and my guide was a determined young woman, a fiery feminist, who led the tour as a crusade to right the wrongs of sexual discrimination. I found that miraculous changes had taken place in nearly all the participants of the drama. A mere sixteen years had been sufficient to partially open the royal closet and alter Henry III from an "immoral travesty as king" (the specific nature of Henry's immorality was never so much as hinted at in the 1970s) to a king who was simply misunderstood by a century that did not fully "appreciate his artistic qualities."

Catherine de' Medici's transformation, during these same sixteen years, was far more extreme than her son's. Although dead for four centuries, Catherine underwent, in the hands of this feminist guide, as drastic a restoration as the very walls and fireplaces of the château itself when nineteenth-century neo-Romantics restored the structure.

On my 1974 tour, the description of Catherine was the one traditionally given by historians. She was, as she had always been, the fat, unattractive, scheming, Sinister Queen of bourgeois descent, whom Francis I had brought to the court of France to marry not his beloved eldest son and expected successor but merely a second son. Her plumpness was said to have disgusted that son, who became Henry II. (Henry remained a morose and taciturn man until he made the shapely and charming Diane de Poitiers his mistress—but more about Diane at Chenonceau.) Catherine's poor French accent and bourgeois blood horrified the sixteenth-century aristocracy. ("They have smirched the Valois lilies with a mercantile alliance!" cried the emperor Charles V. "Bah! It is only the shopkeeper's daughter!" scoffed Henry's mistress, Diane, to a member of the court.) According to the traditional version, Catherine's use of poison, massacre, and Machiavellian cunning paved her way to thirty years of power.

Not so in 1990. My feminist guide, convinced that Catherine de' Medici had been maligned by male historians, took us on a tour of the château designed to revise our view of the Sinister Queen's reputation. She first ennobled Catherine's blood by describing her not as a "shopkeeper queen," as my earlier guide had done, but as "a descendant of Il Magnifico," the great Florentine patron of the arts.

My guide mentioned neither Catherine's portly figure nor Henry's humiliation over her habit of publicly stuffing herself with food "until she almost burst." She concentrated on Catherine's achievements in freeing women from dining in private, and in bringing Italian cuisine to France with the Italian chefs who accompanied her to prepare the tournedos, artichoke hearts, and quenelles with which she gorged herself. (There were, however, reasons why women tried to eat in private in the sixteenth century: their teeth were often rotten; the food was mostly very tough meat; the fork was used only by "fops" and "jackanapes"; and the rules of etiquette stated, "Do not stuff too large mouthfuls in both cheeks" and "Do not keep your hand too long in the platter and put it in only when the other has withdrawn his hand from the dish." Therefore, knowing that they were not at their daintiest when eating, and that their faces were distorted by chewing, women tried to eat in private to maintain their allure—and their place at court—in a rather promiscuous society.) Henry was so disgusted by Catherine's eating habits, and by her, that he ate very little and tried to play tennis every day to keep himself slim; his mistress, Diane, kept slim by riding at dawn every morning without fail, even when she was seventy years old.

On both tours of the château, when we reached Catherine de' Medici's study, both guides pointed out the beauty of the 237 carved and painted wooden panels lining the sixteenth-century room, which escaped destruction of the Revolution and the restoration. And both guides opened a number of secret panels by pressing a hidden pedal on the floor. It was at that point, however, that the similarities between the two tours ended. My guide of 1974 explained (as do many books on the period) how the Sinister Queen hid behind these panels poisons that she used, Borgia style, on the people who seemed to die all around her as she schemed and intrigued her way to power. It was poison brought by an Italian cupbearer that killed off Francis I's favorite and elder son and made Catherine's husband, Henry, dauphin and, eventually, king.

As an illustration of Catherine's nefarious use of poisons, my 1974 guide related the mysterious circumstances surrounding the death of the Queen of Navarre, Jeanne d'Albret, mother of Henry IV. Catherine had summoned the fierce Huguenot queen from her small kingdom in the Pyrénées to discuss a political marriage between the Valois Princess Marguerite and Jeanne's son, Henry of Navarre. During the course of the negotiations the Huguenot queen, who was opposed to the marriage, wrote to her son that Marguerite was pretty enough but overly painted. In general, she found the society at Blois depraved, and wanted no union with the Valois dynasty. Her opposition to the marriage ended with her death—which occurred after she donned a pair of leather gloves that had been a gift from Catherine. It was rumored that the Florentine leather had been poisoned.

When I toured Blois in 1990, this entire tale was dismissed as male chauvinist fiction. To my feminist guide, the secret panels (and I guess the secret panels in Catherine de' Medici's study at Chenonceau as well) were used not to hide poisons but merely as safes for jewels and money. There has never been any real evidence to support the contentions that Catherine employed poisons, the guide adamantly said. (She never explained why people who disagreed with the queen mother kept mysteriously dying.) The death of Jeanne d'Albret? A heart attack. And the marriage between Marguerite and Henry of Navarre, which followed Jeanne's death, was an act of statesmanship on Catherine's part, designed to hold the monarchy together. (One sidelight of her daughter's wedding was the murder of the previously elusive Huguenot wedding guests as they slept off the wedding festivities. This act of statesmanship is generally referred to as the Saint Bartholomew's Day Massacre.)

As for Francis's beloved eldest son, who stood between Catherine and the throne of France, his death was caused not by poison but by ice water. (The French, of course, are acutely aware of the dangerous properties of ice water, as any American knows who has attempted to ask a French waiter for a glass.)

The dramatic content of the tour received another blow from my feminist crusader when we reached a room connected to Catherine's study. A large hole in the center of this room, the hole through which the doomed Cardinal of Lorraine had been thrown, suffered a drastic change in function. In 1974 I was told that Catherine, ignored and detested by her husband, had a succession of secret lovers, each of whom she murdered black widow style, discreetly disposing of the bodies down this hole. Alas, according to the 1990 guide, the queen mother was too occupied with affairs of state and preserving the monarchy to have time for lovers (and for that I am quite sorry, given the humiliating nature of her marriage), and this hole, like similar holes in castles throughout France, was merely a relic of the medieval past, used to connect the king's quarters with the guard room on a lower floor and to raise and lower food when the castle was under siege and cordoned off.

But regardless of distortions that are the inevitable by-product of time, both the charming town of Blois and its famous and majestic château are tourist's treasures whose value increases each time Blois is either revisited or remembered. It is a wonderful place to begin a journey through the early Renaissance of France that will continue on to Villesavin, Chambord, and Chenonceau.

THE CHÂTEAU OF
Villesavin

Villesavin is a work of genius, an absolute Renaissance jewel. And although it was undergoing the tribulations of restoration when we visited it in 1990, it is so evocative of the era of Francis I, whose bust greets you in the courtyard, that once you pass through the medieval wall, you feel you are entering the ghostly world of a Renaissance courtier. The château was built between 1527 and 1537 by Jean Le Breton, the squire of Villandry and the financial secretary to Francis I. He was in charge of overseeing the construction of Chambord and found that Villandry was too far for a daily commute. In building Villesavin he diverted to its construction some of the materials, as well as the artisans and Italian masters, that Francis I had gathered to create Chambord itself. Its style is that of the period, a central loge with wings enclosing a court of honor. It has the spirit of an artist's sketch, which is sometimes lost in a finished painting, and is therefore the perfect place to visit after seeing Blois, with which Francis I was dissatisfied, and before visiting Chambord, which was in the process of being created.

When we arrived at the château, no one seemed to be there. The parking lot was empty. After a few minutes an elderly and rather cranky gentleman walking a dog appeared, took our money, and grumbled directions to the château. Our guide for the day was a charming, erudite gray-haired woman who pointed out frescoes and carvings with her gold-handled cane. She spoke elegant French, enunciating each word so that her two American tourists could understand, and she would occasionally, and politely, interject words in English to make sure we understood.

First, she pointed to the château's roof and told us that it was once made of gilded lead but that the lead was removed by Napoleon to make bullets for his soldiers. She noted sadly that there would never be enough money to restore it to its original condition. Then she showed us a fountain of Carrara marble in the center of the courtyard and told us it was the creation of one of the Italian masters brought to France by Francis I. She pointed out four beautifully carved lion masks and pointed her polished wooden cane to numerous carved figures, all of which had lost their noses during the Revolution. Angry peasants, she told us, had chopped them off. Then she led us to the dovecote, where no fewer than three thousand pigeons had been kept during the reign of Francis I, and slowed our tour until she was sure that we understood the relationship of the three thousand pigeons to the anger of the peasants. "Only a very important person could possess a dovecote of this size," she noted. "These pigeons were allowed to eat the corn growing in the fields of the peasants, and the peasants were not allowed to molest them." She looked at us, and it was obvious we had not understood the full implications of what she was saying. "Two pigeons," she added, "could eat a hectare of corn." Clear sharp eyes in a wrinkled face looked at two Americans who did not comprehend the significance of three thousand pigeons being allowed to eat all the peasants' food while the peasants starved. "This was the privilege of the aristocracy," she emphasized. "This privilege ended with the Revolution." I understood at last and hoped the noses would not be restored.

We were then led to a tiny chapel where the privileged few could take communion without mixing with the masses. The walls were covered with frescoes, the work of the school of Primaticcio, one of the Italian Renaissance painters whom Francis I brought to France, and the ceiling, like those we would see at Chambord, were also painted. Our guide noted that the ceiling was low so that the room could be more easily warmed. Then she leisurely led us through the château, its kitchen, its carriage room.

After dinner that evening at the Domaine des Hauts de Loire, my innkeeper, Monsieur Bonigal, told us that our gracious and elegant guide, who had made our day so pleasant, was Villesavin's owner, a countess hoping to maintain her château on tips. The crotchety gentleman who took the money when we parked our car was her husband. Bonigal was delightfully sympathetic to the countess's plight as he explained that it was far easier for *him* to work, since his family had always been bourgeois, than it was for the countess. It was the tradition of the middle class to work hard, but the aristocracy had always had servants. He then told us of another countess who had opened her château to paying guests and who actually did the cooking. Although I never would have done so, I had the urge to hug Monsieur Bonigal. This man, who had taken a run-down hunting lodge and created what is perhaps one of the most perfect and hospitable Relais & Châteaux inns in France,* was in awe of a member of the aristocracy. And much to my surprise, so was I.

---

*We have been staying at the Domaine des Hauts de Loire for over sixteen years. In fact, I believe we stayed there the first year it was opened to tourists. On our initial visit to France, we had stayed across the river at Monsieur Bonigal's father's inn, but since there were no rooms available when we returned, he suggested we stay at his son's place, and we have been going back there ever since. Words cannot describe the pleasure I have experienced at the Domaine des Hauts de Loire. I have watched the grounds become a serene park, the tennis court fill with the scent of roses, a barn become luxurious country suites. One year, a room not being available, we stayed at another Relais & Châteaux hotel (Le Prieuré), perhaps more beautifully located, but its rooms lacked the taste in decoration, and its help lacked the hospitality I have found so enjoyable at the Domaine des Hauts de Loire.

Chambord

Chambord is Francis I's Renaissance castle. It is the monumental man-ifestation of his dreams of empire and beauty realized in stone. The first sight of it is an overwhelming experience, which evokes an under-standing that, with Francis, the monarchy had reached a new level of power. The king now stood not only above all nobles but above the Church, ordained by God and holding his power by divine right. Moreover, if you have visited Chinon, Loches, Langeais, Amboise, and Blois—the châteaux of successive kings—and now arrive at Chambord, you h seen the evolu-tion toward the absolute power of kings reflected in the evolving architec-ture, as each château became less and less a château of a feudal lord, or first among equals, and more the palace of a supreme monarch.

When, in the sixteenth century, the ambassador from Venice saw Chambord for the first time, he wrote:

> I have seen in my life a number of magnificent buildings but none more beautiful nor more opulent. The park in which the château stands is full of forests, lakes, streams, pasture, and hunting grounds. And in the middle stands this fine building with its gilded battlements, its lead-roofed wings, its pavilions, its terraces, and its galleries...When we left we were stunned or, more exactly, dumfounded.

Choosing the middle of a vast expanse of flat land where there was nothing but a hunting lodge and a marsh, Francis was able to build the palace worthy of a Renaissance king that he and the aging Leonardo da Vinci, who died in his arms, had planned. Its six towers, each as immense as either of the two at Amboise that allowed carriages to circle their way up into the castle, seem even more massive because you see them all at once, and also because you see their size doubled in a reflecting pool. You are surprised to learn not that the château has 440 rooms but that it doesn't have more.

While Chambord is called a Renaissance château because of its appearance of symmetry and harmony and the overlay of Greek and Roman designs, its architecture is as symbolic as the windows of a Gothic church. Like those windows, it was intended to be read by all who entered. You approach Chambord today, as Francis intended, from a lane arched by nature with the branches of trees searching out the sun. At first, from the distance, only the trees are visible. Then, the fleur-de-lis, the symbol of the French monarchy—and not the cross—is seen above the trees. As you come closer, the lantern dome—the Church's symbol of heaven—comes into view beneath the fleur-de-lis, announcing in stone what the Pope had already conceded in 1516 in the Concordat of Bologna, that the king controlled the Church in France. And then, beneath the symbols of both king and Church, across a reflecting pool, rises the spectacular array of massive towers, the symbols of the feudal rights of the aristocracy.

Inside the château, I climbed the great double staircase under the lantern dome and walked out onto a rooftop terrace designed by Leonardo da Vinci, where I was thrilled by a cityscape of whimsical chimneys and turrets before me. From a distance they make Chambord look, as Chateaubriand wrote, "like a woman with wind-tossed hair." Seeing the infinite variety of their shapes and ornamentations—Moorish, medieval, and Renaissance—all so different, so diverse, but existing together in a harmony of design, I felt closer to Francis's dream: an empire in which all men could exist and freely exchange ideas—Muslim, Lutheran, and Catholic—under one rule, *his rule,* held together by loyalty and allegiance to their king.

Visiting Chambord today, the crowds of tourists melt away in endless acres of parks and endless empty rooms of the château, where Francis's symbol, the carved salamander, and his initial, F, seem to be everywhere. But inside, I was unable to find the lingering presence of the young king, whose deeds of chivalry on the battlefield, whose prowess in the hunt, whose charming banter at the dinner table, and whose poetry in captivity made him beloved in all the courts of Europe. I tried to imagine the gallant knight setting off to conquer Italy and feeling, as one Italian city after another fell before his sword, that it soon would be his. Yet this young Caesar, as his mother called him from the time he was born, was betrayed in 1525 by a French noble at the Battle of Pavia. As he was being led into captivity, he wrote to his mother, "All is lost, but honor and life are still safe." For a year he was held prisoner in a dungeon in Madrid by Charles V, Holy Roman Emperor and King of Spain, the man who would thwart all of Francis's foreign ambitions. His treatment was unusually harsh; despite his youth, he nearly died. His sister, Marguerite, hearing he was near death, rushed by carriage across the Pyrénées to be at his bedside and begged the emperor for his release. (The Huguenots, whom Louise, his mother, wanted to burn at the stake during Francis's captivity, were especially anxious for his return. Francis, caught up in the paganism of the Renaissance, was not himself particularly religious, but, as he said, "any other religion than that of the Holy Church would prejudice my estate." Upon his return to France, he would burn only as many Protestants as he felt necessary to maintain the well-being of his realm, which was being enriched by the Church's gold since the signing of the Concordat of Bologna.)

But Charles V would not release Francis until he agreed to cede Burgundy. And for a year Francis refused. In captivity his poignant poetry, his courage, and his defiance of the emperor's demands won the hearts of all Europe. In France he was compared to Charlemagne and Roland. In England his plight inspired comparisons with Richard the Lion-Hearted. Suleiman, the Sultan of Turkey, likened him to Bajazet, his country's hero, and wrote to the imprisoned king, "My horse is always saddled and my sword by day and night is girded on," to show his brotherhood with the open-minded king who had opened trade with his country. The romantic Spaniards, who hated their cold Austrian king, idealized the chivalrous young ruler held hostage in their country and compared him to Amadis of Gaul. Even the emperor's sister fell in love with him. In a letter to Francis's mother, she wrote, "Would that it were in my power to deliver the King!" She begged her brother to set him free and to let her marry him. Francis did marry her, saying, rather ungallantly, "On the faith of a gentleman, I'd marry Charles's mule, if necessary, to be again in France." But in gaining his freedom he lost the love of Europe. Instead of dying honorably in prison, he agreed to the surrender of Burgundy—which refused to be surrendered—and gave to Charles two of his young sons as hostages in exchange for himself.

When he returned to France, Francis was no longer the handsome young knight who had set out to conquer the world, but a sick and disheartened man. He poured money into building Chambord, employing eighteen hundred workers each year, and found funds to induce some of the greatest Italian Renaissance artists—Benvenuto Cellini, Francesco Primaticcio, and Il Rosso among them—to come to France. (Andrea del Sarto refused to leave his mistress, but Francis left money with the artist's banker in Rome, just in case he changed his mind.) Yet for four years he said he could not find two million gold crowns to ransom his sons. Henry VIII of England advised Francis to forget about them, since he had a third son, and to renege on his promise to cede Burgundy. Francis I of France (1494–1547), Emperor Charles V of Spain (1500–1558), and Henry VIII of England (1491–1547) had come to their respective thrones at almost the same time, practically as teenagers, and throughout their reigns they played their games of war on the chessboard of Europe. A diplomat who knew the three kings summed up their personal feelings toward one another: "Charles V greatly injured Francis and disliked him little, Francis hated him and loved Henry VIII, by whom he was hated and who was jealous of him." Francis took Henry's advice about Burgundy, breaking his promise as soon as he was safely home, and delayed ransoming his sons for four years.

In 1539 Charles asked permission to cross French territory with his troops to subdue a rebellion in the Low Countries. Much to the shock of his courtiers and the rage of his son Henry, who had spent four years as the emperor's captive, Francis not only granted the emperor permission but entertained him lavishly. Young girls dressed as Greek goddesses threw flower petals on the ground to lead the emperor to the palace. The only reference Francis made at dinner to his captivity in Madrid was dessert: a pastry concoction baked in the shape of the dungeon where he had been held captive. Although Charles was suitably impressed with Chambord, calling it "the epitome of human endeavor," he was not so impressed that he refrained from enticing Francis's mistress, Madame d'Étampes, to intrigue in his behalf.

Beautiful Chenonceau

Sister Irene Mahoney, an Ursuline nun who worked at a desk next to Bob in the Frederick Lewis Allen Room at the New York Public Library, was writing a biography of Catherine de' Medici when we set off for France for the first time. She had traveled extensively around France, researching the life of the Queen Mother who ruled as regent for her three sons after the death of her husband, Henry II. One of the places she told us we must not miss on our trip was Chenonceau, the château which Henry II had given to his mistress, Diane de Poitiers, and which Catherine plotted to have as her own.

Even though Irene had told us it was the most beautiful château in France, I was not prepared for just how beautiful it was. I remember how stunned we both were when, on a misty day, we saw it rising like an enchanted castle from the middle of the silvery waters of the River Cher, a feudal fortress that had become a fairy-tale fantasy design. The four perfectly proportioned and delightful Renaissance turrets adorning the corners of the chateau are miniatures of the somber massive keep, which is all that remains of the medieval fortress. This stolid tower now stands guard by the bridge leading to this priceless Renaissance jewel. Unlike the thick walls of the tower, the stone walls of Chenonceau are open with double-mullioned windows, so that the gardens on the riverbanks become floral tapestries for those inside. The unique beauty of Chenonceau is created by a three-story gallery resting on a bridge connected to the château and spanning the Cher. On a gloomy day the dark still waters of the river create the impression of a medieval defensive moat guarding a snow-white castle, but on a sunny day the water is transformed into a silvery reflecting pool, in which the five arches of the bridge become ovals and the château above becomes a whimsical dream. When, twenty years ago, Bob and I crossed the little bridge to the château and walked through large open rooms whose walls were filled with tapestries and portraits of Diane and Catherine, and then came across the small secretive paneled study Catherine had added on, we suddenly found ourselves alone in this elegant gallery built across the Cher. Renaissance music was playing, so, of course, we danced together down the long hall, on the marble floor of black and white squares arranged in a diamond pattern. As we whirled around, we felt we were being joined by the courtiers Irene had told us about; we could see their faces, carved life-sized, in medallions on the walls separating the large arched windows. And through those windows we saw the river, as Diane must have envisioned it when she conceived of a terraced gallery built in such a way that those inside could see the river as they danced. It was a magic moment, and I dearly wish I hadn't gone back to refresh my memory—alone, and on a Sunday. There are many things you can do alone, but coming to romantic Chenonceau is not one of them. Here I was, all by myself in the gallery Catherine de' Medici had completed (she eliminated the terrace from Diane's designs), and I felt as Catherine must have felt after she finally had driven her rival from Chenonceau. The château was hers at last, but Henry was dead and she was alone with her horrid sons, just as I was alone with horrid busloads of tourists.

While I wish I could say my fascination with Chenonceau arose because it is the most breathtakingly beautiful château I have ever seen, which it is, or because at Chenonceau the Italian Renaissance and the French Gothic styles merge to create the most exquisitely romantic fantasy castle imaginable, which they do, or because Chenonceau represents the culmination of the early Renaissance in France, which it does, I cannot do so. My interest has not been aesthetic, architectural, or historical; rather, it has sprung from a fascination with the king's mistress, Diane de Poitiers, which peaked when I learned that she was twenty years older than her lover. Specifically, I was concerned with the question of how—in a time when kings generally had successive mistresses, each of them quickly replaced as she became wrinkled, toothless, or obese—Diane kept Henry so desperately in love with her for twenty-one years, from the time he was seventeen until he died at thirty-eight, that he hardly slept with another woman (except when Diane urged him to do so), had her image, not Catherine's, on the reverse side of the coins minted during his reign, turned over to her not only Chenonceau and the Duchy of Valentinois but the crown jewels as well, leveled her dreary château at Anet so that she could build, at his expense and with his architect, a temple to herself, referred to by the poet Joachim du Bellay as "Paradise Anet," and, in effect, made her the uncrowned Queen of France for the twelve years of his reign. She was, in fact, a combination of what Madame de Maintenon, during the reign of Louis XIV, and Madame de Pompadour, during the reign of Louis XV, would be—ruler of both king and country. "No woman in France of her condition had ever before amassed so much," wrote one contemporary historian. While it wasn't unusual, in an age when marriages were political alliances, for a king to have a mistress—Henry's father, Francis I, had scores—it was unusual for a king to have only one. And since women in the sixteenth century didn't age particularly well, it was also unusual for a thirty-eight-year-old king to have a mistress who was almost sixty. It was also unusual for a king to have as his mistress a woman who may have been the mistress of his father. I say "may" because there is little agreement on this point.

There is, however, no disagreement over the fact that Diane was beautiful. You can see for yourself just how beautiful she was by looking at her portrait in the Francis I Room at Chenonceau, painted by Primaticcio during the period she owned the château. In this painting, and in another by Veronese, the classic features of her exquisite face are framed by a crown of golden hair. You can also see her curved and graceful body, arm resting voluptuously around the neck of a stag (one of the symbols of the king), by traveling to Anet, where a copy of Jean Goujon's statue *Diane Chasseresse* is in the garden.* It is also related that when Cellini searched for the perfect model, a woman with the graceful body of an athlete, for his *Nymph of Fontainebleau,* he passed over Madame d'Étampes, Francis's mistress, and chose Diane. The best description of Diane's beauty, I believe, was written by my friend Irene Mahoney in her biography *Madame Catherine:*

> Despite her age (she was nearing fifty), Diane's beauty remained unmarred. The milky glow of her skin, her features at once soft and classical, the high, firm breasts, the exquisite grace of her neck, had not lost their loveliness . . . When her hair began to gray, she did nothing to hide it but let its silver add something gentle and wise to her beauty. Age did not frighten her . . . Her dress remained as simple and elegant as ever, the black and white of her gowns acting as the perfect mounting for the king's jewels, which she wore not in defiance but as her right.

Diane's life began drearily enough. On March 29, 1514, at the age of fifteen, she was married to Louis de Brézé, the governor of Normandy (the grand seneschal), known as "one of the ugliest men of his time." Since he was the son of Charlotte of France (daughter of Charles VII and Agnès Sorel) and Jacques de Brézé, he must have been at least thirty-seven years old at the time of their marriage, because his mother had died thirty-seven years before, when his father surprised her in bed with a lover and stabbed each of them over a hundred times.

Except for the birth of two daughters, the eldest of whom was named

*The original is in the Louvre.

Françoise after the king, the first nine years of Diane's marriage were un-eventful. Then, in 1523, Diane's father, implicated in a plot to overthrow Francis, was arrested for treason. There seems to be no question of her father's complicity. He was captured, tried, and condemned to die. He was first held prisoner at Foulques Nerra's gloomy dungeon at Loches, where he wrote to his daughter: "Madame la Grande Sénéchale, I have arrived at the Château of Loches, as badly treated as a poor prisoner could be." It is with this episode that the legend of Diane de Poitiers began.

Diane sought and was granted an interview with Francis. Since the king had spent three weeks hunting at Anet as a guest of her and her husband, she was no stranger to him. The interview took place at Blois the day before her father was to be executed. By then he had already been moved from the dungeon at Loches to Paris. After the interview was concluded, an archer of the king's guard carrying the king's pardon galloped at full speed from Blois to Paris. According to a contemporary historian, her father was already on the scaffold when his pardon arrived. It is the nature of the argument Diane used to secure her father's pardon that has led to centuries of historical speculation: whether or not she exchanged her "virtue" for her father's life.

The nature of Diane's relationship with Francis is unclear and falls into the rumor category until after the death of her husband, in 1531. She then left her dreary feudal castle at Anet and became a member of Francis's nomadic royal court, traveling back and forth between Saint-Germain, Fontainebleau, Blois, Amboise, Chambord, and Chenonceau. As a sign of mourning for her late husband, she dressed always in black—which accentuated the gold of her hair and enhanced rather than detracted from her beauty. Court gossipers marveled at how beautiful she still was, although she was already thirty-three, by which time, in the sixteenth century, most women had already lost their teeth and figures and were considered middle-aged. Her enemy at court, Madame d'Étampes, Francis's mistress, had the court poet compose a verse, "The Wrinkled One," which mocked Diane for being in the "autumn" of her life. Conjecturing that Diane had to be a sorceress using witchcraft to preserve her youth well into old age, Madame d'Étampes said she drank a magic potion containing the essence of gold and bathed in asses' milk. Actually,

Diane believed it was her bath in ice-cold spring water each day after her three-hour ride that preserved her milky-white complexion. I have actually given a lot of thought to this, more than I should have; rejecting "essence of gold" and "asses' milk," I have concluded that it was her frugal diet, devoid of sweets (which enabled her to keep her teeth), plus a combination of the icy baths and exercise, which preserved her youthfulness and attracted the young king to her.

When she first arrived at court, it was rumored that she was having a secret affair with Francis. According to the Venetian ambassador at court: "Having been left a widow, young and beautiful, she was loved and tasted by the King Francis and by others also, according to what everyone says. Then she passed into the hands of the present King when he was only a Dauphin." Whether or not King Francis, as the ambassador so deliciously put it, "tasted" Diane, I have no idea. Madame d'Étampes certainly hated Diane enough to strongly suggest that possibility. Looking back from the twentieth century, the issue of Diane's virtue seems far less clear-cut or significant. While sleeping with the king was one of the few ways a woman in the sixteenth century could gain wealth and power, a secret affair would not have benefited Diane; and Diane did very little, if anything, that did not benefit herself. It is, however, possible to hypothesize a case either way. On the one hand, Francis loved beautiful women, and his love was not usually platonic. According to the chronicler Brantôme, Francis "loved too wildly and too much: for being young and free, he became involved first with one, then with another, for in that time a man was not considered much of a gallant unless he whored every place without distinction." On the other hand, having been brought up by two powerful and intelligent women, his mother and sister, whom he greatly respected, Francis had greater regard for the intelligence of women than did most men of the period. And not only was Diane intelligent, but she shared Francis's passion for both hunting and art. She was a woman of great taste, with a discerning eye for artistic talent, who would continue Francis's patronage of artists during the reign of Henry II. The keenness of her eye was revealed when, after her husband died, she decided to leave a magnificent tomb at the Cathedral of Rouen in his memory. To create the perfect memorial, she searched for the perfect sculptor and settled on a sixteen-year-old boy. He was none other than Jean Goujon, considered today to be "one of the greatest French sculptors of the Renaissance." (Diane, thinking of her own immortality, had herself included in the memorial.)

While I don't believe it, perhaps Francis was intrigued only by Diane's elegance, wit, and intelligence. For when, after his eldest son died, his second son, Henry, became dauphin, Francis turned to Diane, whom he referred to as the "lovesome ladye of the Court," to "polish him a little." Francis had never liked Henry, who lacked the easy charm and gaiety that Francis considered so essential for a Frenchman and a member of his court. It was Henry and his older brother who, years before, were sent to Spain in trade for their father, held captive in Madrid by Emperor Charles V. The young princes had assumed that their father would ransom them quickly, but instead he used available funds to build Chambord. The two boys returned from four years in captivity with their spirits crushed; worse, Henry, who had been guarded only by Spanish soldiers, was no long able to speak French. When Francis met the young princes on their return to France, he turned away from them, declaring, "I do not care for dreamy, sullen, sleepy children," and lavished his affection on a third son, who, like himself, was witty and charming, a sparkling conversationalist. Francis thought so little of Henry that he married him to Catherine de' Medici for her dowry. Her great-grandfather may have been Lorenzo the Magnificent, but to Henry, to whom bloodlines were more important than money, she was always "the shopkeeper's daughter." Already harboring ill feelings toward his father for the years he had spent in captivity, he was insulted that his father chose as his bride a member of the bourgeoisie. Most of the French aristocracy shared his sentiments, as did Charles V, who commented, "They have smirched the Valois lilies with a mercantile alliance." Then Henry's older brother was poisoned by an Italian—some say at Catherine's instigation—and Henry became dauphin. According to some sources, Francis, finding Henry so unsuited to be king, asked the thirty-six-year-old Diane to educate the sixteen-year-old prince in the ways of a courtier.

Henry is described in all court memoirs as being somber and withdrawn until his affair with Diane began. She was successful in changing the dauphin from a timid, taciturn, awkward young prince into a dignified, gracious, and tactful king. In the process, Henry fell helplessly in love with her, with a passion that lasted until his death and inspired jealousy in his wife, Catherine, who was driven to drilling a hole in the ceiling of Diane's bedroom at Saint-Germain to see what was going on.

It is difficult to know how Diane felt about Henry. She instructed him to burn all her letters to him, all the while trying to create the impression that their relationship was platonic. Historians, perhaps finding it difficult to accept a love affair between a young man and a woman so much older, have concluded that her feelings for Henry were maternal; others, citing Henry's loss of his mother while he was still a child and his rejection by Francis, suggest that Henry's feelings were of a reciprocal nature. Henry's letters and actions, however, prove otherwise. In one letter, written to Diane, when she was recuperating after a fall from her horse at Chenonceau, Henry wrote:

> In truth, I cannot live long without seeing you. Because I am not afraid to risk the loss of my father's favor in order to be with you, honor me, I pray you, by granting my deep desire to serve you. I assure you that I shall know little peace of mind until my courier returns bringing me news of your health. I beg you, therefore, to send me a true word as to how you do and when you will be able to depart. I think that you understand full well how little pleasure I have at Fontainebleau when I may not see you and that there is little happiness in life for me when I am absent from the one upon whom all my happiness depends. Now I am not only unhappy but afraid that this letter be so long as to weary you in reading it, so that I commend to your indulgent care my humble homage which I beg you to cherish forever.

During her life at court, Diane, famous as a horsewoman and huntress (she had ridden since she was six), strove to identify herself with Diana, goddess of the moon and the chase, simultaneously the symbol of both chastity and fertility. She chose as her symbol the crescent moon. The young prince, enchanted, not only adopted her colors of black and white but made the crescent moon his emblem as well. He designed a monogram, the interlocking HD, which became the symbol of their eternal love and passion; we can see hundreds of the monograms today carved in stone at Chenonceau and Anet and on the great façade of the Louvre.

Diane's education of Henry remains as compelling as her legendary beauty. She and the young prince would read together each afternoon the chivalrous and romantic adventures of Amadis of Gaul. In the many volumes of this series, the last two volumes of which were dedicated to Diane, the knight is true and constant to his lady, the fair Oriana, for whom he conquers giants and breaks sorcerers' spells. (These medieval stories remained popular in France for almost a century, even in Paris, until Cervantes satirized them in *Don Quixote.*) Henry, romantic and impressionable, took these romantic stories quite seriously and used them as a model for his court. Like the hero Amadis, Henry continually jousted in the numerous tournaments that took place during his reign, and, like Amadis, he continually made love. What I find fascinating is that Diane succeeded in having him identify her with both Diana, goddess of the moon, and Oriana, the perfect knight's one true love. When he was king, he wrote to her, "Remember him who has never known but one God and one love."

And it wasn't just Henry who was enthralled by Diane. One of the great celebrations of the time was a king's formal entry into a city of his realm. When Henry entered Lyon, it was the lovely Diane who sat beside him on the barge; Henry had instructed the portly Catherine not to arrive until after dark. The celebration, prepared by the citizens of Lyon, included a girl representing the goddess of the chase, with a bow in her hand and a quiver on her shoulder. She held a tame lion by a silver chain, which she begged Henry to accept. It was as if Diane had enchanted not only the young king and his court but all of France as well.

Diane felt confident that she could keep her lover "true and constant" as long as Henry was married to Catherine. The epithet "shopkeeper's daughter" was Diane's. Henry was disgusted by Catherine's obesity and her gluttony. Although the ladies of the court had begun dining in the privacy of their own rooms, Catherine, fancying herself a gourmet, did not share their notion of delicacy. On the day she was crowned queen, she stuffed herself with artichokes; at a round of royal feasts in 1576, one observer remarked that she "ate so much that she almost burst and was terribly ill with diarrhea." And unlike Diane, who bathed every day, Catherine smelled. Another woman, practically any other woman, might have presented a threat to Diane's total control of the young prince. When Catherine, after several years of marriage, had not produced an heir, her father-in-law, King Francis, began considering an annulment. Diane shrewdly persuaded Henry to spend nights with his wife. Eventually Catherine produced ten children, and Diane became their governess. It was Diane, not Catherine, who chose their nurses. And it is from Diane's letters that we learn about Henry's children. Perhaps because he had been unloved as a child, Henry was, unlike most men of the age, a very devoted father.

It was a strange threesome. Catherine was always cordial to Diane because, as she wrote some years after Henry's death, "if I was cheerful toward Madame de Valentinois, it was the King that I really was entertaining: and furthermore I always made him understand that I was doing it against the grain since never did a woman who loved her husband love his mistress." But her true feelings may be revealed in an incident related by Brantôme:

> Having complained to one of her favorite ladies, she plotted with her to find some means whereby she might spy through an aperture at the sports in which her husband and his lady might together indulge. Accordingly, she had a number of holes pierced in the ceiling of the said lady's bedchamber, to see what manner of life they led there. They placed themselves to watch the spectacle, but they saw nothing that was not very meet, for they perceived a very beautiful woman, white, exquisite, and very fresh, half-clothed by her shift and half-naked, giving to her lover every sort of caress which he returned. Then this lady of rank, who had witnessed everything, fell into weeping, sighing in her distress that her husband never used her in the manner nor played such frolics as she had seen him do with the other . . . yet she renewed this pastime of spying as often as she could.

Almost from the time she arrived at court, Catherine had suffered humiliation at Diane's hands. Not only did Diane take her place as queen—

in bed, at ceremonies, and with the royal children—but when Catherine almost died of scarlet fever, it was Diane who nursed her back to health, so Catherine owed Diane her life. It is not hard for me to believe the rumor, current at the time, that she plotted unsuccessfully for years to have the Duke of Nemours arrange for acid to be thrown in Diane's beautiful face.

Diane's personality is revealed in her acquisition of Chenonceau. It had once been owned by one of Francis I's finance officers, Thomas Bohier. It was his wife who had leveled all but one tower of a feudal fortress and built the charming square château in the middle of the Cher on the piers of an existing mill. Francis, in need of money, ordered an audit of his financial minister in 1527. And, as in each case when the affairs of the king's financial minister were investigated, whether it was Jacques Coeur in the fifteenth century or Nicolas Fouquet in the seventeenth century, major discrepancies and debts to the crown were discovered. Francis liked Chenonceau so much that he accepted it in payment for all Bohier's debts, and Chenonceau became crown property. When Henry became king, Diane requested and was given Chenonceau. Some sources say that trees and gardens were immediately planted, but that was not the case. Diane was aware that if Henry died or if he replaced her as his formal mistress—she was already forty-seven at the time of the gift—Chenonceau, being royal property, would revert back to the crown. Everyone at court was well aware of the fate of Françoise de Châteaubriant, Francis's mistress before Madame d'Étampes. When Francis tired of her, he asked for the return of the jewels he had given her. (She returned them, but only after having the settings melted down.) She then had no alternative but to return to Brittany and her husband, an unforgiving man, who had her killed. And no one knew better than Diane the fate of Madame d'Étampes's estates, which Henry had given to her.

Diane realized that if Chenonceau was to be hers permanently, it could not remain crown property, so she had Henry return Chenonceau to Bohier's heir, along with all his father's debts, the debts canceled by Francis, and forced the young man to auction off Chenonceau to pay them. Since no one dared to bid against Diane, Chenonceau was hers. It was then that the trees and gardens were planted and other improvements begun. This financial arrangement was so disadvantageous to the young Bohier that he was forced to flee to Italy. Male historians note this incident as proof of lack of feeling on Diane's part, a coldness in her personality. I think it shows a great deal more.

For the twelve years that Henry II was king, Diane practically ruled France, maintaining her power (as Catherine de' Medici would after Henry died) by balancing two opposing factions—the House of Guise against the Duke of Montmorency. Then, during a tournament near the Place des Vosges in Paris, Henry was accidentally killed in a jousting match, at the age of thirty-eight. In an instant the fairy-tale romance was over. Because Diane had wisely married her younger daughter into the powerful House of Guise, Catherine, who needed the Guises politically, could not destroy Diane completely. Diane immediately returned the crown jewels to Catherine, hoping to keep her beloved Chenonceau. But it was no use. Catherine illegally took Chenonceau and gave Diane the gloomy feudal château of Chaumont in exchange. Diane chose to return to Anet. There she could lie in the bed that she and Henry had shared and listen to the soothing sound of the waterfall through the window. There she could walk on ceramic floors that bore their interlaced initials. There her symbol of the crescent moon was everywhere. She could walk through the gardens and see Goujon's statue of her as a young huntress, or pray in the domed chapel Henry had built for her, with its floor of colored marble taken from the villas of Roman emperors. Although some of Anet, outside Paris, has been destroyed, it is a lovely place to visit on a Sunday afternoon. If I couldn't live at Chenonceau, I too would have gone to Anet.

The Île-de-France

The Age of Louis XIV

I felt a sense of relief as we drove away from the Loire Valley, where, at last, the King of France was ensconced in a palace suitable for an absolute monarch. It had taken many centuries and many miles to get him there, yet my relief was not in the king's achievement but in my own.

Before leaving for this trip, I had assured Bob that it would be possible to travel through almost two thousand years of French history on a summer vacation while driving northwest from Provence to Paris. I had mapped out the trip down to finding centrally located hotels with swimming pools and tennis courts where we could stay while visiting the different ages of France—provincial Rome in Provence, medieval France and the Age of Faith in Languedoc, the beginning of the Hundred Years

War in the Dordogne Valley, the rise of the middle class and cathedrals in Bourges, the end of the Hundred Years War and the evolution of the French king from an elected first among equals to an absolute monarch in the Loire Valley. Although my plan of following history in a rented car had seemed like a great idea, I hadn't been quite as certain that the vacation itself would be enjoyable, and that, as we traveled, we would really feel the passage of the centuries. But to my amazement, so far it had worked: the first sixteen hundred years of the vacation had been magical, and the only day of boredom was spent at a Peugeot repair shop waiting for our time machine to have its air conditioner fixed.

We had started by seeing the foundation on which France grew: the marble cities in Provence that retired Roman veterans had founded along the French coast of the Mediterranean, the inland sea that was the center of the Roman Empire. Then we climbed the rugged hills of the Alpilles to see the caves to which, after five centuries of the Pax Romana in France, fourth-century ascetics had fled as the barbarian hordes—Ostrogoths, Huns, Franks, Saracens, and Vikings—swept down the Valley of the Rhône and sacked those marble cities, dismantled the Roman Empire in the West, and plunged France into the Dark Ages, the beginning of the thousand-year-long Middle Ages. Then we drove west, deeper into the Middle Ages, as we visited the isolated Romanesque monastery of Fontfroide in the wastelands of Languedoc and, sitting in its serene cloister, looking up at the circle of protecting hills, felt the sense of escape from the chaotic world of the time into another world, closer to God, that men of the early Middle Ages must have felt as their social order crumbled.

Then, still in Languedoc, we traveled northwest to watch the Middle Ages evolve. We watched cities change. Getting off at one exit on the autoroute, we saw Narbonne, a great Roman commercial hub that, some centuries after the fall of Rome, remained linked to other cities by the Mediterranean and by a network of rivers and roads. By the ninth century, however, the Saracens had closed off the Mediterranean to trade, and cities were no longer commercial entities, but centers of a self-contained agricultural society, each with its marketplace and its residence for the bishop—cities closed off to the world. Cities became walled, fortified places of sanctuary for the surrounding countryside. So, getting off at another exit, we went to see the immense battlements of Carcassonne.

Then, to see the next step in the evolution of the Middle Ages and of France—the rise of a dynasty of central kings, the Capetians, who, starting in 987, allied themselves with the Roman Catholic Church and began to absorb the local rulers—we turned our car north to Albi. That city symbolizes for me a central event in the long alliance between the King of France and the Church: the Albigensian Crusade of 1209. Albi's architecture is so powerful and the events that took place there so tragic that the city's fortified cathedral still evokes today the "Crusade's" massacres, the ruthless Inquisition, and the addition of the domains of the Viscount of Carcassonne and the Count of Toulouse to the royal realm. So many history books talk about the growth of royal power only from the point of view of the king, but by the time Bob and I left Languedoc, we felt this growth from the other side. We saw what that concentration of power meant to those who *lost* their power—some of the local counts, barons, and dukes who had been beloved by people before the rise of the Kings of France.

This portion of the Middle Ages was also the Age of Faith, and, traveling north again, we visited two recommended stops (recommended both in the thirteenth and twentieth centuries) along the Pilgrims' Path, where medieval travelers stayed the night as they headed south through France on their way to Jerusalem, Rome, or Compostela, the age's three great pilgrimage destinations. From a distant cliff we watched modern tourists wind their way up the cliff to Rocamadour to see the "Black Virgin," just as medieval pilgrims had once done.

Turning northwest, we entered the fourteenth century and the beginning of the Hundred Years War when we reached the Valley of the Dordogne, the river that then divided the lands of barons loyal to French kings from those loyal to the English. There, mighty French and English fortresses still face each other from opposing banks. And not only had England remained in France in the fourteenth century, but even French territory was not yet unified—as we could imagine when we stood behind the crenelated battlements at Beynac and looked out at other castles, each the self-sufficient stronghold of a nobleman trying to add to his territory and his position in the feudal hierarchy.

Farther north again, we arrived at Bourges, in central France, one of the cathedral cities of the late Middle Ages, when soaring Gothic towers rose as the economy revived, and burghers, proud of their prosperous cities and filled with civic spirit, contributed freely to their beautification. And here we visited the palace not of a nobleman but of France's first great entrepreneur, Jacques Coeur.

North of Bourges was the golden Loire, the Valley of Kings. Driving back and forth through the valley, we saw—in the châteaux of each successive king during the fifteenth and sixteenth centuries, after the English were driven from France by Joan of Arc—how the monarch had changed: from a feudal lord in a feudal fortress, merely an elected first among equals, to a national figure, and then to an absolute monarch presiding over his courtiers in a Renaissance palace.

And we saw this historical evolution in the architectural evolution of the châteaux of the Loire. The kings who built Chinon, Loches, and Amboise were still struggling to assert their authority within France, and their châteaux still had defensive towers and battlements. But by the time the Blois we see today was built, internal threats to the monarch had disappeared—and so had the defensive fortifications. The king's château at Blois was the center around which the aristocracy had built *their* châteaux. At Chambord, built by Francis I in the first half of the sixteenth century, the monarchy reached a new height, as the château's forest of domes, chimneys, and towers makes clear. The fleur-de-lis, the symbol of the monarchy, rested on Chambord's lantern dome, the symbol of the Church, just as the king's divine right to rule rested on the sanction of the Church.

But the appearance of absolutism at Chambord—all its extravagance, pomp, and ceremony—was an illusion, as was revealed by the outbreak of the Wars of Religion. These wars, really rebellions waged by an aristocracy seeking to regain power and independence, were brought to a close by Henry IV, the former leader of the Huguenots. While he accepted Catholicism in order to become king, he began to shift the base of royal power away from the aristocracy to an alliance with the emerging middle class.

And now we were going to travel to the climax of this history and to see France in all its glory. For we were headed north one more time, to the Île-de-France, the region around Paris carved out by four rivers: the Seine, the Aisne, the Oise, and the Marne. The Île-de-France is an area stamped indelibly by the king who represented all that France was proud of: Louis XIV, the Sun King, the Grand Monarch.

Louis was born in 1638, became king at five, and ruled for seventy-two years. His reign is known as the Age of Louis XIV—also the Grand Siècle, the Golden Age of France. Because of his extraordinary encouragement of writers and sculptors and artists and architects, Voltaire called it "the most enlightened age there has ever been," a time when, as R. R. Palmer writes in *A History of the Modern World:* "French language, French thought and literature, French architecture and landscape gardens, French styles in clothes, cooking, and etiquette became the accepted standard for Europe. France seemed to be the land of light."

It was an age of epic dramas, of biting wit and satire, of magical animal fables and fairy tales such as "Sleeping Beauty," and of literary salons. It was the age of Corneille, Racine, Molière, La Fontaine, La Rochefoucauld, Madame de Sévigné, Mademoiselle de Scudéry, and Charles Perrault.

It was an age that responded to Copernicus's revelation—that the apparent revolving of the solar system around the earth was an illusion—with a distrust of nature and the senses and a corresponding reliance on reason and geometry. In painting, this distrust of the senses manifested itself in a demand for historical and mythological themes, in an emphasis on subject matter and on drawing, which appealed to the intellect, and a corresponding subordination of color, which appealed to the senses. It was the age of Simon Vouet, Nicolas Poussin, Claude Lorrain, and Charles Le Brun. It was an age in which the French classical garden was created by one man, André Le Nôtre, who designed the gardens at Sceaux, Saint-Germain-en-Laye, Dampierre, Fontainebleau, Vaux-le-Vicomte, Chantilly, Saint-Cloud, the Tuileries, Maintenon, the Champs-Élysées, and Versailles. Under Le Nôtre's direction, gardens became increasingly formal, controlled, and geometrical; flowers, whose color and smell appealed to the senses, were regarded with contempt. It was an age that began by copying the art of the ancient Greeks and Romans, and ended by creating an art distinctly and elegantly French. It was the age in which Descartes said, "I think, therefore I am," and in which Louis XIV thought, but did not say, "The state is me." It was an age that believed in order, rejected anarchy in nature, art, and government, and accepted man's tyranny in all. It was an age that believed in man's ability to control his destiny by reason rather than by faith.

So profound was the impact of this age on Western civilization that not only did most of the contemporary world try to model their cultures on the French—the elite of Peter the Great's Russia spoke French, aped the styles of the Île-de-France, and were ordered to build palaces around Saint Petersburg as the French aristocracy had around Paris—but future generations tried to do so as well. (In far-off New Jersey, three hundred years after Louis XIV's explorers set sail from Honfleur and settled Louisiana, I, as a teenager, sat on a Louis XIV–style dining room chair reading about the salons of the Marquise de Rambouillet and Madame de Sévigné and determined that, while the chairs around my adult dinner table would not be Louis XIV, they would be filled with writers, artists, and musicians and would center not so much on pot roast as on witty, elegant, enlightened conversation like that which sparkled in the salons of the Place des Vosges.)

On the Île-de-France, Louis built the immense palace—Versailles—that is most associated with him in the public's mind. Versailles evokes the height of absolutism in France, when art and architecture were devoted to the glory and the service of the king. And the palace also speaks of Louis's political genius, with which he once and for all broke the power of the aristocracy. Nobles who formerly were independent and powerful in their isolated castles were brought to Versailles, where they spent their lives elegantly dressed and meticulously performing meaningless rituals.

Under Louis's encouragement and patronage, hundreds of châteaux blossomed in the countryside around Paris during France's most splendid age. Since Louis XIV would chastise any member of his court who built a home he considered in poor taste, or which he felt did not enhance the beauty of France, many of these châteaux are masterpieces, including Maisons-Laffitte, the structure created by François Mansart which is considered by architectural historians to best illustrate the point in French architectural history at which Greco-Roman classicism became "uniquely and unmistakably French," and Dampierre, a château typical of the hundreds of châteaux which Louis XIV encouraged the aristocracy to build throughout the Île-de-France. At Sceaux, the château and park built by Louis XIV's minister Jean-Baptiste Colbert, there is a cascade that once provided the elegant setting for the Nights of Sceaux, festivities epitomizing the "loose morals and strict etiquette" of the age. And the Île-de-France contains Saint-Germain-en-Laye, where Louis was born and spent the first twenty years of his reign, and where he was driven when the rebellion called the "Fronde" forced him from Paris.

And the Île-de-France contains Vaux-le-Vicomte.

During the seventeenth century French architects assimilated the elements of Greco-Roman classical architecture—Greek orders of columns and pilasters, pediments and entablatures, Roman arches and domes—the way a growing child assimilates the vocabulary of language, and they finally created a poetry of architecture, a new style, that is elegantly, divinely, totally French. It was the age of François Mansart, Louis Le Vau, Charles Perrault, and Jules Hardouin-Mansart.

Because I had concentrated on medieval history while in college, I had never studied this period, but now I couldn't wait to see it. My plan for touring it was simple. We would make one short sortie to Paris to see the church built to celebrate the Sun King's birth, and then we would rent a car, leave Paris, and head out into the Île-de-France, which we would tour as we had toured the other regions on our trip: driving from château to château, staying at hotels near the sites we were visiting.

However, unlike Louis XIV, who could carry out his plans regardless of the consequences, I found my plan totally upset when we were lent an apartment in Paris and simply could not tear ourselves away. I decided to see whether I could stay in Paris and follow Louis XIV's life from conception to death by making day trips to each of these places by Métro, or subway, and the suburban railway line known as the RER. I discovered not only that it was possible but that it was an inexpensive and totally enjoyable way of touring.

Paris:

THE SUMMER OF 1991

During a conversation with a friend who was advising me where to buy a summer house, she said, "Location is everything." While I ignored the advice at the time, some years later I found how right she was when, in the summer of 1991, we were given use of an apartment on the Left Bank in Paris, right on the Quai des Grands Augustins. Its eighty-five-foot balcony—Bob measured it with his feet—overlooked the Seine between the Pont des Arts and the Pont Neuf. The master bedroom faced a quiet courtyard, so we could sleep undisturbed by the laughter and noise from along the river. It didn't bother me that most of the very grand rooms were empty of furniture—I hate clutter. It bothered me even less that I was unable to work its space-age stove. We had intended to stay only a week or less, since it was July and stiflingly hot when we arrived. But we stayed and stayed, because that was the summer I fell in love with Paris.

I had always found Paris quite nice before, but I had never really understood what all the fuss was about, preferring the French countryside, where people were politer, the food was fresher, and everything was less expensive. That summer, though, I learned what everyone else apparently already knew; and I never wanted to go home, because, just as my friend had said, "Location is everything," and we were located not only on the Left Bank but in the most perfect spot in Paris, which may be the most perfect spot in the whole world.

A few blocks to our left was the Musée d'Orsay; behind our apartment, narrow, winding cobblestoned lanes, seemingly untouched since the Middle Ages, led to a lively market with two fruit stands, bakeries, charcuteries, and a cheese shop that seemed to sell all of the more than four hundred cheeses made in France; a few blocks to our right was the Île Saint-Louis and Notre-Dame; and right across the river was the Louvre. Always gray on our visits before, that summer the Louvre, recently cleaned, looked as it should, like a palace fit for kings. Its white pilasters gleamed, as did its rows of frilly Corinthian columns, its bas-reliefs, and its statues, whose faces were visible now that they were free of dirt and grime. In fact, everywhere we looked in Paris, dirt was being wiped away. Every palace and church seemed to sparkle in the sun and glow in the moonlight.

That month we saw from our balcony sights a New Yorker never sees: a municipal worker in a green uniform took a rag and shined a garbage can, stood back, and proudly looked at his work; a truck with a boom raised and lowered its "bucket" so that the man standing in it could soap the top of all the lampposts along the avenue and wash the poles from top to bottom with his long-handled brush; a "caninette," a three-wheeled motorized vacuum cleaner, chugged along the streets cleaning up after dogs, so that tourists could look up—and looking up at the carved pediments, ornamented dormers, and mansard roofs of Parisian rooftops is more pleasurable than looking down to see where you have to step.*

---

*Garbage is picked up seven days a week. Never, in all my trips to Paris, have I passed the large piles of garbage waiting for pickup that one sees in New York. I understood why when, the following spring, living in an apartment on the Avenue Gabriel, I watched our concierge. She waited in our courtyard with the garbage behind the gate, looked at her watch, then, a few minutes before the garbage truck arrived, a time she knew in advance, rushed the bags to the street.

And everywhere we went, there was music. Under the arcades that line the four sides of the Place des Vosges, we listened to a young string quartet play Mozart, Bach, and Hungarian Rhapsodies each Sunday; in the Métro station Étoile, where the acoustics are superb, we listened to the exotic sounds of a Peruvian band; at the plaza in front of Notre-Dame we had our choice of folk singers with guitars; at tea in the elegant marble salon of the Hôtel de Crillon, we listened to a sedate harpist; at a dreadful restaurant on the Rue de Grégoire de Tours, one of the ancient cobblestoned streets behind our apartment, we listened through an open window to a beret-capped man, dressed in a tight blue-and-white-striped T-shirt with a red scarf around his neck, sing French love songs. As he sang, he ground out tunes on a hand-painted Art Nouveau organ embossed with red and yellow flowers. And though the food in that restaurant was truly awful and his outfit corny, I kept leaning out the window to tip him so that he wouldn't go away—and I might even have eaten in the restaurant again if he had returned. Because we ate at restaurants that did not serve decorator food, and only one of which had a star, I didn't lose my appetite when I saw the prices. We ate lunch at a sidewalk table at Chez Paul, where we could watch men playing bocci on the grass square of the Place Dauphine; dinner at little bistros like Rôtisserie d'en Face, Chez Pauline, and Vivario, a tiny Corsican restaurant that made absolutely perfect roast pigeon and roast goat.

Usually we would see an early evening movie—the French love old films as much as we do and always have festivals of old classics—and then around nine, with the sun still casting that lingering, luminous Parisian light, we would walk to dinner along the river. And after dinner each evening we walked home past Notre-Dame, each time, it seemed, noticing a beautiful detail of the cathedral we had somehow overlooked before. The experience of slowly coming to know something exquisitely beautiful, whether a cathedral or another person's soul, is a gift that must be God-given, because passing Notre-Dame each evening in the moonlight, waiting for the floodlights of tour boats to make it even whiter against the black sky, we became more and more intimate with its beauty as we fell more and more in love with it, with Paris, and with each other. To end each evening, we sat on a bench on the Pont des Arts, a pedestrian bridge filled with painters by day and lovers by night, sometimes looking at Henry IV's medieval Pont Neuf, sometimes across the river at the Louvre's seventeenth-century Cour Carrée, built by Louis XIV, or the dome of the College of Four Nations, founded by Louis XIV's minister Cardinal Mazarin.

It's hard to say what made Paris so wonderful that summer: the cleanliness, lunch at the Place Dauphine, tea at the Crillon, the long warm summer nights, our moonlit walks past Notre-Dame, classical music under the arcade of the Place des Vosges, the river, a huge ornate apartment free of belongings with a stove I couldn't work. Whatever it was, I decided that I wanted to stay in Paris while I visited the life of Louis XIV. And that entailed not having a car.

I know my inadequacies, and even though I have been driving a car since I was sixteen, they include not being able to drive in and out of Paris. Around the city, guarding it like a medieval moat filled with lions, is a thing called the Périphérique, on which cars, each of which seems to be attached to the rear fender of the car in front of it, travel at speeds suitable only on a deserted Texas highway. And there seem to be as many of them as jam the Long Island Expressway in New York. To exit correctly, you need the eyes of a bird-watcher to see the signs before they fly by and the reflexes of a teenage tennis star to reach the exit after seeing the sign. (Staying in the right lane is no help. Lanes appear on your right where there were none, and, worse, some exits are from the left lane.) Bob now contends that he has no trouble whatsoever driving in Paris, and on our last trip, after only fourteen years of horrible experiences, he did admirably at finding his way into Paris and to our apartment. My single experience driving in Paris, on the other hand, on a trip I had taken without Bob, was filled with terror comparable only, I believed at the time, to Joan of Arc's trip on horseback from Domrémy through enemy lines south to Chinon. And Joan at least had three saints to guide her, while I was all alone. I hadn't wanted to go to Paris. I had taken a wrong turn and found myself inexorably headed for it in three lanes of speeding bumper-to-bumper rush hour traffic. Where I wanted to be was on the road to Orléans, whose three empty lanes leading south I could see across the barrier. Ever since, I have avoided driving in

Paris by simply renting a car at a properly chosen airport—Orly when heading south, Charles de Gaulle when heading north, Nice for the Côte d'Azur, Bordeaux for the Dordogne, and Lyon for Burgundy—or better yet, taking a high-speed train and renting a car near our destination.

Val-de-Grâce

AND ANNE OF AUSTRIA

Val-de-Grâce was built to thank God for the birth of Louis XIV. During the first twenty-two years of his reign, Louis XIII had not done the one thing required of all French kings for there to be a peaceful succession: produce an heir to the throne. In 1637 his queen, Anne of Austria, feared having her marriage annulled and being dispatched from France (probably to a convent) on the grounds of infertility. Although she had been married to Louis when she was only fourteen, their marriage had not gone well; the king had been a reluctant lover from the start. First, two royal cousins—a man and a woman—tried to show him how it was done, but he seemed notably reluctant to imitate the process. Finally, he had to be carried by a faithful friend, kicking and crying, to the bed of his young wife to consummate the marriage. This ridiculous royal procession, described by biographer Vincent Cronin, marched down the halls of the Louvre led by a valet de chambre, a candle clutched ceremoniously in both hands, to Anne's room.

During the years that followed, Louis generally refused to visit the queen's bedchamber, complaining that she dined too heavily and retired too late, as was the custom in Spain. Her affair with the Duke of Buckingham, which became the scandal of the day when Buckingham, not caring that Anne's courtiers were watching, pushed his way into her private quarters, did not help the royal relationship. (The affair inspired Alexandre Dumas's *The Three Musketeers*.) The relationship was also not helped by the fact that Anne was a sister of the King of Spain and belonged to the House of Hapsburg, the dynasty with which French kings had been intermittently at war for more than a century. As a young boy, Louis XIII had seen his father, Henry IV, forced to convict and sentence to prison his beloved mistress, Henriette d'Entragues, for conspiring with the Spanish.

Louis XIII had grown up in a palace in which sexual mores were so loose that the Florentine ambassador exclaimed, "Never has there been anything more like a brothel than this court!" Louis's father, Henry IV, a famous gallant, kept the children of all his mistresses at court. But Louis grew to manhood a prude, disliking even an off-color joke. The one woman he asked to be his mistress, Louise de La Fayette, hastily entered a convent instead. In fact, his love life in general did not go well. Cinq-Mars, a young man of whom Louis was fond, thought the king was so enamored of him that he could literally get away with treason, and Louis was forced to have him beheaded. (Louis was so furious at Cinq-Mars that he lopped off the tops of his feudal towers at Cinq-Mars's Loire castle as well.)

Anne, as the years passed, spent increasingly more time at the Val-de-Grâce convent, now a church and hospital on the Boulevard de Port Royal, not far from the Luxembourg Gardens. Spies of Cardinal Richelieu discovered she was writing letters there to her brother, which appeared treasonous to both Richelieu and her husband. They seemed confirmation of Louis's suspicions that she was feeding the Spanish king secrets of state.

Given the king's suspicions of his queen, and the infrequency of his visits to her bed, it was not surprising that Anne was queen for twenty-two years before producing a son. The real surprise was Louis XIV. Anne was already thirty-seven; time was running out for her, and since she preferred the court to a convent, she dreaded the threatened annulment. She prayed for a son, and promised Val-de-Grâce a church if she was granted one. When Louis was born, in 1638, she called him "Dieudonné," or "God-given." (Considering that the king had not slept with her for seven years before the night the boy was conceived, the birth did seem almost a miracle to the French people.) And Val-de-Grâce was built to thank God.

In 1645, in fulfillment of her promise, Anne of Austria commissioned François Mansart (1598–1666), one of the greatest architects in the history of France, to build Val-de-Grâce. The church was planned to echo the great basilica of Saint Peter's in Rome. Its dome is very much like that of Saint Peter's, and the baldachino over the high altar resembles the high altar of the tomb in Rome. Mansart, however, was never to finish the project. He was a temperamental artist, unable to compromise or to conceal his contempt for the opinions of patrons, no matter what their rank, and he could not summon up the deference to which royalty was accustomed. His work was all that mattered to him, and he insisted on its integrity as he saw it. Moreover, he insisted on the right to tear down a structure after construction had begun if it did not meet his standards of perfection. He had a reckless disregard for expense. For example, when Colbert asked him to complete the Louvre (what is now the Cour Carrée), "he was unwilling to undertake this commission unless he had freedom to reconstruct parts of the edifice which seemed to him defective when he had completed them." After the construction of Val-de-Grâce had been under way for just a year, he was fired; only the crypt and the lower story had been built.

Mansart was replaced by Jacques Lemercier, who is considered a competent designer but one, according to art historian Anthony Blunt, "lacking Mansart's subtlety and ingenuity." Lemercier is said to have followed Mansart's plan for the construction, but given Mansart's history of changing his mind, we will never know how Mansart's Val-de-Grâce would have looked. The building has been criticized for not melding French and Italian styles, and the façade of the present church frankly does look strange to me: the upper level, ornate and exuberant, seems out of keeping with the restraint of the lower. However, it was in keeping with the taste of the time, which slavishly adored anything Greek or Roman, and contemporary society thought it quite wonderful. The Gothic churches of the Middle Ages were, during the seventeenth century, considered barbarous. Molière summed up the feeling of the age by calling them "odious monsters of ignorant ages."

The inside of Val-de-Grâce is very beautiful. I particularly like the coffered ceiling and the use of black, white, and red marble inlays. The dome was painted by Pierre Mignard, an artist so highly regarded that Louis XIV selected him to do the portrait of his favorite mistress. (Molière would refer to Raphael and Michelangelo as "the Mignards of their century.")

It is the queen's church. You see her name carved in stone, her portrait in oil. There is now a painting of Anne of Austria where once her heart—removed during the French Revolution—had been. But more important for me as a traveler through history, trying to get an impression of the generations living before me, was the unmistakable aura I felt as I walked through the church, with depictions of the Virgin Mary and Christ that seemed, if not interchangeable with Anne and her God-given heir, at least indicative of how close the royal family felt its relation to God to be.

Val-de-Grâce is a depiction in stone of the concept underlying the reign of Louis XIII and his great son: the divine right of kings. According to this belief, the body of the king, his physical person, is sacred; the royal power has been bestowed directly by God and is therefore absolute; and the king is responsible only to the Almighty. (Of course, anyone who resists the king's authority will be eternally damned.) Walking beneath the beautiful dome of Val-de-Grâce, I was startled to see Hebrew letters carved in the stone walls. But I should not have been. Charlemagne was called David by his courtiers and the King of France considered himself both "the successor of the Caesars" and "heir to the power of David and Solomon, anointed of God." Indeed, the experience of being in Val-de-

Grâce clarifies for a twentieth-century visitor—to whom the divine right of kings is hopefully an irrelevant abstraction—something Louis XIV wrote to his son. God, he said, is "a superior power of which our royal power is part...God appoints kings the sole guardians of the public weal. [Kings are] God's vicars here below." Once, after a military defeat, Louis blurted out, "God seems to have forgotten all I have done for him."

Versailles

B ob and I visited Versailles on our first trip to France. I suppose everyone does. We visited it again eleven years later, in 1985. Both visits had
exhausted my supply of superlatives. We had taken the guided tour, which
I thought wonderful. We had seen the king's antechamber, where, we were
informed, Louis XIV dined alone while twenty-four violins played. We
were taken to his bedchamber, where a hundred courtiers were given the
honor of attending the morning ritual of *lever* and another hundred the
evening ritual of *coucher.* When these descendants of fighting knights
donned *their* armor, they were probably heading off not to battle but to one
of the innumerable costume parties that set the immense palace glittering
in the evenings.

In the Hall of Mirrors, the Galerie des Glaces, we saw busts of Roman emperors in porphyry and marble, antique statues of Greek gods—and, under a vaulted ceiling painted by Le Brun, crystal-and-silver chandeliers, and gilt-and-crystal candelabra reflected in seventeen arched mirrors. Now, in 1991, fondly remembering the hall—and Versailles as a whole—as I planned this journey through France's history, I felt it would be the perfect prism through which to see the Age of Louis XIV. The silver furniture that once sparkled in the light of four thousand candles may have been melted down to pay for Louis's wars—and Louis's vases of gold, inlaid with diamonds, agate, emeralds, turquoise, jade, and pearls, may have been transferred to the Louvre—but, remembering my earlier visits, I felt that the splendor and magnificence of this hall encapsulate for the tourist France's Golden Age. The arcade of seventeen arched mirrors reflects more than the seventeen arched windows, more than the chandeliers and candelabra or the splendor of the Grand Siècle; it illuminates also the socioeconomic foundation that lay beneath the gilt. For example, the mirrors at Versailles were manufactured in France. Previously, fine mirrors had been imported from Italy, because no one in France knew how to make them properly. Louis XIV and his minister Colbert were determined that France be economically self sufficient, but they could not simply begin to manufacture mirrors. Venice made the finest glass in the world, so Venetian artisans were enticed to France by extravagant salaries and perquisites to teach the art; then Venetian foremen were recruited to set up a factory in Paris. Economic competition in the seventeenth century was not taken lightly, and when Italian authorities learned that two of the best mirror artisans had been lured to France, the authorities had them poisoned before they were able to teach their secrets to French apprentices. As soon as the industry was in place, the tariff on imported mirrors was doubled, thereby discouraging imports. By the end of Louis's reign the finest mirrors in the world were made in France, and Voltaire could write, "The fine mirrors made in our own factories, which now decorate our houses, cost far less than did the little ones that used to be imported from Venice." Louis and Colbert did the same for other industries, encouraging high quality by awarding prizes to the French master craftsmen who produced the finest-quality products (or "master pieces"). "We have beautiful and ornamental materials that are both cheaper and better than those brought from abroad," Voltaire wrote.

Other incentives were used. "In order to establish the manufacture of tar in France," Colbert later recalled, "the king brought from Sweden a certain Elias Hal. This man, after three or four years' work, informed me of his desire to settle in France. His Majesty ordered me to take the trouble of arranging marriage for him—he gave him two thousand écus for use at his marriage and disposed two thousand livres of appointments for him annually, which has always been regularly paid. I found a girl at Bordeaux who brought him a very honorable marriage."

Colbert desired not merely to limit imports but to increase exports, so Versailles was designed in part as a showcase, displaying to ambassadors and foreign visitors French products of such excellent quality and taste that they returned home wanting to buy the products themselves and singing their praises throughout the world. Foreign dignitaries attending state functions held at night in the Hall of Mirrors could hardly help being impressed by the reflected glow of four thousand candles—and by the silver furniture, the Savonnerie carpets, the Gobelin tapestries, and by the vases, the laces, the marble from Languedoc used throughout the palace.

Look up at the ceiling painted by Le Brun for the Hall of Mirrors. It glorifies Louis's victories in a war with Holland, the country most competitive with France. If normal means of commercial competition proved inadequate, Louis and Colbert went to war. Descartes, the French philosopher, who lived in Holland, wrote that "everybody but myself is in business and so engrossed with his profits that I could live here all my life without being noticed by anyone ... All their toil helps to adorn the place of my abode, and supplies all my wants ... the vessels arrive which bring an abundance of all the produce of the Indies and all that is rare in Europe." Louis said the Dutch "absorb nearly all the profits of trade in all parts of the world and leave only a very small portion to the other nations." The last straw was an embargo that the Dutch placed on French wine and brandy. Louis declared war on them in 1672.

In planning this journey through French history, I had expected, when we reached the Age of Louis XIV, to recommend Versailles as a magical place to visit the pinnacle of monarchy. I had felt, moreover, that the twentieth-century visitor, viewing the Sun King's bedroom, visualizing there the crowd of dukes and counts—men who once were independent masters of fiefdoms like Carcassonne, Beynac, and Castelnaud, but who now filled their hours with useless court functions, waiting around to watch the king get into or out of bed, helping him put on his clothes—would see how under Louis the king's favor had become the sole source of power in France.

And a visit to Versailles, I had felt, would reveal the tyranny of Louis XIV not only over his courtiers but over the arts as well. The function of art, to Louis, was simple: his glorification. He was being quite candid when he told the members of the French Academy, "I entrust to you the most precious thing on earth—my fame." (The artists proved faithful trustees—not that they had much choice. Molière may have mocked the rest of society, but he never mocked Louis XIV. One gentleman who ventured to criticize the length of a prologue praising Louis XIV promptly found himself in jail.) For twenty years Louis XIV was the primary patron of the arts, and for twenty years Le Brun, director of the French Academy, saw to it that the arts were devoted to enhancing the splendor of Louis XIV's palace and glorifying his image. It was Le Brun's identification of Louis XIV with Apollo—an identification evident throughout Versailles—that created for posterity the image of the Sun King that Louis desired.

In August of 1991, Bob and I were concluding a test tour of the places I wanted to include in this book, to check whether those I had fallen in love with over a period of twenty years were still as I remembered them. Arriving at Versailles on a beautiful summer day, we found the parking lot in front of the palace filled with a herd of large tour buses, and the line to purchase tickets to visit the palace far longer than either of us had the patience to endure. Not wanting to spoil our memory of Versailles, we went back to Paris without visiting the palace. Without Versailles, however, I was afraid the plan of my book would be incomplete. I told myself that August, the month the French go on vacation, was not the time to visit Versailles or, indeed, any place in France. We would, I decided, go to Versailles before Easter, not only before the French vacation but before colleges and schools let out for the summer. We returned on a rainy day in early April 1992.

We took the Métro to the Invalides station, where there is a connection with the RER to Versailles/Rive Gauche. (The train to Versailles Chantier does not go to the palace.) The ride was only thirty-eight minutes. Versailles is easy to get to—perhaps too easy.

It was a Tuesday morning, cold, overcast, and intermittently rainy. But again the lot was filled with buses, huge single-deckers and even larger double-deckers. I counted over thirty-five of them—and then stopped counting. When we arrived at the gilt-and-black wrought-iron gate leading to the courtyard, the serpentine line of tourists waiting to visit the palace extended past the gate curving around Bernini's equestrian statue of Louis and across the entire length of the enormous courtyard. In 1985 I had been overwhelmed by the beauty of what I saw; this time I was overwhelmed by the crowds. Oh, well, I thought bitterly, even in the Age of Louis XIV, Versailles had been commercial.

Giving up on seeing the inside of the palace, we retreated to the gardens. The long line of visitors queued up to take a little train to the Trianons was so long that the train would have had to make four or five trips to transport the people already on line. And even as we watched, the line was getting longer.

One of the greatest things about the gardens at Versailles is the fountains. An aqueduct and the Marly Machine were built to bring water four miles to fill the fourteen hundred fountains. (One reason contemporaries were so opposed to Louis's construction project at Versailles was the lack of an adequate water supply nearby.) The fountains, however, were silent during our visit. I later found out they are so expensive to operate that they are rarely turned on.

Descending into the gardens, we sat down on the edge of Le Brun's Fountain of Apollo. Bob, having noticed that I hadn't spoken for quite some time, tried to whip up some enthusiasm by pointing out the geometric beauty of the terrace, the arc of dark green hedges in a great horseshoe behind it, and the arcs of Grecian urns and Grecian statues framed by the hedges circling the Fountain of the Sun God—and, behind it, the palace of the Sun King. Someone, I thought, had been a seventeenth-century public relations genius. At the time Louis was king, over a hundred years had passed since Copernicus had shaken the foundations of the medieval world by proving that the earth revolved around the sun. To the subconscious mind of some seventeenth-century visitors, the garden of Louis's palace must have suggested that the planets revolved not around the sun but around the Sun King.

I turned to my book on gardens and read once again that Le Nôtre had designed the gardens here to be an earthly paradise—the Elysian Fields that the Greeks had imagined. But I had to confront the fact that Versailles was no paradise to me. Originally built to destroy the independence of the nobility, in the twentieth century it may work just as well to destroy the tourist's desire ever to tour again. It creates a curious dilemma: Versailles is so sumptuous and magnificent that you ask yourself, "How can I not visit it?" But after I had visited it, I began to consider buying a summer house, my desire to tour having been totally dissipated. My advice is to buy *Versailles: Complete Guide of the Tour of the Château and Gardens* in Paris and read it in the gardens at Vaux-le-Vicomte, Rambouillet, Dampierre, or Sceaux. I recommend that you skip Versailles.

In 1992 it was no longer possible to sit in, or even to enter, the wonderful Colonnade, the circle of thirty-two arches supported by columns of blue and pink marble from Languedoc, which, after my earlier trips, I would have suggested as a particularly lovely place to sit while reading a book. The whole Colonnade was now fenced off. When I saw a VIP being given a private tour, I became truly annoyed. I was angry at Bob, too. I could have arranged for a special tour of Versailles and many of the other places I was visiting, but Bob had asked me when I started doing the research for this book, "How can you write honestly about places where you are given special treatment and the average traveler isn't?" So I had come to Versailles as an ordinary tourist and the experience had been truly unpleasant. When I glared at Bob, he had no idea why. Exercising my divine right to leave, I headed for Les Trois Marches, a charming, romantic restaurant in the town, where in 1985 we had enjoyed a meal whose asparagus wrapped in pastry I still remembered melting in my mouth—but the restaurant had moved, probably to larger quarters to accommodate more tourists.

When, hungry and tired, I settled back in my comfortable seat on the train for the ride back to Paris, I heard the sighs of other people settling into theirs. Don't get me wrong: these were not sighs of contentment but of relief—of escape from a truly enervating and depressing experience. The train was packed with tourists, and the gloomy atmosphere of disappointment reminded me of a subway ride I had taken many years before from Giants Stadium after the loss of a championship football game.

. . .

Since I always like to travel with someone from the century I am visiting, I had stuck Voltaire's *The Age of Louis XIV* in my oversized purse along with my camera. On our trip back to Paris I sat silently reading it for a second time. I was amused to see how, within a few hours, my reading of this paean to Louis XIV had changed. On the trip to Versailles, hoping to experience the brilliance and splendor of the Sun King's court by visiting the setting of the endless round of feasts, ballets, masked balls, and hunts that all of Europe wanted to emulate, I had approvingly underlined: *"it seems clear that one of Louis XIV's main preoccupations was to inspire, in every field, that spirit of emulation without which all enterprise languishes."* On the way back, being in a nasty mood, I found a bit of malicious pleasure in recalling that Voltaire's book had not been well received. It was published twenty years after the Sun King's death, and the king at the time, Louis XV, considered Voltaire's praise of Louis XIV's reign to be a criticism of his own. In addition, a line I had read right over on the way to Versailles now stuck in my mind: *"if he had spent . . . a fifth of what it cost to force nature at Versailles on embellishing his capital, Paris today would be, throughout its whole extent, as beautiful as is the area around the Tuileries and the Pont-Royal, and would have become the most magnificent city in the Universe."*

As we emerged from the Métro station, the good thing, I thought, about our trip to Versailles was that it was still early in the afternoon and we had plenty of time that day to spend in Paris.

Saint-Germain-en-Laye:

GETTING THERE BY RER

The next afternoon Bob and I took the RER to Saint-Germain-en-Laye. Just as the Métro is one of the easiest ways to get around Paris, the RER (the Regional Express Network), or suburban line, is the easiest way to reach places just outside Paris, like Saint-Germain-en-Laye, Maisons-Laffitte, Sceaux, Versailles, and Malmaison.* For places a little farther away, like Rambouillet, Chartres, and Bourges, you can take the regular train; and for more distant cities, like Dijon and Toulouse, you can take the TGV, a high-speed, highly enjoyable train. Mass transit in France is, on the whole, an agreeable and relatively inexpensive experience.

*The town of Rueil-Malmaison is about ten minutes by the same RER that takes you to Saint-Germain-en-Laye, plus a healthy walk or a taxi ride. An estate built at the beginning of the seventeenth century, Malmaison served as the retreat of Napoleon and Josephine before he became emperor.

The first thing to remember about taking the Métro is that the No. 1 Métro line (the M1), which runs under the Champs-Élysées, was built first. Every other Métro and RER line leading to the rest of Paris either connects or "corresponds" to one of the stops along the route of the M1. To know the direction you want to go, look at a Métro map, find your stop, and then locate the last stop along the line you are taking. For example, if you are at the Franklin Roosevelt station on the M1 and want to go to the Étoile stop, look for La Défense, the last stop on the line in the direction you want to go. Château de Vincennes (Mazarin's château) is the last stop in the other. The signs directing you to platforms will not mention your stop but will indicate the direction of the train by saying Direction La Défense or Direction Château de Vincennes. Once on the train, you will see a sign above the windows listing, in order, all the stops and *correspondences* with other lines. There is a sense of freedom in not being dependent on taxis and in knowing you can easily get around Paris by Métro if you are unable to get a taxi, as is usually the case when it is raining.

We had taken the Métro since our very first trip to Paris but had never ventured forth on the RER. On this trip we did. The following details are probably unnecessary, but since I was so nervous and unsure about how to take the RER to Saint-Germain-en-Laye, I figure that anyone else who has never taken the RER will feel much the same way.

We took the Métro M1 to the Charles de Gaulle Étoile station, from which the A1 RER train to Saint-Germain left. We followed the *correspondence* signs through various tunnels to the RER. At its entrance you can buy a ticket at a booth or from a *billet* machine. The machine is easier and far more polite. You need either change or a Visa card (Carte Blue) to use the machine. While I don't generally get along well with machines, I found this contraption quite easy to use. It is covered with buttons of different colors and words. First, look for the little buttons with the names of different places; we selected and punched the one labeled "St-Germain-en-Laye." Then, using "Nombre de Titres," we selected two tickets. Then the machine tells you how much money to put in; if you comply, the machine produces the number of tickets you requested. After getting our tickets, we placed them in a turnstile and followed the signs to Saint-Germain. (Keep your ticket, however, because, unlike the Metro, the RER requires it when you leave the station at your destination.) When you get to the platform, you will know whether you are on the right one, because above your head is an electronic sign listing the stops made by trains leaving from that platform. However, don't relax yet. Next to some station stops is a square orange light. That means that this train, or the one about to arrive at the platform, stops at all the stations lit up and at none of the stations that are not. Our station was not lit up, so we sat on one of the marble benches and waited for five minutes, at which time the square for our station lit up and our train arrived. The ride from the Charles de Gaulle Étoile station to Saint-Germain-en-Laye took twenty-two minutes.

As the train made its way through the suburbs to Saint-Germain, I became enraged as I looked out the window by the amount of graffiti covering the buildings of Paris. Calling it "the scourge of barbarism defacing the most civilized city in the world," I suggested to Bob that the perpetrators of this misdeed should be hanged. Bob burst out laughing and calmly suggested, "Perhaps they should be spray-painted instead."

Saint-Germain-en-Laye

AND THE BIRTH OF LOUIS XIV

I wanted to go to Saint-Germain-en-Laye because, while Versailles has become practically synonymous with Louis XIV in a tourist's vocabulary, Saint-Germain-en-Laye is the château where Louis XIV was born and in which he lived for more than twenty years before moving his court to Versailles. French monarchs had been living at Saint-Germain since the time of the first Capetian kings. Louis the Fat (1108–1137) had ordered the hasty marriage of his pious son to Eleanor of Aquitaine there; Louis IX (Saint Louis, 1226–1270) had set off to crusade against the infidel after praying in the chapel he built there. Francis I (1515–1547) had found Saint-Germain so pleasant that he built a Renaissance château right on top of the existing ancient feudal fortress. Today it houses an excellent museum of prehistoric and Gallo-Roman artifacts.

After leaving the train at the Saint-Germain stop, we were directed by signs to a very long and very steep escalator. Although a woman at the tourist office in Paris had assured me that the château was near the station, I was worried that I would be faced with a long walk. But as the escalator ascended, in the square of blue sky at the top there suddenly appeared a beautifully carved Renaissance balustrade, which I recognized from pictures—the balustrade of the château. Then, beneath it, there appeared stone-and-brick arches enclosing tall windows. As the escalator slowly brought us up into the sunlight, there right in front of us was the foundation of the medieval fortress on which the Renaissance château had been built. It was separated from us only by the château's long-dry moat. A short Métro ride, then twenty-two minutes on the RER—and I was at the château where the Sun King had been born.

Since it was lunchtime, we walked past the château into a park designed by Le Nôtre. At its end is an escarpment beyond which lies the long, low spread of the city of Paris. At the edge of the escarpment is a small brick building, topped by a dome, that was originally part of a much larger structure, the Château Neuf, which was finished by Henry IV at the end of the sixteenth century, thirty years after Henry II began it.

This is the building in which Louis XIV was born. Anne of Austria had moved the twelve miles outside Paris, to Saint-Germain-en-Laye, for her confinement because the Louvre was considered unhealthy. The streets of Paris were mostly unpaved, muddy, filled with garbage, and used as giant outdoor toilets. People in the cities of France were still dying of the plague.

Since the small building is now part of a hotel and restaurant, the Pavillon Henry IV, it had not closed for lunch, so we could visit it. Passing through a tall wrought-iron gate, above which was an arch bearing the words *"Ici Naquit Louis XIV,"* we saw on a brick wall a medallion with a bas-relief of a cradle. (On another wall is a much more impressive brass plaque commemorating another event of historical significance to the French: the creation of béarnaise sauce, in the same building, in 1847. The name of the sauce, created, the plaque informs us, by "Le Grand Chef" Collinet, honors Henry IV, sometimes known, because he was born in Béarn, as "Le Béarnais.")

The room in which Louis XIV was born is mildly interesting architecturally, but fascinating if you know a little of the gossip of history. It is a square room, about twenty by twenty of my feet (size seven shoe), with white walls decorated with pilasters and medallions and topped by a high, domed octagonal ceiling; it is quite small, considering the number of people it had to accommodate. Because the body of the king's first-born son—and no other body in all the world—was sacred and imbued with the divine right to rule, witnesses were on hand to observe that the child born was a son and that no substitutions (such as a live infant if the heir was stillborn) were made.

The witness with the most riding on this baby's sex and health was Louis XIII's younger brother, Gaston d'Orléans, who had been borrowing money in the expectation that he would one day be king. The birth of a boy could, in fact, be said to have saved the fabulous staircase we admired in the courtyard at Blois. Gaston, whose domain included Blois, was remodeling the château; his architect, Mansart, was tearing it down and rebuilding it wing by wing, and the wing with the staircase was next. With the birth of a male heir, and the consequent abrupt cancelation of Gaston's credit line, the remodeling was over. If Louis had been born one year later, the staircase would probably be gone.

The guest list of witnesses on the night of September 4, 1638, and the following morning was glittering. Princesses, duchesses, and countesses rushed out from Paris at the first news of Anne's labor pains, crowded into the little room, and stayed through the night and early morning to watch the queen grasp the bars at the head of the royal birthing bed as she ushered in the Grand Siècle. And the importance of the witnesses was to become apparent five years later, when Louis XIII died. Scheming to discredit Anne and Cardinal Mazarin, whom she had appointed to rule France in her name, and thereby to obtain power for themselves, Gaston and Mazarin's rival, Cardinal de Retz, published a pamphlet (printed secretly in the Netherlands and smuggled into Paris) that alleged that Louis had an *older* twin brother, who had been secretly whisked away at the moment of his birth. According to another rumor, the twins were fathered not by Louis XIII, who was thought to be too "weak and languid, and sapped moreover by secret poison . . . not . . . able to beget heirs," but by Mazarin himself, who was alleged to be the queen's lover. (These rumors provided the inspiration for Mark Twain's *The Prince and the Pauper* and Alexandre Dumas's *The Man in the Iron Mask.*) The stories spread widely because Mazarin was hated for his tax increases. The firstborn, and therefore the rightful heir to the throne, was said to have been hidden away by Mazarin at a place that only he knew so that he could later blackmail the imposter king, who lacked the divine right to rule. According to the rumors, the queen had been told that the first child was stillborn.

Louis's birth touched off a national celebration. The birth of an heir meant that France was spared the chaos and civil war that had followed both occasions when the direct line of the Capetian dynasty was broken. From an obelisk placed on the escarpment outside the Pavillon Henry IV, free wine flowed to celebrate the birth of an heir to the throne. For six days, cannons were fired, *Te Deums* were sung, people danced in the streets, and fireworks lit the skies at night. Two years later Anne of Austria, who had taken twenty-two years to conceive her first child, gave birth to another, Philippe, known as "Monsieur."

The Saint-Germain-en-Laye where Louis spent his childhood was far different from today's. The pavilion in which Louis XIV was born has been altered beyond recognition. The theater castle built for Henry IV is gone. The beautiful gardens that once adorned the slopes leading down to the river, where Louis XIV played as a child, are now scarred by twentieth-century homes and threatened by the construction of a highway. Henry IV had wanted his palace built as close as possible to the edge of the escarpment—the medieval view of sixteenth-century Paris being better then than today—but was informed that the ground could not support a structure; too much stone had been quarried from the hill beneath to build the old château. Therefore, while Henry was solidifying his hold on France, he was also busy solidifying and fortifying the hill on which he would build his château. His military engineers, who had been using their new hydraulic skills (learned from the Arabs) to bring water to besieged castles, used them now, during the twelve peaceful years of Henry IV's twenty-five-year reign, to create gardens, cascades, and hydraulically powered moving statues. Caves and tunnels in the Saint-Germain hill were not only reinforced but turned into fabulous grottoes. A series of six rectangular terraces with stairways and cascades descended down to the River Seine. Seen from across the river, the terraced gardens leading up to the domed pleasure palace looked like, and were compared to, the Hanging Gardens of Babylon.

The caves created by the quarrying were lined with marble, mother-of-pearl, and seashells. Each grotto was named and adorned for the pagan god or hero whose statue was placed there. Beside a square pond in the Grotto of Orpheus stood a life-sized bronze likeness of the musician, his arms and head moving so that he appeared to play tunes on his lyre while a tiger and a ram came out of adjacent tunnels to listen to the music and then return. Water spouted up from snail shells and cascaded down the side of the cave, which was lined with trees. (Louis XIII, as a child, was frightened by this statue, which clanked when it moved, and by an apparatus that unexpectedly squirted the child with water; Henry IV thought it was hilarious to surprise visitors with an unexpected soaking. Louis refused to go near the cave unless assured by servants that the mechanism had been turned off.)

When he visited Saint-Germain in 1629, the philosopher René Descartes marveled at "the grottoes and fountains in the gardens" and at "the force that makes the water leap from its source [and] is able of itself to move diverse machines and even to make them play certain instruments ... according to the various arrangements of the tubes through which the water is conducted."

In one cave, Perseus, larger than life, struck the head of a dragon, which then sank beneath the water of a pond. In another, Bacchus was seated on a rock, holding a cup from which water fell and set in motion craftsmen plying their trades. In the Neptune Grotto, lined with seashells (sixteen barrels of them), the statue of the god was in the center of a pond, and other statues circled the rock on which he sat. In yet another cave, lined with rare marble, Hercules, the warrior who could not be defeated, sat on a lonely rock.

The view from the restaurant's terrace is of Paris. The Red Michelin classifies it as a *vue exceptionelle,* and in the seventeenth century Saint-Simon called it "marvelous." But I don't like it—the view from the terrace today is of the drab suburbs that have spread out from the city—and neither did Louis XIV, possibly because that view prominently included (as it does today) the Cathedral of Saint-Denis, where Louis knew he would one day be buried, an unfortunate reminder that even a Sun King was mortal. It was, in fact, at least partly to escape from the view that Louis built Versailles. Walking along the terrace overlooking Paris, and jabbing a royal finger in the direction of the cathedral, the King growled to his mistress, Athénaïs de Montespan, "That, Madame, is a gloomy, funereal view, which makes me displeased and disgusted with this residence, fine though it be."

Madame de Montespan replied, "Sire, in no other spot could a more magnificent view be found. Yonder river winding afar through the vast plain, that noble forest divided by hunting road into squares, that Calvary poised high in the air, those bridges placed here and there to add to the attractiveness of the landscape, those flowery meadows set in the foreground as a rest to the eye, the broad stream of the Seine, which seemingly is fain to flow at a slower rate below your palace windows—I do not think that any more charming combination of objects could be met with elsewhere, unless one went a long way from the capital.*

But Louis said, "The view of Saint-Denis spoils all these pleasant landscapes for me. I shall enlarge Versailles and withdraw thither. At Versailles fewer objects confront the eye . . . I shall make Versailles a delightful resort, for which France will be grateful to me, and which my successors can neither neglect nor destroy without bringing to themselves dishonor."

For a table with a view from the restaurant's terrace, you need a reservation. Not liking the view, however, I thought it would be just as pleasant to "withdraw thither" and eat at a table without a view. Since I have a weakness for crêpes à sucre, and a Breton woman was making fresh crêpes at an outdoor stand in the park, Bob and I withdrew totally thither, out of the hotel and into the park, for our lunch.

When, at two o'clock, Bob and I crossed the moat and entered the old château, we found the first floor filled with an exhibition dealing with the House of Stuart. Louis XIV was a very young king, himself recently driven

*Paris is the opposite of New York. New York looks like a jewel from the distance, out the window of a plane or through the windows of a skyscraper or from across the reservoir of Central Park, but Paris, because of its exquisite human-scale buildings, looks best from the ground, from the middle of a bridge crossing the Seine, from the Pont des Arts, or from the street as you walk along, where you can't see the twentieth-century skyscrapers on the outskirts.

into exile at Saint-Germain by the Fronde, when, in 1649, his cousin King Charles I of England was beheaded and the Stuarts were exiled from England. An ardent believer in the divine right of kings, Louis was horrified to learn of his relative's fate, and after having abandoned Saint-Germain for Versailles, he turned the château over to the exiled Stuarts in 1688.

The château is now a museum of prehistory and Gallo-Roman France, and very little of it recalls the reign of Louis XIV. You can visit what is now called the Mars Room—but called the Comedy Room when Louis XIV was king—and see where Louis, who was quite graceful, danced the ballet and watched plays by Molière. But, like interiors of other châteaux that have not been lived in for many years, this one has little spirit, and aside from the etchings of court life, there are few indications of the lavish seventeenth-century court that once existed here.

Nonetheless, I found the museum wonderful, and so, I noticed, did the many children present, who were enthralled by the prehistory exhibits. I found the Roman exhibits fascinating and rationalized spending time with them by reminding myself that Louis XIV read Caesar's *Gallic Wars* while he lived at Saint-Germain-en-Laye. By this convoluted reasoning I told myself I was seeing exhibits of what Louis was reading about, such as Caesar's battle at Alesia against Vercingetorix. Bob, being a purist, left early and went back to Paris.

Louis XIV was forced to spend so much time at Saint-Germain because of the Fronde (1648–1653), a revolt against Mazarin's taxes, which erupted in Paris and threatened the monarchy. It got its name, according to Cardinal de Retz, because a mob of throwers *(frondeurs)* massed at the Louvre carrying slings *(frondes)*. Louis and his mother were forced to flee from the Louvre to the safety of the fortress here at Saint-Germain-en-Laye. Madame de Motteville relates that on the night the royal family left Paris, the ten-year-old king was put to bed as usual so that no one would suspect that their flight was imminent. At three in the morning he and his little brother were awakened and brought down a secret staircase to the garden, and then the royal party set off in the dark for Saint-Germain. It was still dark when they arrived in the palace courtyard. It was still the custom to bring furniture, tapestries, carpets, and linens when the royal family moved from château to château, but sending furniture would have aroused suspicion, so when they arrived at Saint-Germain, it was as empty of beds and chairs as it is today.

It was here, looking at Paris from this cliff, that Louis XIV learned to hate his capital. He is described as growing tall at Saint-Germain-en-Laye, while being too poor to replace his green velvet squirrel-lined dressing gown, which year by year grew shorter as he grew taller. Throughout his life Louis preferred the country, and he lived in Paris infrequently.

Later that afternoon I walked through the town of Saint-Germain-en-Laye to the Priory Museum. In 1678 Athénaïs de Montespan purchased the building for a poorhouse. Her motivation seems to have been not so much altruism as a desire to clear the streets of Saint-Germain, frequented by members of the court, of the unattractive sight of beggars. Louis would later construct poorhouses, such as La Salpêtrière in Paris, in many French cities. Maurice Denis, whose paintings are now displayed at the museum, found the house charming. Perhaps I had seen too much already that day, because I did not.

Maisons-Laffitte

The following day the RER took Bob and me to a town about ten miles northwest of Paris called "Maisons," where we saw a château—called Maisons-Laffitte since the nineteenth century—that is generally considered one of the greatest masterpieces of François Mansart and one of the supreme examples of French architecture during the Age of Louis XIV.

The man responsible for the creation of Maisons-Laffitte in the middle of the seventeenth century was René de Longueil, *président à mortier* of the Parlement of Paris, scion of a family that boasted an old lineage but had never been part of the high aristocracy. During the Fronde, Longueil remained loyal to Mazarin and the young Louis, and as reward, he was made France's superintendent of finances in 1650. Aware that if the King visited his home, his social standing would be raised, he used the vast wealth that came with his new post to commission the famous Mansart to design a château lavish enough to induce the king to stop there for refreshments during the hunt. As far as I know, that was the only instruction given to the temperamental artist. Mansart, the architect even a queen found too expensive, was given total artistic freedom and unlimited financing.

The train, a different line from the one to Saint-Germain although the two towns are not far apart, left from the same platform as the one we had taken the previous day. After a fifteen-minute ride we arrived in a friendly little suburb whose tourist office is right across from the RER station. We walked down its main street into a park, and then, after a brief walk, turned right onto a suburban street lined with nineteenth-century houses. At the end of the street we saw Mansart's masterpiece. The houses that line the street, though charming, interfere with the view of the château. Mansart, I am sure, if allowed to return to earth, would tear them down in a rage.

But when you get close enough to see the façade whole—and even more, when you walk around to the rear of the château, where it is surrounded by a park so large that you can walk back far enough to see it whole—there before you is the climax of the two thousand-year evolution of French architecture that we have been following all the way up from Provence.

The design of Maisons-Laffitte is based on the classical Greek orders of columns and pilasters—Doric below, then Ionic, and atop them Corinthian—but the classical columns are combined in a monumental architectural composition that is quintessentially French in spirit. The long façade is topped by a tall, high-pitched roof of the distinctive design that bears Mansart's name, a roof that for me is the final evolution of all the gray-blue turrets and towers that we saw in the Loire Valley. Atop the roof are tall chimneys, and the façade is broken by columns, by an entablature with a dramatic gap in its center, and by two round windows with delicate caps. The whole expanse of Doric, Ionic, and Corinthian orders is not only arranged with perfect proportion and harmony but combined in a composition whose delicacy, restraint, elegance, and orderly severity are unmistakably Gallic.

The history of this magnificent structure serves to explain why the Île-de-France contains hundreds of seventeenth- and early-eighteenth-century châteaux, not many as beautiful as Maisons but many just as lavish, and why the Île-de-France is where France reached the height of its architectural, historical, and cultural glory. René de Longueil was able to commission so costly a building because he was one of the great new officials of the centralized, all-powerful government appointed during Louis XIV's minority by Cardinal Mazarin, and, after Louis assumed the full royal authority, by the king himself. Most of the owners of these châteaux were not, as the art historian Anthony Blunt has pointed out, the old aristocratic families (the *noblesse d'épée*) but the "great officers of the Crown, particularly those who were connected with the Treasury," the new nobility (the *noblesse de robe),* former bourgeois "who had enriched themselves, often with suspicious rapidity, in the service of State and the collection of taxes." It was an aristocracy whose only aim was to please its king, each of the new noblemen and ministers vying with the others to build a château that would add to the splendor and glory of France.

The story behind Maisons-Laffitte is a microcosm of this development. The system under which a superintendent of finances such as René de Longueil could accumulate such vast wealth was the archaic system of taxation, and the discontent over taxes was one of the main causes of the Fronde. The old aristocracy paid no taxes at all. Peasants, on the other hand, were taxed so heavily that, as one member of Parlement of Paris declared, "the peasantry must sleep upon straw, for their effects have been sold to pay taxes . . . owning nothing but their souls—and that merely because nobody has devised a means to put them up for sale." As for the middle class, Mazarin's taxes on commerce had alienated them, too. And most governmental offices were purchased by fees, or *paulettes,* paid to the crown. (At the time of the Fronde the price of an office was 33,000 pounds.) When Mazarin proposed increasing the *paulettes,* members of the Parlement, joined by the middle class and the peasants, revolted against Mazarin and Anne of Austria.

During the course of the Fronde, Mazarin had bargained for Longueil's support, and Longueil, unlike most Parlementarians, sided with the king. A year after his appointment as superintendent of finances, his "no expense spared" château was ready to receive the king. Soon after

Louis's visit, Longueil, who was efficient at filling his own but not the royal coffers, was removed from his post.

The Longueil family owned the land on which the château was built—not through a centuries-old grant from a long-dead monarch but because they had purchased it—and when their money went, their land went as well. Eventually, Maisons and the vast acres around it (the Longueil land extended all the way to the Seine, and across it to an island on which the axis of the château was continued in a broad avenue) were purchased by the Comte d'Artois, who loved horses and racing and who coveted the stables Mansart had built at Maisons—themselves an architectural triumph. Then Maisons was sold to a famous banker, Jacques Laffitte, who lost *his* money and had to sell off most of Maisons's park, including the land on which the stables stood, to a developer; he razed the stables and erected the nineteenth-century town houses that now spoil the approach to the château.

From the rear of Maisons-Laffitte you can still get some idea of the original harmony of gardens and château when you see them across the large, round reflecting pool. A balustraded terrace, with gracefully curved steps, leads to the gardens and to the reflecting pool in their center. Aside from the roof, we had seen all the elements used in the façade—the Doric, Ionic, and Corinthian columns, for example—when we visited the Roman theaters, triumphal arches, coliseums, and temples whose ruins we saw in the Rhône Valley. All the elements referred to in architectural jargon as the "Greco-Roman vocabulary" were used as well in the Church of Val de Grâce. But here at Maisons-Laffitte they and the spirit of the ancient world and the classical French were blended. The "dignified proportions" that the Roman architect Vitruvius—resurrected and worshiped in the seventeenth century—said were so important in any structure are seen here both in the relationship of the three wings and in the harmony of all the parts. Looking across the pond at the château, I understood the phrases used to describe the work of Mansart: "cool rationality" and "absolute control of design elements."

The park behind the great château belongs to the town now, and townspeople were using it. Little children were playing as their mothers watched them; two or three elderly couples were strolling. And towering over all of them as they played or strolled—almost filling the horizon at one end of the park—was that magnificent monumental façade of columns and pilasters and entablatures and pediments and noble roof—the façade created three and a half centuries before by France's greatest architect. To Bob, the wonderful thing about the scene was that the château was so familiar to the townspeople that they weren't paying any attention to it. It was just part of their lives, something they took for granted, probably as their parents and grandparents had taken it for granted—this supreme symbol of another, a Golden, Age. And yet, Bob felt, whether they paid attention to it or not, whether they consciously even noticed it, the château was part of their lives, an evocation of history that must have had some influence, however unconscious, on those lives.

When Bob said that, I knew what he meant. It is that mixing of history—a great and splendid history—with the daily life of the present which is so distinctive a feature of France and which adds to life there a dimension not much evident in the United States. It is part of what makes traveling through France so rich an experience for me.

I have to admit that architecture was not the only attraction that had drawn me to Maisons. I have loved going to racetracks ever since—years ago— Bob and I went to the track at Saratoga, in New York State, and, placing my two-dollar bets, I won one race after another. And while the Comte d'Artois's stables may be gone, his racetrack isn't. I had scheduled our visit to Maisons-Laffitte on a day the track was open, and after visiting the château, we walked back to the RER station and caught the bus to the track.

Since that glorious day at Saratoga, hardly any horse I have bet on has won, and never has even one of my picks won in France, where the horses run in the wrong direction. Nevertheless, I love going to the track, especially in France, where I can lose while enjoying a delightful meal. No matter what the activity, in France it is always accompanied by a delightful meal, and no matter how small the track, it always seems to contain a pleasant restaurant. I can study my racing form in comfort at a table overlooking the finish line while a waiter serves me wine, pâté, and lunch; place my ten-franc bet on a horse whose name appeals to me (which is usually something like "Good Review" or "Publisher's Delight"); and then, when the race begins, sedately walk out onto a terrace reserved for diners and scream my head off in the sun if my horse comes close to winning.

It must run in the family. I have an uncle, sort of the black sheep of the family, who is now in his early nineties and during the winter is a snowbird living somewhere near Hialeah, a racetrack in Miami. In the summer he returns to his home in New Jersey and makes at least one trip a week to the casinos at Atlantic City. While I was growing up, I was told that Uncle Ben "played the horses." I never knew what else he did. I was reminded of him because the track at Maisons-Laffitte was filled with men who looked like French Uncle Bens. They looked like him when he was thirty, forty, fifty— in fact, they looked like Uncle Ben at every stage of his life.

Dampierre

The following day we took a trip that turned out to be one of those magical days in France, the kind I had thought only possible when touring by car. I had wanted to visit Dampierre because both the château and gardens exist today pretty much the way they did in the seventeenth century and give an impression of what a château belonging to a member of the old aristocracy would have been like during the Age of Louis XIV.

Since there was no train from Paris to Dampierre, we took one to the nearest station, Rambouillet. This train leaves frequently from the Montparnasse station, and the trip takes either a half hour or an hour depending on whether you take the local or express. (It is the same train that goes on

to Chartres.*) Before leaving Paris, I had called the tourist bureau in Ram-
bouillet† and asked for the name of a radio taxi. I then called the taxi and
arranged for the driver to meet us at the station, which he did. He drove us
to Dampierre and agreed to pick us up several hours later. Luckily we arrived at lunchtime, and the château was closed. I say "luckily" because we
were forced to eat at the Auberge du Château, which we might not have
done had the château been open.

It was hard to believe that this inn, with its white stucco walls and ancient, blackened oak beams and friendly service, was only a few miles outside Paris, not deep in the heart of provincial France. The smiling proprietor led us through a formal country dining room to a sunny porch
enclosed on three sides by floor-to-ceiling French windows. Our table had
an excellent view of the château, and from my tapestried high-backed chair
I could, in comfort, see the iron fence guarding Dampierre from the three
tourists who had massed at the gate. I could also see most of the *cour d'hon-
neur* created by the central château, flanked by two elegant arcaded pavilions. All three buildings were the same height, were constructed of the
same creamy stone masonry trimmed with deep pink brick, and were
topped with silver-gray mansard roofs. On one of the four grassy parterres
in front of the château, a leather-booted man was raising a gun at a bird I
couldn't see, but at which his black-and-white hunting dog was pointing.
As I began to nibble at a leek pâté, which was unexpectedly delicious, I was
reminded that I enjoyed touring best over a lazy afternoon meal. I liked my
meal and the Auberge so much that before we made our way across the
street to the château, I took a tour of the inn, selecting either room 9 or
room 12 in which to stay when we returned. Both were light and airy and
had views of the château.

Dampierre was designed by Jules Hardouin-Mansart, a nephew of
François Mansart, who, unlike his prickly uncle, knew how to get along
with aristocracy and royalty. He had taken both his uncle's last name and
his dusty, unused, uncommissioned plans and used them to good advan-

---

*Chartres makes an equally pleasant day trip from Paris. Arrange the day before with the Chartres tourist office to
take a tour with Malcolm Miller through the cathedral and to have lunch at La Vieille Maison.
†You can easily find the telephone number of any tourist office in any town by simply looking in the Red Michelin.
No matter what language you speak, there is generally someone to assist you. They will provide you with the numbers of several radio cabs. If you are staying at a hotel, the concierge can make the arrangement for you.

tage at Dampierre. As at Maisons-Laffitte, the château is surrounded by a moat, but Dampierre's moat is filled with water. Even so, the château is high enough to let light enter the lower floors. A dam separates the moat from a lake on one side and from delightful gardens and a tiny cascade in the rear.

The château was built with Colbert's money for his daughter and his fancy son-in-law, the Duke of Chevreuse, who had initially considered the Colbert family beneath him. He was, however, gracious enough to accept Colbert's money to raze his mother's Renaissance château and construct this elegant Baroque one in its place. Colbert, Louis XIV's great minister, was himself ashamed of his lineage and did what he could to improve it. Born the son of a draper, he accepted a title from the king and then attempted to rewrite his genealogy, sanding off the word "wool" from his grandfather's tombstone and simultaneously depositing forged deeds to "prove" his descent from Scottish kings and a saint.

We took the tour of the château, which has beautifully preserved seventeenth- and eighteenth-century furniture, as well as paintings of many of the Grand Siècle courtiers I had been reading about. In the downstairs salon there was a portrait of the Duchess of Chevreuse.

Although the duchess ("La Grande Amazone") had actually taken up arms against Mazarin and the royalist forces at Orléans during the Fronde, and had been in semi-exile from court at Dampierre ever since, she had been, when young, the closest of friends with Anne of Austria—with whom she may (or may not, depending on which book you read) have shared the Duke of Buckingham as a lover. She was a woman whom Anne, now queen mother, respected and trusted. In her youth she was beautiful, and, according to the Duchess of Orléans, "her wit was so brilliant and so full of wisdom that the greatest men of the age would not have been ashamed of it," but when Anne made her visit to Dampierre on June 27, 1661, both women were old. In fact, a cruel remark referring to the duchess's former love affairs was circulating in society at the time: "Chevreuse is an ancient fortress, now completely in ruins—the citadel had been destroyed by many sieges. They say it often surrenders unconditionally." I could have lingered in the salon looking at her portrait and at the gardens framed by the windows; at Dampierre, however, the guided tour moves not at your pleasure and pace but at the guide's, and our tiny group of five was taken away to see the rest of the château.

I don't want to mislead you into thinking that you are hustled through the château. To the contrary, unless you have an extraordinary interest in seventeenth- and eighteenth-century furniture, you may find the tour a bit lengthy. There is one absolutely mind-boggling reception room on the second floor (the French first floor). Created during the Restoration, it contains a Greek temple with a ten-foot-high gold-and-ivory copy of Phidias's statue of the Greek goddess Minerva. It should not be missed.

You should save time to enjoy the lake and the seventy acres of gardens designed by Le Nôtre before going on to Rambouillet.

Rambouillet

Our taxi was waiting for us when we finished our tour of Dampierre and took us to the château at Rambouillet, where the driver left us, explaining that we could easily walk to the train station.

The château at Rambouillet is now the country home of the President of the French Republic, and before scheduling a visit, you should take the precaution of calling the Rambouillet tourist bureau to make sure he is not in residence that day; if he is, the château is closed to visitors. It is definitely worth the trouble of rescheduling. The architecture is not what I would call beautiful or thrilling, but there is something about Rambouillet that made Francis I want to come here to die, Catherine de' Medici and her sons Charles IX and Henry III come here to hide during the Wars of Religion, Molière select it as the site of *Le Misanthrope,* Napoleon spend his last night here before leaving for exile on Saint Helena, Charles X abdicate here, and the twentieth-century Presidents of the Republic choose it, of all the châteaux of France, as their country home, and Bob and me return for a second and third visit.

Rambouillet's recorded history begins in the year 768, when Pepin the Short, Charlemagne's father, gave monks the land near the brook named Rambo for a monastery. Over the years the château and surrounding forests acquired the name Rambouillet. Records show that in 774 Charlemagne confirmed the grant his father had made. Rambouillet faded in and out of history until 1052, when Amaury de Montfort became the seigneur. Then it became the fief of Simon de Montfort, the bloodthirsty leader of the crusade against the Albigensians. For three centuries thereafter it was the fief of the Angennes family and was in their hands when, in 1547, Francis I, making his way from Chambord to Saint-Germain-en-Laye, rode up to the gate, ill and dying. He had spent the previous day at Dampierre, hunting with the Count of Tavannes, despite his illness. He came to Rambouillet because he had had so many happy days hunting there in the past. A few days later, unable to rise from his bed and knowing he was about to die, he sent for the dauphin—who was to become Henry II—to give him his last words of advice: never to trust either the Duc de Guise (leader of the Catholic League) or the Duke of Montmorency (the king's minister, whose sympathies were with the Huguenots). He then died in the château's massive central tower. Henry, who hated his father, ignored his advice—and both France and Rambouillet fell into ruins during the Wars of Religion.

Louis XIV gave Rambouillet to his twenty-seven-year-old son, the Count of Toulouse. He had already given him the domains of the once-independent Count of Toulouse. (Toulouse, like the Duc du Maine, was a legitimized bastard by Athénaïs de Montespan. After Louis's mother died, he insisted his bastards be treated as legitimate princes of the blood.) Toulouse turned Rambouillet into a "little Versailles" but left untouched the tower where Francis I had died. As we toured the inside of Rambouillet, we suddenly came upon an outside wall of this tower, where the remains of a portcullis are still visible. When the Count of Toulouse built his "modern" château, he built it right around the feudal tower, incorporating

France's past into its (then) present. Every piece of furniture, every Gobelin tapestry, every Aubusson rug, every mirror, every chandelier is of museum quality. But Rambouillet is not a museum. It is alive. Because it is used by France's heads of state, it has been constantly lived in and lovingly cared for, maintained without regard for expense, so that when you walk through the château, the spirit of power and richness, of kings, emperors, and presidents pervades the rooms. And unlike Versailles or Vaux-le-Vicomte, where lavish expenditures were made to impress others, here each item seems to have been chosen for the enjoyment of those living here.

As we walked through the château, we came to a white-paneled room with exquisite boiserie bearing the carved initials MVS—those of Marie Victoire Sophie de Noailles, the forty-five-year-old widow whom the young Count of Toulouse fell in love with and then married, much to his father's displeasure. (Marrying for love rather than for advancement or money was quite unusual in the seventeenth century.) The paneling of this room is so beautiful that it alone is worth the trip to Rambouillet.

The bedroom where Louis XIV and Madame de Maintenon stayed when they visited the Count of Toulouse, from October 1712 to July 1713, is now the dining room. The chandelier, because of the way in which the mirrors are hung, is reflected a hundred times, and the seventeenth-century tapestries decorating the room are of a rare and beautiful quality, so beautiful to me that my eyes filled with tears when I saw them.

As Bob and I walked through the gardens, where hundreds of workers were busy restoring them to their seventeenth-century condition, we tried to figure out why Francis I had chosen a feudal tower in which to die; even then it was not the best room in the château. Perhaps it was fitting that the last King of France to embody the values of chivalry and knighthood should die in a structure that symbolized the feudal world from which those values arose.

Le Nôtre's Gardens

AT SCEAUX

It was an overcast Sunday morning when I dragged Bob off to Sceaux—not the perfect day to admire a park, but, I realized, the only day left during our stay in Paris that the famous cascades André Le Nôtre built at Sceaux would be in operation, and I didn't want to go there without seeing them.

We took the Métro to the Châtelet Les Halles station, where we boarded the RER train to the Parc Sceaux station. (Beware! There is another train marked simply "Sceaux"; do not take that.) This was my third trip on the RER, and I was now able to purchase my ticket from the machine with an ease that made me feel as independent and free as if I were a girl taking off alone on a bike for the first time. So many places on the Île-de-France were now open to me, unrestricted by limits of scheduling, since the trains ran so frequently (the train to Parc Sceaux, for instance, left every five minutes); unrestricted by the bother and expense of rented or chauffeured cars (the round-trip cost of a train trip to Sceaux was only twelve francs, the duration only fifteen minutes); and free of the endless chatter of strangers on a guided tour. The Métro and RER allowed me to go where I wanted, whenever I felt like it, without any arrangements other than making sure my destination was open that day.

Arriving at Sceaux, we found the plaza around the station marked by graffiti, and I was initially apprehensive about the area we would have to walk through to reach the park. However, the graffiti were confined to the station plaza, and the ten-minute walk to the park was along streets lined with cherry trees (beautiful in April) in a pleasant upper-middle-class neighborhood.

I wasn't quite sure what to expect at Sceaux. I knew that the original Baroque château and park were gone, razed and turned into farmland by a wealthy nineteenth-century businessman who replaced a masterpiece with the ordinary and uninviting structure that now houses the Musée de l'Île-de-France. Sceaux had once been the creation of the combined talents of some of the greatest artists of the Age of Louis XIV: Le Nôtre, landscape architect; Claude Perrault, architect; Le Brun, painter; and Coysevox and Girardon, sculptors. Working as a team, they created a château and surrounding gardens that exemplified the qualities of order, regularity, and unity characteristic of the age. As a result, the château and grounds together—like Maisons-Laffitte—were a harmonious unit of art, one part complementing another. Commissioned by Louis XIV's great minister Colbert at a time when the king encouraged the aristocracy to build homes that would embellish France—and sternly admonished them when he felt they showed poor taste—it and other châteaux constructed throughout the Île-de-France emulated the grandeur and splendor of the Sun King, around whose palace at Versailles their lives orbited. The seventeenth-century attitude toward construction and its place in the life of society is revealed by Louis XIV's court historian in a paragraph, written about Henry IV's building projects at Saint-Germain-en-Laye, that could just have well been written about Louis XIV:

For by raising these proud edifices he [Henry IV] leaves the fair marks of his greatness and riches to posterity; he embellishes his kingdom, attracts the admiration of his people, makes strangers know that his coffers swell with treasure, gives life and bread to a great number of poor workmen, labors profitably for his own convenience and for that of his successors, and last, but not least, makes architecture, sculpture, and painting flourish, which have ever been highly esteemed by all the most polite nations of the world.

Some idea of the proportions and classical beauty of Colbert's château at Sceaux can still be seen in the small domed Pavilion of the Rising Sun, which somehow survived the château's destruction. When you see the pavilion in its perfect little park, you get some hint of what was destroyed. This gem of a building, some distance from the main château, was where the children were kept. (Seventeenth-century parents liked their children out of the way; even children from the most aristocratic homes were generally ignored and neglected. Though Colbert may have encouraged parents to produce large families—any father siring ten or more children was exempted from taxes—he was motivated by a desire to fill his factories with workers.)

When Colbert died, Louis XIV considered the château fine enough to purchase for his favorite son, the Duc du Maine. Maine was a precocious child who had inherited the looks, charm, and conspiratorial nature of his mother, Athénaïs de Montespan. In an age when ten of the seventeen children sired by Louis died, Maine had somehow miraculously survived polio, though he was left with one leg paralyzed. His governess, Madame de Maintenon, nursed him back to health so lovingly that the king, observing her care, said, "Madame de Maintenon knows how to love. There would be great pleasure in being loved by her." Unlike the dauphin, who was terrified of his father, Maine was always totally at ease with the king and amused him by doing hilarious imitations of members of the court as he relayed court gossip. The king may have found Maine wildly funny, but the rest of the court did not; he was feared and hated for the very gossip the king found so entertaining. If the portrait that emerges from the memoirs of the period is accurate, he was treacherous and scheming. For example, he loved his governess, Madame de Maintenon, more than his own mother. At a time when Athénaïs de Montespan, having already given birth to numerous royal bastards, was growing fat and the king, for the first time, was beginning to feel guilty about sleeping with a married woman, Maine conspired to install his governess in his father's bed in place of his mother. According to the king's sister-in-law, the Duchess of Orléans:

> The Duc du Maine persuaded his mother to retire from Court for a short time in order that the King might recall her. Being fond of her son, and believing him to be honest in the advice he gave her, she went to Paris, and wrote the King that she would never come back. The Duc du Maine immediately sent off all her packages after her without her knowledge; he even had her furniture thrown out the window, so that she could not come back to Versailles. She had treated the King so ill and so unkindly that he was delighted at being rid of her, and did not care by what means.

When the queen died, Louis secretly married the governess, but, alas, the tender love he had observed Madame de Maintenon bestow on Maine—and desired for himself—was reserved for his bastard son. According to the Duchess of Orléans, the "old sorceress never loved anyone but her favorite, the Duc du Maine." Saint-Simon agrees that Madame de Maintenon "had eyes only for him."

Louis was opposed to Maine's marriage and to what he foresaw as a rival royal line, but he was persuaded by Madame de Maintenon to arrange a union between Maine and a princess of the blood, the tiny granddaughter of the Grand Condé. Maine's wife was "no bigger than a child of ten," so small, in fact, that according to the Duchess of Orléans, her headdress was said to weigh more than she. She was nicknamed "Dona Salpetria," perhaps because of her temper or perhaps because of the fireworks she continually set off at her pleasure parties and famous nightlong feasts, the "Nights of Sceaux," in which even the austere Knights of Malta participated. Maine was infatuated with the petite princess, although, according to court gossip, she whipped him. Her numerous affairs included one with the Cardinal de Polignac, whom she invited to visit her at Sceaux in these words: "We are going into the country tomorrow; and I shall so arrange the apartment that your chamber shall be next to mine. Try to manage matters as well as you did the last time and we shall be very happy."

There is not much left at Sceaux of this luxurious and scandalous seventeenth-century world. All that remain are a couple of statues of animals by Coysevox, which greet you as you enter the Court of Honor; an orangerie that once sheltered the orange trees Louis loved; and the tiny pavilion where the children were raised. When you pass through the main gate, you are confronted with the very ordinary-looking Musée de l'Île-de-France. Even the cascades are not original, though their marvelous reconstruction faithfully followed the designs of Le Nôtre.

Indeed, the cascades and the fountains are worth the visit, even on an overcast day, and they are in the gardens where the duchess reigned like a tiny goddess, putting on ballets, operas, and plays for the king's entertainment, and holding assignations for her own.

André Le Nôtre, who designed the gardens, is considered the greatest landscape architect of the seventeenth century, the man responsible for the direction that the formal French garden would take. He designed not only the gardens here at Sceaux but also those at Saint-Germain-en-Laye, Dampierre, Fontainebleau, Vaux-le-Vicomte, Chantilly, Saint-Cloud, the Tuileries, Maintenon, and, of course, Versailles. As a boy, he had worked with his father, the king's gardener at the Tuileries. Early on, he displayed a talent for painting, and his father sent him off as an apprentice in the workshop of Simon Vouet, where he met and became friends with Charles Le Brun, then a young, unknown painter. The two artists would work together throughout their lives.

Unimpressed by titles, Le Nôtre declined an offer of one from Louis, who adored him. He was the exact opposite of Colbert, the man for whom he designed the gardens at Sceaux and who went to great lengths to artificially improve his ancestry.

Certain elements basic to Le Nôtre's designs can be seen at each of his surviving or reconstructed parks. He liked to create broad, sweeping, elongated vistas that could be seen from the center of a château's terrace—giving the illusion that everything was visible from there—and he would then form a cross by placing a great canal at right angles to this central axis. In addition, he alleviated the boredom of a strictly symmetrical plan by creating secondary axes off the first (and by providing delightful surprises for the person actually walking through the garden). The whole constituted a unified geometric design, in contrast to the medieval garden, whose parterres were unrelated to one another.

While most memoirists of the period adored this warm, affectionate, unaffected man, not every member of the court shared Le Nôtre's view of gardening. The king's cousin, the Grand Mademoiselle, who owned a château at Choissy, did not. Receiving a visit from Le Nôtre, she wrote to Athénaïs de Montespan:

> M. Le Nôtre came here for a little; he wanted to cut and destroy, and upset and disarrange, as with the King at Versailles. But I am a different mold to my cousin; I am not to be surprised with big words. I saw that Le Nôtre thought only of expenditure and tyranny; I thanked him for his good intentions, and prayed him not to put himself out for me. I found there thickets already made of an indescribable charm; he wanted, on the instant, to clear them away, so that one could testify that all this new park was his. If you please, madam, tell His Majesty that M. Le Nôtre is the sworn enemy of Nature; that he sees only the pleasure of proprietorship in the future, and promises us cover and shade at that epoch of our life when we shall only ask for sunshine in which to warm ourselves.

Le Nôtre may not have been "the enemy of Nature," but he certainly wanted to exercise total, rational control over it. Some social historians have suggested that this "tyranny" was an extension of the political and social tyranny exercised by Louis XIV; others have suggested that it resulted from Copernicus's heliocentric view of the planets, whereby the intelligentsia realized that it was an illusion that the universe revolved around the earth, and therefore trusted reason rather than their senses. (Although today's gardens at Sceaux contain flowers, Le Nôtre, contemptuous of any appeal to the senses, did not include them in his original designs.) But what you see at Sceaux is Le Nôtre's genius in *creating* illusion.

As we walked toward the cascade, the first thing we saw was a single graceful plume of water in a small circular pond beyond which a broad sweeping green flat meadow appeared to rise to the horizon. As we came closer, we saw what looked like an alley lined by two privet hedges. Then, when we were right on top of the cascade, we suddenly realized that the privet hedges were not hedges at all but the tops of two columns of tall plane trees, pruned to look like hedges and supported by perfectly uniform tree trunks lining a steeply descending alley. Then I saw the cascade. At first I was disappointed. "Cascade" had conjured up in my American mind the wild rush of frothy water plunging down a rocky cliff, as at Yosemite Falls in California. Here the water sedately made its way down a water staircase, pausing like a genteel lady in a lacy hoop skirt in each of twelve semicircular pools as it descended, level by level, into the large octagonal pond in the valley between the two slopes. At each of the twelve levels, a pair of fountains sent up graceful plumes of water. For a brief moment in our visit, the sun came out and magically turned the plumes into a sparkling crystal fence. Only after we began to descend did we see the source of the cascading water—the mouths of marvelous, somewhat humorous faces *(mascarons)* designed by Rodin, which replaced the original statues by Girardon and Coysevox. At the base, looking upward, we saw the strictly ordered and elegant descent of water, a visual expression in landscape design of the belief, held by the artist in the Age of Louis XIV, of man's ability to control nature. The waterfall had the same formality, restraint, and proportions I had seen in the architecture at Maisons-Laffitte.

Vaux-le-Vicomte

AND NICOLAS FOUQUET

There may be more beautiful places than Vaux-le-Vicomte, but I haven't seen them. It is today, as the king's mistress exclaimed when she saw it for the first time over three hundred years ago, a "veritable fairy palace." It is a palace that was built with an extravagance that astounded a very extravagant king.

While both Vaux-le-Vicomte and Versailles were built to impress—and they do—and both palaces were designed by the same team of artists, Vaux is to Versailles as an artist's sketch is to a ponderous finished oil painting. Vaux is human in scale, "of superb and elegant proportions," while Versailles is intentionally overwhelming. In addition to possessing that sense of grandeur and splendor associated with the Age of Louis XIV, Vaux is filled with life and with a sensuous vitality I have found nowhere else.

Seen from the gardens, this domed Baroque palace, which seems to float upon the square reflecting pool, is a gem. And walking inside the château is, for me, like walking inside a many-faceted jewel. Its rooms are elaborately ornamented in a form of decoration first hinted at in Fontainebleau: a breathtaking combination of stucco, gilding, and painting. The subjects are mythological in an idealized, rational, classical landscape. In the Room of the Muses, where Molière's plays were performed for Nicolas Fouquet, and Voltaire's performed a generation later, eight muses luxuriously recline in pairs at the corners of the ceiling. Clio, the Muse of History, with Prudence and Fidelity at her side, occupies the center, holding a key: meaning that the past is the key to the future. Thalia, the Muse of Comedy, draped in blue velvet, holds a smiling mask in her hand, and a garland of red flowers flows from her hair; above her, an eagle holds a banner with Fouquet's motto *("Quo non ascendum"*—"How high shall I not climb?") in his beak. Euterpe, the Muse of Music, is playing the flute. Terpsichore, the Muse of Dance, is holding a lute; Calliope, the Muse of Oratory, a book; Urania, the Muse of Astronomy, a compass and a globe. The goddess of night, dressed in a film of black, is drawn through the clouds by two black horses. The carvings, unable to contain their joy at being at Vaux, seem to burst out of the Baroque frames created to hold them.

Notably unfinished is the domed grand salon, far more Roman and Imperial than the rest of the château. On its ceiling, now an empty sky, Le Brun was to have painted symbolic pictures of Fouquet's accomplishments.

The gardens at Vaux and those at Versailles were both designed by Le Nôtre, and both were based on the principles of geometry, perspective, illusion, and control of nature by man. As is the case with all Le Nôtre's gardens, they were designed so as not to interfere with the view of the palace, but to enhance it and to harmonize with it. The major differences between the gardens at Vaux and at Versailles are the scale and the thematic treatments. The scale is much grander at Versailles. At Vaux, the park, with its statues of mythological Greek gods, succeeds in creating what the ancient Greeks once envisioned: the Elysian Fields, the pagan paradise that only those favored by the gods could enter. At Versailles, on the other hand, the central theme compares Louis XIV to Apollo, the Sun God, around whom the universe is in orbit.

Visiting Vaux the first time, after having just seen Le Nôtre's gardens at Dampierre and Sceaux, I understood the theme and variations of his designs. Nearest the château on either side of the central allée are two long parterres with intricate swirling designs, which are laid out on the landscape like two elegantly woven oriental carpets. The central allée leads from the center of the château terrace into the distance, to a huge statue of the Farnese Hercules, the Greek hero who could not be defeated. Along the way are green parterres crossed by gravel paths and by canals—first two small canals and then the Grand Canal. Each difference in gradation creates illusion and surprise. Carefully pruned shrubs look more carved than real. Rather than colorful flowers, there are graceful plumes of water spouting from a multitude of elaborate fountains. The gardens must be seen when the fountains are in operation, and they are best seen when you look back at the château from the Hercules statue, which stands in the center of a long, sweeping vista bordered by forests on both sides. (It takes about a half hour to walk from the château to the statue.) When Louis XIV walked from the palace to the canal, he passed through crystal walls of water, spouting from a hundred jets, such as those seen today at Sceaux. A seventeenth-century visitor to Vaux commented, "The air was filled with the sounds of a thousand fountains falling into marvelously fashioned basins, as if it were the throne of Neptune." From the Farnese Hercules you can see the cascades, invisible from the château, where Madame de Sévigné liked to bathe beneath the watchful eyes of the Greek river gods, who recline in hidden grottoes. As I stood here, with the pagan gods in careful attendance, it did appear, as my little book on gardens suggested, that I was in an earthly paradise, and I wished with all my heart to be swimming where Madame de Sévigné swam.

The story of Vaux-le-Vicomte is inseparable from the story of the great party its creator, Nicolas Fouquet, gave there—the party he gave for Louis XIV which so angered the king that he imprisoned the host for the rest of his life.

Fouquet was one of the most unscrupulous, and perhaps the most ambitious, of all Louis XIV's unscrupulous and ambitious ministers. Born in

1615, the descendant of a long line of wealthy judges, he was sent to study with the Jesuits, but his father, soon realizing that his second son was ill-suited for the priesthood, purchased for him, when Nicolas was only sixteen, the position of *avocat* at the Parlement of Paris. From that time on, thanks to the nimbleness of his mind and his boundless energy, his rise was unmarred by setbacks of any kind. At eighteen he was *conseiller* to the Parlement of Metz; at twenty-one, *maître des requêtes*. At thirty-five he purchased the post of *procureur général*, the chief prosecuting officer of the Parlement of Paris. At thirty-six he married Marie-Madeleine Jeannin de Castille, whose immense dowry was added to his growing fortune. Serving as an official in the royal army, he became the cardinal's protégé; when Mazarin was sent into exile during the Fronde, Fouquet protected the cardinal's interests and property until he returned to power in 1653. Mazarin rewarded Fouquet with the post of superintendent of finances, recommending him to the young king by saying, "If they could get women and building out of his head, great things might be done with him."

The great things Fouquet did, however, were at least as much in his own behalf as in the king's. As superintendent of finances, he paid the government's bills partly by borrowing on his own credit, but in the process hopelessly intermingled the public purse with his own; he successfully kept the royal armies outfitted and provisioned and the royal coffers filled, but more successfully, and fraudulently, filled his own. His position as *procureur général* (attorney general) shielded him from investigation, as did Mazarin's favor. Fouquet, noted Louis's mistress Athénaïs de Montespan, was,

> envied by a thousand, provoked indeed a certain amount of spite; yet all such vain efforts . . . to slander him troubled him but little. My lord the Cardinal was his support, and so long as the main column stood firm, M. Fouquet, lavish of gifts to his protector, had really nothing to fear.

But eventually even Mazarin became alarmed at the extent to which Fouquet was diverting the nation's taxes. About to launch an inquiry into Fouquet's activities, however, the aging cardinal realized that the investigation would reveal the immense gifts his protégé had made to *him*—and he let Fouquet off with a warning.

But Fouquet was much more than a financier. He was also a remarkable patron of the arts, a man of superb taste, possessing an uncanny ability to recognize and inspire great talent—in both young and old—in all the arts. He seems to have thought of himself as a seventeenth-century Maecenas, the ancient Roman patron of the arts who, like himself, was both an adviser to a great ruler (Maecenas to the emperor Augustus) and the most renowned literary patron of his day (among Maecenas's protégés were Horace and Virgil). Comparing the Age of Louis XIV to the Age of Augustus was not uncommon—and there are indeed similarities. It wasn't merely that Voltaire, writing less than a generation later, compared the Grand Siècle to the Augustan Age, or that, as a twentieth-century historian of Louis's reign wrote, "Not since Augustus had any monarchy been so adorned with great writers, painters, sculptors, and architects." The people who lived during France's Golden Age saw themselves as the embodiment of all that was to be admired in the ancient world. Louis XIV certainly saw himself as a modern Augustus, and so did artists of his age. In the statue of Louis by Girardon at Vaux, the king is dressed as a Roman emperor, as he is in the painting by Mignard, and the statue in the Venus Drawing Room and the carved medallion in the War Room at Versailles. Louis considered the wall of the Roman Theater of Orange, the one containing the statue of Augustus, "the finest wall in my kingdom." When he tore down the medieval walls surrounding Paris, he built at the entrance to the city a series of triumphal arches, such as Augustus had built at the entrances to Roman cities.*

Fouquet gathered around his table, for which the food was prepared by the renowned chef Vatel, France's most celebrated artists and authors, such as Jean de La Fontaine, Paul Scarron, Mademoiselle de Scudéry, Madame de Sévigné. And he was attracted not merely by fame but by talent. The reputation of playwright Pierre Corneille, who did not adhere to the Aristotelian unities of time, place, and action that the Academy considered indispensable in the Golden Age, was so low in 1659 that, unable to bear the

*After having dinner near the Porte Saint-Denis, at a restaurant noted for its Art Nouveau decorations, we stumbled upon one of the two arches still extant in Paris. Built in 1672, it is decorated with friezes of Louis's victories on the Rhine.

prospect of more vicious attacks by French literary critics, he had not written a play in eight years, and, impoverished and depressed, was determined never to write again. Fouquet, however, recognized Corneille's greatness and gave him both a pension and praise—as well as an idea for a new play. He kept encouraging Corneille until he began writing again. Watching Fouquet provide artists with pensions, private rooms in his château, meals prepared by a great chef, and scintillating conversation, an admirer wrote that he had the "true fiber of humanity: he could touch its spring in others and they would answer to him." The artists themselves adored him. For example, from 1654 on, he gave the absentminded La Fontaine a thousand livres a year, the condition being that every three months he was to present Fouquet with a new poem. Books were dedicated to Fouquet, and he appeared as a character in Mademoiselle de Scudéry's novel *Clélie,* in which he is described as a "man who makes nothing but what is great, and whose mind by its vast range cannot conceive little designs."

All of Nicolas Fouquet's love for the arts was poured into Vaux-le-Vicomte.

At the time he bought the property, it held only a tiny fortress and three little villages. The first thing he did was raze them. The second was to plant a forest where they had stood. In the seventeenth century a forest signified more than trees to a man intent on rising above his station. Like the feudal tower, which was a symbol of feudal authority, the forest was a symbol of a feudal lord's rights, a place where he could hunt and cut down trees for firewood, while the peasantry was forbidden to do so. And Fouquet—whose motto was "How high shall I not climb?"—was very intent upon rising above his station. Then he instructed Le Nôtre to design a park so that it seemed to be carved out of the forest.

To build Vaux he brought together a team of relatively unknown young men whose work had caught his keen eye: the architect Louis Le Vau; the painter Charles Le Brun; and Gilles Guérin and Thibault Poissant for sculpture. Le Brun had a talent for organizing groups of artists. He suggested to Fouquet that André Le Nôtre, with whom he had developed a friendship while an apprentice in the workshop of Simon Vouet, join the team to design the gardens, and Fouquet agreed. Fouquet gave Le Brun the opportunity to deploy his full artistic talents in the decoration of his château, and Le Brun never again painted as sensuously and movingly as he did at Vaux. His work at Versailles is generally agreed to lack the vitality it has here. The allegorical paintings at Vaux are by his own brush; he provided the designs for the garden sculptures and for the decorative sculptures in the château; and he drew the cartoons for tapestries, which were manufactured at Maincy, where a factory was created to supply Fouquet's needs. Eighteen thousand men worked on building Vaux and its gardens.

Fouquet commissioned and oversaw every detail of construction. You know this, for example, when you look at Le Nôtre's planned landscape designs, now hanging on a wall in the château, and then see Fouquet's alterations in the actual gardens. He filled Vaux's library with 38,544 manuscripts, many of them very rare. Ancient Greek marble statues, seventeenth-century busts of Socrates and Seneca, tables of porphyry, rare mosaics, a copy of the Talmud, several old copies of the Bible, and other treasures filled its rooms.

When the château was completed, he invited the king and his entire court—all the hundreds of courtiers—to a great fête in the king's honor, to take place at Vaux on August 17, 1661. Louis accepted the invitation, but he had already become suspicious of the methods by which his superintendent of finances had obtained the funds to build Vaux. He was beginning to wonder how high Fouquet's ultimate ambitions might reach, and, in fact, had begun subtly to undermine the sources of his power.

Louis's suspicions had been awakened a few months before, when, on March 9, 1661, the dying Mazarin had warned the twenty-two-year-old king about Fouquet's financial manipulations and had recommended another young minister, Colbert, as a safeguard against them.

Colbert found six million livres Mazarin had squirreled away in various places in the Château of Vincennes (that was in addition to the fortune, estimated to be as high as forty million livres, he left his nieces) and shrewdly turned the money over to Louis. From that moment, Louis trusted him implicitly; he would write in his memoirs, "To keep an eye on Fouquet, I associated with him Colbert . . . in whom I had all possible confidence, for I knew his intelligence and application and honesty." Louis appointed Colbert as Fouquet's "assistant," which meant that every afternoon

Fouquet went over accounts with Louis, and every evening Colbert would show Louis how Fouquet had falsified those accounts.

Colbert began to intrigue against Fouquet—and Fouquet, supremely overconfident, didn't bother to defend himself at first. In the meantime, he had purchased his own island—Belle-Île-en-Mer, off the coast of Brittany—and begun repairing the existing ramparts to create a fortress there. And under the pretext of nurturing an infant sardine industry, he was in effect creating his own fleet by purchasing armed vessels from Holland, which he added to his whaling fleet.

But Louis XIV, although certain Fouquet was guilty of embezzlement, did not yet feel in a position to arrest his financial minister. He was too powerful and too popular. His popularity extended from the Parlement of Paris, where his position as *procureur général* protected him from investigation, to the coterie of artists he subsidized, and, most important, to Louis's own mother, Anne of Austria, whom Fouquet had often supplied with funds and who was very fond of him.

But Anne's fondness was about to be destroyed—by her old friend the Duchess of Chevreuse. When, on June 27, 1661, the queen mother visited the duchess at Dampierre, Colbert was there; his daughter was about to marry the duchess's son, bringing with her a large dowry, and Colbert and the duchess had become allies. They told Anne how Fouquet was extending his power, buying the support of members of the Parlement and promoting his friends and relatives by means of public money. By the time the queen mother completed her visit to Dampierre, her mind was so poisoned she was ready to accept Fouquet's arrest.

When he learned from spies of Colbert's success in turning the queen mother against him, Fouquet tried to persuade Louis's mistress, Louise de La Vallière, to intercede with the king on his behalf, using a technique that had proved successful with other women. As the keen-eyed Athénaïs de Montespan, whom Louise had brought to court to amuse the king with her charming banter, reported:

> M. Fouquet has one great defect: he took it into his head that every woman is devoid of willpower and of resistance if only one dazzles her eyes with gold. Another prejudice of his was to believe, as an article of

faith, that, if possessed of gold and jewels, the most ordinary of men can inspire affection.

Making this twofold error his starting point as a principle that was incontestable, he was wont to look upon every beautiful woman who happened to appear on the horizon as his property acquired in advance.

This time, however, the technique failed, although the offer—twenty thousand pistoles, if Louise would speak highly of Fouquet to the king—was certainly generous. Madame de Montespan reported:

> To his extreme astonishment, this young beauty declined to understand such language. Couched in other terms, he renewed his suit, yet apparently was no whit less obscure than on the first occasion. Such a scandal as this well-nigh put him to the blush, and he was obliged to admit that this modest maiden wither affected to be, or really was, utterly extraordinary.

Finally, according to Louis's biographer, Vincent Cronin, Louise replied, "with scorn in her voice," that " 'not for a quarter of a million pistoles would she commit such an indiscretion,' " and she complained to Louis that Fouquet had insulted her.

Fouquet also underestimated the young king. Although Louis XIV had told Fouquet at Mazarin's death that he would be his own chief minister, *("Il est temps que je les gouverne moi-même"),* Fouquet, knowing Louis's passion for women, hunting, and the ballet—Louis was an enthusiastic and graceful dancer—had not taken him seriously, had not taken the measure of the man with whom he was dealing. Louis, however, understood Fouquet all too well. The king now tricked him into selling the position of *procureur général,* which protected him from investigation, by hinting that he would appoint Fouquet to Mazarin's old post as head of government if only a conflict of interest between his position with the Parlement and his potential position as minister could be resolved. When he learned that Fouquet had decided to sell, Louis informed Colbert, "He is digging his own grave."

The great fête at Vaux was the last straw.

Fouquet's building of a grand château at Vaux was not unusual, nor was his invitation to the king. Both Cardinals Richelieu and Mazarin had built sumptuous châteaux while they were ministers to the king. René de Longueil had built Maisons-Laffitte while he was superintendent of finances, and had entertained Louis when the king hunted in the forests of Saint-Germain-en-Laye. And Colbert, of course, built Sceaux. But this party went beyond the others.

Historians say it was equaled by only one or two celebrations over the entire history of France. Meals were served on solid gold plates; there were ballets, concerts, and a play written by Molière for the occasion. Molière dressed in everyday clothes and greeted the assembled courtiers opposite the cascade, saying he had no actors and no time to prepare the entertainment that was expected, unless some unforeseen help was forthcoming. A shell thereupon opened to reveal a naiad and actors dressed as statues came to life, and *Les Fâcheux* was presented.

Since Athénaïs de Montespan was there, I will let her speak:

On reaching Vaux-le-Vicomte, how great and general was our amazement! It was not the well-appointed residence of a minister, it was not a human habitation that presented itself to our view—it was a veritable fairy palace. All in this brilliant dwelling was stamped with the mark of opulence and of exquisite taste in art. Marbles, balustrades, vast staircases, columns, statues, groups, bas-reliefs, vases, and pictures were scattered here and there in rich profusion, besides cascades and fountains innumerable. The large salon, octagonal in shape, had a high vaulted ceiling, and its flooring of mosaic looked like a rich carpet embellished with birds, butterflies, arabesques, fruits and flowers.

On either side of the main edifice, and somewhat in the rear, the architect had placed smaller buildings, yet all of them ornamented in the same sumptuous fashion; and these served to throw the château itself into relief. In these adjoining pavilions there were baths, a theater, a paume ground [tennis court], swings, a chapel, billiard rooms, and other salons.

One noticed magnificent gilt roulette tables and sedan chairs of the very best make. There were elegant stalls at which trinkets were distributed to the guests—notebooks, pocket mirrors, gloves, knives, scissors, purses, fans, sweetmeats, scents, pastilles, and perfumes of all kinds.

But to Louis, aware by this time of Fouquet's financial manipulations, such extravagance was proof of how much his minister had stolen from him. As Athénaïs put it:

It was as if some evil fairy had prompted the imprudent minister to act in this way, who, eager and impatient for his own ruin, had summoned the King to witness his appalling systems of plunder in its entirety, and had invited chastisement.

And finally there was the incident of the forest. The king liked the view from the balcony of his apartment at Vaux—except for one large, rather barren-looking clearing. He mentioned this to his host, who, while the king slept, put hundreds of peasants to work. When Louis awoke the next morning and stepped out on the balcony, the clearing was completely filled with full-grown trees. Recounted Athénaïs:

Fouquet, with airy presumption, expected thanks and praise. This, however, was what he had to hear: "I am shocked at such expense!"

Louis, infuriated, wanted to arrest Fouquet on the spot, but his mother persuaded him that this would be unseemly behavior for a guest. So he waited for nineteen days, and then, as Fouquet left the royal presence, had him arrested by D'Artagnan, the most trusted of the royal musketeers.

The trial that followed lasted three years. The artists Fouquet had supported now supported him and, as Madame de Sévigné wrote to him, "count chances on their fingers, melt with pity, with apprehension, hoping, hating, admiring; some of us are sad, some of us are overwhelmed. In short, my dear sir, the state in which we live is an extraordinary one, but the resignation and courage of our dear sufferer are almost more than human." It was what she wrote on November 20, after attending his trial, that made me cry:

> As he was returning by the arsenal on foot for exercise, M. Fouquet asked who were those workmen he perceived. He was told that they were people altering the basin of a fountain. He went up to them and gave his advice; and then turning to D'Artagnan [said,] "Do you wonder that I should interfere? I was formerly considered clever at these sorts of things."

While most of the judges were in favor of merely exiling Fouquet from France, the king intervened and increased the sentence from exile to life imprisonment. Fouquet, who loved beauty and women, would spend the rest of his life under heavy guard in a cold, damp dungeon in the Pignerol fortress in the Alps.

(Various theories arose to explain the harshness of Fouquet's sentence. One suggested a link to the Man in the Iron Mask, Louis's supposed twin brother and a threat to his throne; this explanation provided Alexandre Dumas with the story line for *Le Vicomte de Bragelonne*. Those preferring a soap opera version saw Fouquet's imprisonment as the result of his attempted seduction of Louise de La Vallière, the king's mistress. Others claimed that Louis, who had been forced to melt his silver to pay for his wars, became furious when served a sumptuous supper on gold plates.)

Louis XIV arrested Fouquet three weeks after seeing Vaux-le-Vicomte, but he entertained no animosity toward the artists who had created it. Instead, the entire team assembled by Fouquet to create Vaux (along with several hundred of Fouquet's orange trees) were brought to Versailles to create the great palace that Louis XIV had envisioned while standing on the escarpment at Saint-Germain-en-Laye.

Bob and I have been to Vaux-le-Vicomte a number of times. It is not far from Orly, and whenever we rent a car at the airport, we try to stop at Vaux before making our way south.

We have visited Vaux both on days when the fountains are in operation and on days when they are not. I highly advise making sure they are on before visiting the gardens.

. . .

On our last day in France, we decided to visit Louis XIV in Paris. We began at the Louvre, which had been his palace for the first twenty-eight years of his reign, the years he was transforming France into the most powerful and civilized country in Europe. There, in the Louis XIV Galleries, we could see the furniture he used, the Savonnerie carpets he walked on, the Gobelin tapestries and Le Brun paintings that hung on his walls, and the sculptures by Girardon and Coysevox he chose to have near him. We entered the palace grounds as Louis XIV would have wanted—through the pavilion he commissioned. He wanted the pavilion to possess a grand and impressive façade, which would tell the world they were entering the palace of a great king. Voltaire felt he had succeeded, calling this façade "one of the most august monuments of architecture in the world," adding that "no palace in Rome has an entrance comparable." I had seen it before—the whole previous summer I had routinely passed through it on my way somewhere else. I confess, however, I hadn't taken much notice of it. As I stood there looking at it, I realized that it reminded me of something, that its design echoed the style of the Maison Carrée, that perfect Roman temple which had left me totally unimpressed in Nîmes. While I now understood that I could never share Voltaire's ecstatic reaction to the façade— the style is not to my taste—I was nonetheless impressed with the young king who oversaw its construction. The leading architect of the day, the sixty-six-year-old Bernini, who had just completed Saint Peter's Square in Rome, was commissioned to design this façade. Louis XIV, only twenty-seven at the time, demonstrating those aesthetic qualities which set such uncompromising standards for the art of his age, rejected the revered old man's designs. The Baroque pavilion Bernini envisioned would have been inconsistent both with the elegant architecture of Louis's age and with the preexisting pavilions at the Louvre.

Once I was in the Cour Carrée, surrounded by the gleaming white stone and frilly Corinthian columns, the caryatides supporting the dome of the Clock Pavilion, the friezes of cherubs and garlands, it was not difficult to imagine being in the royal courtyard of a palace. I was reminded of the places I had been and kings I had visited on my journey through France

when I saw the initials carved in the stone of the four pavilions: the inter-
twined "H" and "D" of Henry II and his mistress Diane that I had seen at
Chenonceau and Anet (initials that Catherine de' Medici, acting as regent
after Henry's death, contended were an "H" and a reversed "C"); the solitary "H" of Henry III, Catherine's transvestite son, the last of the Valois
line, whom I had visited at Blois; the "H D B" of Henry IV, the first of the
Bourbon line, and his initial again, this time joined by the "G" of his favorite mistress, Gabrielle d'Estrées, whose children played at court with the
dauphin, the future Louis XIII; and the "LA" for Louis XIII and Anne of
Austria, whose union finally produced Louis XIV and the age I had just
briefly visited.

Later that day we left the Louvre through the Court of Napoleon and
found ourselves facing the Arc de Triomphe du Carrousel, which
Napoleon commissioned to commemorate his victories of 1805. It is a triple
arch, like the Roman arch at Orange, topped with horses and a chariot, as
that Roman arch once had been. Both arches, after their completion, underwent rededication. The four horses Napoleon placed on top were the
four gilded bronze horses that his troops had removed from Saint Mark's
Cathedral in Venice after he conquered Italy. Those magnificent horses
were returned to Venice after Napoleon's defeat at Waterloo. The reins of
the horses now there are held by a Goddess symbolizing the restoration—
which, after Napoleon's defeat, the arch was then intended to honor. The
arch at Orange had originally commemorated the victories of Caesar's Second Legion but was later rededicated to the Emperor Tiberius's victory
over a Gallic rebellion led by Sacrovir. Napoleon was dissatisfied with this
tiny arch as soon as it was built, and commissioned the Arc de Triomphe to
honor the glory of his Imperial Army. In the distance, we could see, as
Napoleon never would, that grand and monumental arch atop the Étoile
hill, and beyond it, La Défense, the symbol of modern Paris which I wished
would go away.

From the Louvre we walked up the great mall to the Hôtel des Invalides, the last group of buildings in Paris built during the reign of Louis
XIV. Before reading Voltaire, I was unaware that Louis built this immense
hospital and old-age home for his wounded veterans; I associated the Invalides with Napoleon, since it is the Emperor's magnificent tomb that

dominates its domed church, and it is the Emperor's accomplishments that are carved in stone in the crypt encircling the magnificent red porphyry sarcophagus that sits upon a base of green granite. (Just as I had been unaware that the Place Vendôme—dominated by a statue of Napoleon atop a tall column made from twelve hundred cannons he captured in one of his victories—had actually been built by Louis, and was once called "Place Louis Le Grand.")

When we arrived at the Invalides, I remembered at once the helmeted windows in the Mansard roof, which reminded me of a battalion of knights, but was surprised to see prominently carved over the entrance gate a bas-relief equestrian figure of Louis XIV. There he was, standing between Prudence and Justice, but I had somehow missed him on previous visits. In my mind, I had associated Louis XIV with Versailles and Napoleon with the Invalides. I walked through the huge Roman arched entrance into the courtyard with its two tiers of arches marching around its sides, and was reminded of the Pont du Gard and of the arches marching through the wilderness of Languedoc that the Romans had built almost two thousand years before to bring water to the fountains of Nîmes. To me, those arches in the Invalides brought back the smell of wild rosemary and the taste of picnics, but to Louis they meant the glory and power of Rome.

After dinner that night, as we walked back to our apartment, we passed the Place de la Concorde. There, Paris was a collage of monuments to kings and emperors, lit against the sky, vying for posterity's attention. As we came to the Rond-Point, I turned and saw the freshly gilded and illuminated dome of the Invalides. Louis had commissioned the huge, soaring, majestic dome above its church to represent "the glory of my reign." It seemed to float above Paris, a ghostly golden crown in a velvety blue-black sky, regal and majestic, a symbol of the Golden Age of France. I felt Louis was beckoning me to remember the splendor and magnificence of his age, and I was reminded of all the kings before Louis who wore the royal crown.

SELECTED BIBLIOGRAPHY

Most helpful in writing this book was a limited-edition, twenty-volume set entitled *The Secret Court Memoirs,* published by the Grolier Society, which I purchased after our first trip to France. The following volumes were used:

COURT HISTORIAN OF LOUIS XIV. *Memoirs of Henry IV, King of France and Navarre.*

MARGUERITE DE VALOIS. *Memoirs of Marguerite de Valois: Queen of Navarre.*

MONTESPAN, FRANÇOISE ATHÉNAÏS, MARQUISE DE. *Memoirs of Madame la Marquise de Montespan.* 2 vols.

ORLÉANS, DUCHESSE D' (CHARLOTTE ELISABETH OF BAVARIA). *The Secret Memoirs of Louis XIV and of the Regency.*

RETZ, JEAN FRANÇOIS PAUL DE GONDI, CARDINAL DE. *Memoirs of Cardinal de Retz: Containing All the Great Events During the Minority of Louis XIV and the Administration of Cardinal Mazarin.*

Other works consulted include:

*ADAMS, WILLIAM HOWARD. *The French Garden 1500–1800.* New York: George Braziller, 1979.

BABELON, JEAN PIERRE. "François Mansart, dieu de l'architecture," *Bulletin monumental* 133, IV (1975).

BARBER, RICHARD. *The Knight and Chivalry.* New York: Harper & Row, 1974.

BARBIER, PIERRE. *La France féodale: Châteaux-forts et églises fortifiées.* Vol. 1. Saint-Brieuc: Presses Bretonnes, 1968.

BARDON, FRANÇOISE. *Diane de Poitiers et le mythe de Diane.* Paris: Presses Universitaires de France, 1963.

BATTIFOL, LOUIS. *La Duchesse de Chevreuse: Une Vie d'aventure et d'intrigues sous Louis XIII.* Paris: Hachette, 1913.

*BAUMGARTNER, FREDERIC J. *Henry II: King of France 1547–1559.* Durham, N.C.: Duke University Press, 1988.

*BLUNT, ANTHONY. *Art and Architecture in France 1500–1700.* London: Penguin Books, 1988.

BOURGET, PIERRE, and CATTAUI, GEORGES. *Jules Hardouin Mansart.* Paris: Vincent, Fried, 1960.

BRANNER, ROBERT. *The Cathedral of Bourges and Its Place in Gothic Architecture.* New York: Architectural Historic Foundation, 1989.

BRANTÔME, PIERRE DE BOURDEILLES, SEIGNEUR DE. *Mémoires de Messire Pierre de Bourdeilles, Seigneur de Brantôme.* 4 vols. Leyde: Jean Sambix le jeune, 1666.

*BRIFFAULT, ROBERT S. *The Troubadours.* Bloomington: Indiana University Press, 1965.

BROWN, HORATIO. "The Assassination of the Guises," *English Historical Review* X (1895).

BURGESS, GLYN, ed. and trans. *The Song of Roland.* London: Penguin Books, 1990.

BUSSY, ROGER DE RABUTIN, COMTE DE. *Correspondence de Roger Rabutin avec sa famille et ses amis: 1666–1695.* Paris: Charpentier, 1858.

BUTLER, EDWARD CUTHBERT. *Western Mysticism: The Teaching of Augustine, Gregory and Bernard.* London: Constable, 1928.

CAESAR, JULIUS. *The Gallic Wars,* trans. H. J. Edwards. London: Loeb Classical Library, 1917.

*I have starred the books that I found added to the enjoyment of traveling through the history of France.

CELLINI, BENVENUTO. *Autobiography,* trans. George Bull. New York: Penguin Books, 1977.

CHAMSON, ANDRÉ. *Pèlerins et chemins de Saint-Jacques.* Paris: Académie Française, 1965.

CLAPHAM, ALFRED WILLIAM, SIR. *Romanesque Architecture in Western Europe.* Oxford: Clarendon Press, 1936.

CLÉMENT, PIERRE. *Jacques Coeur et Charles VII, ou La France au XVe siècle.* Paris: Guillaumin, 1853.

COIGNET, CLARISSE. *Francis the First and His Times,* trans. Fanny Twemlow. London: Richard Bentley and Son, 1888.

COLLECTION DES CHRONIQUES NATIONALES FRANÇAISES. 10 vols. Paris: J. A. Buchon, 1800.

*CRONIN, VINCENT. *Louis XIV.* London: Collins, Harvill, 1990.

DUBY, GEORGES. *The Age of Cathedrals.* Chicago: University of Chicago Press, 1981.

EINHARD AND NOTKER THE STAMMERER. *Two Lives of Charlemagne,* trans. Lewis Thorpe. New York: Penguin Books, 1969.

FROISSART, JEAN. *Chronicles of England, France and Spain,* trans. Thomas Johnes. 2nd ed. 2 vols. London: Routledge, 1874.

GAUCHERY, ROBERT. *Le Palais Jacques-Coeur.* Bourges: Desquand & Fils, 1949.

GEARY, PATRICK J. *Furta Sacra: Thefts of Relics in the Central Middle Ages.* Princeton: Princeton University Press, 1978.

GREGORY, BISHOP OF TOURS. *History of the Franks,* trans. Ernest Brehaut. New York: W. W. Norton, 1969.

HATT, JEAN-JACQUES. *Celts and Gallo-Romans.* Geneva, Paris: Nagel Publishers, 1970.

HAZLEHURST, FRANKLIN HAMILTON. *Gardens of Illusion: The Genius of André Le Nostre.* Nashville: Vanderbilt University Press, 1980.

HOLT, ELIZABETH G. *A Documentary History of Art.* 2 vols. New York: Doubleday, 1958.

*KELLY, AMY. *Eleanor of Aquitaine and the Four Kings.* Cambridge: Harvard University Press, 1950.

*KERR, ALBERT BOARDMAN. *Jacques Coeur: Merchant Prince of the Middle Ages.* New York, London: Charles Scribner's Sons, 1927.

LESUEUR, FREDERIC. *Le Château de Blois.* Paris: Éditions A & J Picard, 1970.

LEVRON, JACQUES. *Le Château d'Amboise.* Paris: Grenoble, 1949.

LIVY. *The War with Hannibal,* trans. Aubrey de Selincourt. New York: Penguin Books, 1975.

LOPEZ, ROBERT S. *The Commercial Revolution of the Middle Ages, 950–1350.* Cambridge: Cambridge University Press, 1976.

LOUIS XIV. *Manière de montre les jardins de Versailles.* Paris: Éditions de la Réunion des Musées Nationaux, 1992.

————. *Mémoires pour l'instruction du Dauphin.* Paris: Imprimerie Nationale, 1992.

*MACKENDRICK, PAUL. *Roman France.* New York: St. Martin's Press, 1972.

MCLEOD, ENID. *Charles of Orléans: Prince and Poet.* London: Chatto & Windus, 1969.

MADAULE, JACQUES. *The Albigensian Crusade: An Historical Essay,* trans. Barbara Wall. London: Burns & Oates, 1967.

*MAHONEY, IRENE. *Madame Catherine.* New York: Coward, McCann & Geoghegan, 1975.

————. *Royal Cousin: The Life of Henri IV of France.* New York: Doubleday, 1970.

MARTIN, H. I. "What Parisians Read in the Sixteenth Century," *French Humanism,* 1970.

MAWREY, GILLIAN. "The Medieval Gardens at Fontevraud Abbey," *Hortus,* Autumn 1988.

*MELOT, MICHEL. "Politique et architecture: Essai sur Blois et Le Blésois sous Louis XII," *Gazette des beaux-arts* 70 (December 1967).

MITFORD, NANCY. *The Sun King: Louis XIV at Versailles.* London: Sphere Books Limited, 1966.

MORAND, PAUL. *Fouquet, ou Le Soleil offusqué.* Paris: Éditions Gallimard, 1961.

*OLDENBOURG, ZOÉ. *Massacre at Montségur: A History of the Albigensian Crusade,* trans. Peter Green. New York: Pantheon Books, 1961.

ORLIAC, JEHANNE D'. *Francis I: Prince of the Renaissance,* trans. Elizabeth Abbot. Philadelphia: Lippincott, 1932.

————. *The Moon Mistress: The Duchess de Valentinois.* Philadelphia: Lippincott, 1930.

PÉPIN, EUGÉNE. *Chinon.* Paris: Petites Monographies des Grands Édifices de la France, 1963.

PINAULT, RAPHAEL. *Rambouillet: De la grande à la petite histoire.* Paris: Éditions La Bruyère, 1990.

PIRENNE, HENRI. *Mohammed and Charlemagne.* New York: Meridian Books, 1957.

PLUTARCH. *Lives,* trans. John Dryden, rev. Arthur Hugh Clough. New York: Modern Library, reprint of 1864 edition.

POITIERS, DIANE DE. *Lettres inédites de Dianne de Poytiers.* Paris: Jules Renouard, 1866.

RIVET, A. L. F. *Gallia Narbonensis: Southern France in Roman Times.* London: B. T. Batsford, 1988.

*SACKVILLE-WEST, VITA. *Saint Joan of Arc.* Boston: G. K. Hall, 1984.

*SAINT-SIMON, LOUIS DE ROUVROY, DUC DE. *The Age of Magnificence: The Memoirs of the Duc de Saint-Simon,* sel., ed., and trans. Ted Morgan. New York: Paragon House, 1990.

——. *Historical Memoirs of the Duc de Saint-Simon,* trans. Lucy Norton. Vol. 1 (1691–1709), Vol. 2 (1710–1715). New York: McGraw-Hill, 1967, 1968.

SAUSSAYE, L. DE LA. *Blois et ses environs: Guide artistique et historique.* Paris: 1882.

SCHAPIRO, MEYER. *Romanesque Art: Selected Papers.* New York: George Braziller, 1977.

SEDGWICK, HENRY DWIGHT. *The House of Guise.* New York: Bobbs-Merrill, 1942.

SEELY, GRACE HART. *Diane the Huntress: The Life and Times of Diane de Poitiers.* New York: D. Appleton Century Company, 1936.

SÉVIGNÉ, MARIE DE RABUTIN-CHANTAL, MARQUISE DE. *Selected Letters: Madame de Sévigné,* trans. Leonard Tancock. New York: Penguin Books, 1982.

*SEWARD, DESMOND. *The Hundred Years War: The English in France 1337–1453.* New York: Atheneum, 1978.

SHANNON, ALBERT CLEMENT. *The Medieval Inquisition.* Washington, D.C.: Augustinian College Press, 1983.

*STODDARD, WHITNEY S. *Art and Architecture in Medieval France.* New York: Harper & Row, 1972.

STRONG, ROY. *Art and Power: Renaissance Festivals 1450–1650.* Woodbridge, Suffolk: Boydell Press, 1984.

SUMPTION, JONATHAN. *The Albigensian Crusade.* London: Farber & Farber, 1978.

TACITUS. *Historical Works,* trans. Arthur Murphy. London: Everyman's Library, 1908.

TAPIÉ, VICTOR L. *France in the Age of Louis XIII and Richelieu,* trans. D. M. Lockie. New York: Cambridge University Press, 1988.

THEVENOT, CHRISTIAN. *Foulque III Nerra: Comte d'Anjou.* Tours: Nouvelle République du Centre-Ouest, 1987.

TOURAULT, PHILIPPE. *Anne de Bretagne.* Paris: Perrin, 1990.

TOURRASSE, L. DE LA. "Le Château-Neuf de Saint-Germain-en-Laye: Ses terrasses et ses grottes," *Gazette des beaux-arts* 9 (1924).

WARNER, MARINA. *Joan of Arc.* New York: Alfred A. Knopf, 1981.

WHEELER, MORTIMER. *Roman Art and Architecture.* New York: Thames and Hudson, 1964.

*WILLIAMS, HUGH NOEL. *Henri II: His Court and Times.* New York: Charles Scribner's Sons, 1910.

WOLFRAM, HERWIG. *History of the Goths,* trans. Thomas J. Dunlap. Berkeley: University of California Press, 1987.

WOODBRIDGE, KENNETH. *Princely Gardens: The Origins and Development of the French Formal Style.* New York: Rizzoli, 1986.

VAISSIÉRE, PIERRE DE. *Le Château d'Amboise.* Paris. Calmann-Lévy, 1935.

VITRUVIUS POLLIO, MARCUS. *Vitruvius on Architecture.* 2 vols. New York. G. P. Putnam's Sons; 1931–4.

VOLTAIRE. *The Age of Louis XIV and Other Selected Writings,* trans. J. H. Brumfitt. New York: Twayne Publishers, 1963.

INDEX

ABOUT THE AUTHOR

Ina Caro received a master's degree in history, with a concentration in medieval history, from Long Island University. For twenty years she has been the sole research assistant for her husband, Pulitzer Prize–winning biographer Robert A. Caro. She lives in New York City.